# THRESHOLDS OF DIFFERENCE

## Feminist Critique, Native Women's Writings, Postcolonial Theory

In this multi-disciplinary study Julia Emberley offers a critical examination of three related areas of cultural interest: Native women's writings in Canada, Anglo-American feminist theory, and postcolonial
critical theory. Through discussions of various theorists such as Teresa
de Lauretis, Nawal el Saadawi, Edward Said, and Gayatri Chakravorty
Spivak, Emberley explores the conflicting and competing meanings
attached to the value of gender for feminist and postcolonial theories
of difference.

From her readings of Native, Métis, and Inuit women writers Emberley posits a 'double-session' of writing. This doubly directed writing advances towards both a decolonization of feminism, based upon
the critical writings of Native women in Canada, and a feminism of
decolonization, elaborated through a deconstructive materialist feminist critique of gender relations in the discourses of decolonization.

In *Thresholds of Difference* Emberley offers much-needed guidance
about accounting for indigenous experiences and the role of the non-
Native researcher. She sheds light on the relationship between colonizer and colonized, and on the ethnocentrism that underpins Western
neglect of non-European scholarship.

JULIA V. EMBERLEY is currently a member of the Society for the
Humanities, Cornell University. She has taught in the Cultural Studies
Program at Trent University and in the English Department at York
University.

THEORY / CULTURE

General editors
Linda Hutcheon and Paul Perron

# THRESHOLDS OF DIFFERENCE
## Feminist Critique, Native Women's Writings, Postcolonial Theory

Julia V. Emberley

UNIVERSITY OF TORONTO PRESS

Toronto Buffalo London

© University of Toronto Press Incorporated 1993
Toronto Buffalo London
Printed in Canada

ISBN 0-8020-2850-0 (cloth)
ISBN 0-8020-7729-3 (paper)

Printed on acid-free paper

**Canadian Cataloguing in Publication Data**

Emberley, Julia, 1958–
Thresholds of difference : feminist critique,
native women's writings, postcolonial theory

(Theory/culture)
Includes bibliographical references and index.
ISBN 0-8020-2850-0 (bound) ISBN 0-8020-7729-3 (pbk.)

1. Feminism – Canada. 2. Native peoples –
Canada – Women.* 3. Feminist theory. I. Title.
II. Series.

HQ1453.E63 1993     305.48'897071     C92-095726-9

76671

This book has been published with the help of a grant
from the Canadian Federation for the Humanities,
using funds provided by the Social Sciences and
Humanities Research Council of Canada.

to Peter

# Contents

# Acknowledgments

I wish to thank several individuals who read and commented on my PHD dissertation, from which this book emerged: Himani Bannerji, Barry Cameron, Terry Goldie, Atu Sekyi-Otu, Ian Sowtan, and Bill Whitla. I am especially grateful to Barbara Godard, not only for her intellectual support and friendship, but also for her inspiring and energetic commitment to feminist literary theory and criticism in Canada.

I thank friends and colleagues who influenced and supported my work, including Shannon Bell, Gad Horowitz, Donna Landry, Gerald MacLean, Tilottama Rajan, Debbie Simmons, and Colleen Youngs. I owe a special thanks to Linda Hutcheon for her encouragement in bringing this work to publication. Anonymous readers for University of Toronto Press and the Canadian Federation for the Humanities provided helpful suggestions for revisions. Ken Lewis edited the manuscript with care and precision. To all of you, known and unknown, I am grateful for your patience and fine editorial guidance.

I also thank the following group of women, whose generous reception of my work on Native women's writings and feminism at the National Symposium on Aboriginal Women of Canada: Past, Present and Future, held in October 1989, in Lethbridge, Alberta, provided a crucial spirit of comradeship: Jeannette Armstrong, Marie Annharte Baker, Sue Deranger, Linda Jaine, Kim Sawchuk, and Winona Stevenson.

Some of the research and writing of this text was made possible by the Social Sciences and Humanities Research Council of Canada, which provided a post-doctoral fellowship for the 1990–1 and 1991–2 academic years. The English Department at York University provided supplementary funds to do research for the chapter on Native women and the colonial archive.

With the permission of *Cultural Critique* I am reprinting my essay '"A Gift for Languages": Native Women and the Textual Economy of the Colonial Archive.' Chapter 5 contains a few sections which also appear in the article 'Native Women's Writing and the Cultural Politics of Representation,' written for a volume of essays, *Women of the First Nations of Canada*, edited by Christine Miller, Patricia Chuchryk, Marie Smallface Marule, Brenda Eastman, and Cheryl Deering, and soon to be published by University of British Columbia Press. I am grateful to Press Gang Publishers of Vancouver, Canada, for permission to reprint a section from Chrystos's 'Maybe We Shouldn't Meet If There Are No Third World Women Here,' from her *Not Vanishing* poetry collection.

It gives me the greatest pleasure to thank my companion Peter Kulchyski, who contributed enormously to the process of writing this book and to whom this book is dedicated. Not only did Peter read various drafts, offer his commentary and insights, and give generously from his own scholarly work on Native politics in Canada, but he also provided something inestimable – an unsayable call to arms, an embrace without fear.

# (Pre)liminary Fragments

For a deconstructive materialist feminist theory the analytical terms 'subject' and 'discourse' provide new explanatory powers with which to articulate the complex interplay and contradictory antagonisms among race, gender, sexuality, and class differences. Feminist theories of women's oppressions and resistances are currently constituted by the demands of many new social movements, including lesbian and gay movements, animal-rights movements, and anti-racist and anti-imperialist struggles. In an effort to be fully adequate to these and other demands, not to mention in their desire to dispel the previous crimes of subject-exclusions, feminist theorists continue to add terms of investigation to include a critique of racism, heterosexism, and ethnocentrism. This interminable process of listing heavily coded signifiers, such as race, class, gender, sexuality, colonization, and so forth, often produces a false sense of equality and unity within and among the correlative subjects such as Native, Métis, Inuit, lesbian, English Canadian, Woman, Man. While the proliferation of subject-positions and the construction of those positions in the discourses of the human sciences represent increasingly important sites of critical investigation, contradictions and antagonisms would seem to vanish in the striving to create a full presence for the plurality of differences. Jacques Derrida's elaboration of deconstruction in 'Signature Event Context' provides an alternative approach to oppositional critical practices:

Very schematically: an opposition of metaphysical concepts (e.g., speech/writing, presence/absence, etc.) is never the confrontation of two terms, but a hierarchy and the order of a subordination. Deconstruction cannot be restricted or immediately pass to a neutralization: it must, through a double gesture, a double science, a double writing – put into practice a *reversal* of the classical opposition *and* a general *displacement* of the system. It is on that condition alone that deconstruction will provide the means of *intervening* in the field of oppositions it criticizes and that is also a field of non-discursive forces ... Deconstruction does not consist in moving from one concept to another, but in reversing and displacing a conceptual order as well as the non-conceptual order with which it is articulated. (195)

A linear approach to listing successive terms, as a way of accounting for multiplicity and difference, tends to reproduce an implicitly oppositional, and hence, hierarchical relation between those terms and their 'others.' Among those 'others' for an Anglo-American tradition of feminist practices are indigenous women, the women for whom European imperialism has meant the almost complete destruction of their decision-making powers in a gatherer/hunter society.

\* \* \*

In a 'Sesame Street' game called 'One of these things just doesn't belong' four squares are used to represent four 'things.' The object of the game is to pick which object does not belong with the others. Or to phrase it differently, pick out a recognizable conceptual category, which suits three objects, determine the criteria of classification, and remove the fourth image that does not fit. The fourth image or metaphor exists, then, as a disturbance, even though it is entirely necessary, precisely because of its difference, for the homogenization of the other three remaining representations.

As an allegory of reading and interpretation, the literary critic will often start from the position of familiar classification – realist fiction, autobiography, testimonial literatures – determine the place of a text by its assimilating criteria, and marginalize those textual remainders, the disturbing stuff of the fourth box, that cannot be made to fit – all the while ignoring the degree to which the stuff of the fourth box has been instrumental in providing the borders of classification. By focusing on this fourth element, this textual remainder or aberrancy – bringing the margin to the centre, as it were – alternative readings become possible. The literature of experience, like any textual fabric, contains contradictory or paradoxical aspects that cannot be written off as rubbish or waste. And recycling these waste products into the already existing circuit of discursive exchange will not help the critic to unlearn the game of discovering which one of the things just doesn't belong. Learning the game of reading for textual aberrancies is a bit tricky. If there are any rules, they are contained, at least implicitly, in the text. The classification 'Native women's literature' is, on the one hand, a product of the text's aberrant disclosures that cannot be tailored to fit the criteria of the literary industry; on the other hand, the texts written by Native women contain an argument, implicitly, for their constitution as Native women's literature. The use of textual remainders as the stuff for inventing new classifications does little more than recycle difference into a larger mode of unification. While textual disturbances may contest the metaphors of cultural borders, the notion of an 'outside,' a unified field of representation, and the spectre of individual authorship, they can also be reified into bicultural passports of difference, tourist visas to an unknown discursive territory. What texts written by Métis, Inuit, and other Native women do arrange is a multiply conflictual and contradictory assemblage of threads, across which Métis, Inuit, and Native subjects interpellate themselves through socially constituted discursive vacancies. If one such discursive vacancy is 'authenticity,' then that too is a constitutive feature of the textual make-up of autobiographical and semi-autobiographical narrative fictions, in which I would include Jeannette Armstrong's *Slash*, Marie Campbell's *Halfbreed*, Beatrice Culleton's *In Search of April Raintree*, and Minnie Aodla Freeman's *Life among the Qallunaat*.

\* \* \*

In Canada during the 1980s Native women, struggling for self-determination from Canadian colonial interests, challenged the validity of feminist theories and practices. Not only was that challenge directed towards the double blindnesses to racism and ethnocentrism within the tradition of Anglo-American feminism, but Native women also confronted feminisms with the very terms and definitions of gender on which their theoretical knowledge was constructed. Both feminist critical practices and Native women's critique of colonialism, to different degrees of importance and emphasis, have a similar interest in the constructions of female gendering. However, as Native women's writings demonstrate, how female genders are made differs considerably in a society in which gathering and hunting comprise the prevalent modes of production, where exchanges between men and women can be characterized as a form of balanced reciprocity, as compared to a capitalist society in which the exchange of women dominates the very constitution of its social relations. This theoretical insight is predicated

upon a reversal in the usual order of subordination that Native wom-
en encounter in their confrontation with what Valerie Amos and
Pratibha Parmar aptly call 'imperial feminism.' From this reversal I
would posit a 'double-session' of writing which advances towards
both a decolonization of feminism based upon the critical writings of
Native women in Canada and, predicated upon an understanding of
the significance of this literature, a feminism of decolonization elaborated through a deconstructive materialist feminist critique of gender
relations in the discourses of decolonization.

*    *    *

> I have related a story and constructed an interpretation in the hope of
> illustrating the degree to which subversion is most frequently a matter
> of micropolitics, a politics of everyday experience, of speech and ges-
> ture, a politics that leaves few traces, but may be passed on from
> generation to generation through stories or values and may also dis-
> apppear into a backwater eddy of history, not even serving to inspire
> those who bear its spirit of constructive refusal.
>
> Peter Kulchyski, 'Primitive Subversion: Totalization and Resistance in
> Native Canadian Politics,' 190–1

As an English-Canadian woman (caught within the categories I am
trying to subvert) holding a privileged institutional position that re-
wards and supports my research, the reader might well ask, What is
your relationship to Canada's Native struggle for self-determination?
How did you come to write this book?

A personal story: I am a white woman, from a middle-class background, who came from England to Canada with my family at the age
of three. My parents' decision to immigrate to Canada was not an
accidental one. It followed a well-worn history of colonial expectations:
the offer of a new career for my father; the promise of upward mobili-
ty for his children; the achievement of the cultural, racial, and economic conclusion to gaining membership in a newly established white
colonial elite. My mother's stories of relations who braved the voyages
of the Hudson's Bay Company were part of the store of family legend.
As if I were playing a minor role in a Hollywood movie script, I found
myself blithely following the lines of expectations, occasionally fighting for a leading role as a rebellious feminist with a strong, however
undirected, desire to threaten the master narrative of the bourgeois
colonial woman.

In 'A Cyborg Manifesto' Donna Haraway writes that 'for many who share a similar historical location in white, professional middle-class, female, radical, North American, mid-adult bodies – the sources of a crisis in political identity are legion' (155). There is ambivalence in my personal narrative: a desire to become myself – *NOT!* Or in Derridean graphimatics, m~~yself~~: a trace of the 'me' I have told you about, which is no longer 'myself' but a self inescapably altered by coming to terms with the reality effects of a diverse collectivity of Native women's interests, values, and mediations. I/je am (be)coming (a)part from/of the history of an Anglo-American feminist tradition.

\* \* \*

This book sets out to examine a series of articulations among feminist theories, postcolonial criticisms, and Native women's writings in Canada. The shifting limits of this specific constellation of textual practices suggest to me the possibility of a materialist feminism of decolonization and a decolonialist materialist feminism. There are at least two meanings that can be ascribed to an articulation of feminist and decolonialist movements. In a liberal discourse 'to articulate' signals a unified and fully coherent voice protesting its inalienable right to free speech. In his book *Marxism and Deconstruction: A Critical Articulation* Michael Ryan dis-articulates the liberal voice from its 'homogeneous masses': 'A "critical articulation" neither makes similarities into identities nor rigorously maintains distinctions. It is more akin to the weaving together of heterogeneous threads into a new product than to the scholarly and disinterested comparison of homogeneous masses whose distinction is respected' (xiii). In bringing two separate bodies of knowledge together it is possible to find out where they touch each other, interrupt each other, transform each other's assumed values and meanings. A materialist feminism of decolonization and a decolonialist materialist feminism articulate women's resistances to and Native struggles against a phallocentric fetishistic economy.

\* \* \*

What discursive conditions exist with which to formulate a decolonialist theory of gender equality or subordination? Traditionally theory has been the preserve of an intellectual vanguard, to the exclusion of 'the voices of the oppressed.' The current swing to an identity politics in English-Canadian and American feminisms, with subjective authenticity as the code of legitimation, challenges the role of theorists as hegemonic representatives in academic institutions of power. The problem lies, in part, with a conception of theory as a metaphysical game whose principal players – the floating signifiers (academics) – would appear to exist in a field of investigation removed from a ground or clearly defined opposition – the referents (the oppressed). The positing of a fully anti-essentialist discourse is no more nor less than the reinscription of what Derrida criticizes as 'the metaphysics of presence' – however, now in terms of its obverse, the metaphysics of absence. If full presence is not possible, likewise full absence (vacating the essential and authentic as critical categories) is also, aside from impossible, undesirable. A solution to the naïve framing of presumed unmediated 'voices of the oppressed' and the troubling privilege of theory as the exclusive domain of an intellectual vanguard might be found, I would suggest, in the writings of subjects in resistance. The popular fictions, critical essays, testimonials, and poetics of Native women writers engaged in a critique of colonialism already theorize gender equality/subordination and the epistemological effects of colonial violence.

*  *  *

A hypotactic schema of antagonism:
    The classical opposition on which patriarchy founds and funds itself can be re-presented thus:

> (Western) Man
> _____
> (Western) Woman

Equality for English-Canadian woman has been, at times, naïvely based upon a simple cognitive reversal:

> (Western) Woman
> _____
> (Western) Man

The bar or the barrier between these two sets of signifiers is the value-sign of a division of power. The positioning of these two sets is that of an order of subordination, a hierarchical relation.
    The argument for equality has been fought in terms of the struggle over unequal relations, denial of access to material benefits – shelter, food, clothing, education – and a disavowal of participation in decision-making processes through which women assemble to produce the

requirements for their/our needs and desires. These needs and desires have been phrased in the discourse of control over our bodies, of the constitution of our sexuality, of our choice to reproduce or not, and with whom we wish to constitute our social and sexual relations, and of our access to health care and a way of caring that focuses on emotional, intellectual, and spiritual health, as we/women define the parameters of that essential (and not immutable nor intrinsic) difference from men and the essential (that is, the constituted) differences among us/women.

Because we/women/men live in a hierarchical society, in which racism, (hetero)sexism, and class exploitation make up some of its supporting props, a simple reversal, such as the one outlined above, is insufficient for analysing the specific contradictions of epistemological violence among us/women.

I would rewrite the above re(-)presentation of hegemonic relations in the following way:

$$\text{i} \quad \frac{\text{(Western) Man}}{\text{(Western) Woman}} \qquad\qquad \text{ii} \quad \frac{\text{(Western) Woman}}{\text{(Ab/original) Woman}}$$

If I were a mathematician, I might perform here a pseudo-algebraic function of cancellation:

$$\frac{\text{(Western) Man}}{\text{(Western) Woman}} \left| \frac{\text{(Western) Woman}}{\text{(Ab/original) Woman}} \right. = \frac{\text{(Western) Man}}{\text{(Ab/original) Woman}}$$

The violence among women leaves the dominant social relations between men and women intact. Power is displaced onto and dispersed among women.

The historically specific axiological determinations of race, gender, class, and colonialism do not simply blend into, cross over, or parallel each other; they come into conflict with each other. When these conflicts are elided within feminist theories and practices, feminism becomes the bar, the barrier, between which (Western) humanist Man and (Ab/original) Woman are set in a violent relation to each other. (Western) Woman, as this signifier is located within the hypotactic schema of anatagonism, plays the figure of mediation between Eurocentric patriarchy and ab/original women's self-determination. In working towards a critical articulation between feminist and de-colonialist struggles, feminist theories continue to be predicated upon the metaphorical figure of a Woman/Body or its coded metonym 'sexual difference.' As a (pre)liminary moment bordering the centrality of sexual difference in postcolonial feminist modes of social, political, and cultural analysis, the thresholds of gendered colonial difference mark the critical limits for further deconstructive materialist feminist investigations.

# THRESHOLDS OF DIFFERENCE

# Introduction: Articulating Difference(s)

... the sense of a 'world' is the ever-shifting and many-planed converging point of interminable determinations; and even a 'change' conceived of as a restructuring must be called again and again into question.

Gayatri Chakravorty Spivak, 'Three Feminist Readings: McCullers, Drabble, Habermas,' 15

## A Feminism of Decolonization

This book investigates a series of theoretical articulations among materialist feminism, postmodern neocolonial discourse, and Native women's writing in Canada. I am interested as much in drawing points of convergence among these discontinuous critical practices as in deconstructing their foreclosure into a unified, all-encompassing theory. In feminism, for example, the representation of women, sexual difference, and the gendering of male and female subjectivities constitute major sites of investigation, whereas issues of racism, economic dispossession, cultural autonomy, literacy, and self-determination have been, and continue to be, some of the foremost issues in the contemporary discourses of decolonization. The discontinuous relationship between these critical practices produces a double session of theoretical movement: on the one hand, the need to decolonize feminist epistemology, to challenge its underlying imperial assumptions; and, on the other hand, the need for a feminist critique of the unacknowledged gendered assumptions in postmodern neocolonial discourses. A third position, something I would call *a feminism of decolonization*, I read in the literature produced by a diversity of Native women, which posits a different notion of gender formation within gatherer/hunter societies and in relation to dominant capitalist societies.

Native women's writings currently represent an important site of cultural intervention for examining both the ideological contradictions in dominant social formations as well as the various subjugated modes of resistance and alterity that emerge to combat patriarchal, capitalist, and colonial oppressions. A *feminism of decolonization*, produced upon the articulation of feminist and decolonial critical practices, may provide a critical theory that enables a reading of Native women's writings. However, Native women's writings also confront this theoretical body of knowledge with an alternative ideological ground, with interests which run along a different stream of historical and cultural (dis)continuities not necessarily commensurable with that of a paradigmatic feminism of decolonization. The contradictions and clashes within recent Native women's writing in Canada and in relation to Anglo-American feminist and postcolonial theoretical developments in the human sciences are productive sites of struggle, ones that disclose an ideological positioning of Native women as subjects to and of their own historical making.

This introduction examines the theoretical positions adopted in this particular approach to the articulations of postcolonialist and feminist theories. The sections on postcolonialism and materialist feminism summarize some of the critical questions informing these theoretical practices. Subsequent sections on 'Ethnic Diversity or Internal Colonization?' and 'Literature, Politics, and Representation' focus on the relations between and among culture, politics, and interpretation. In the last section of this introduction, 'Confronting Racism: A "Personal" Polemic,' I have tried to account for how my readings of Native women's issues and experiences have affected my understanding of feminism as a critical practice.

## Postcolonialism

Edward Said's *Orientalism* represents a major text in the formation of postcolonial discourse. In this work Said shows how the 'West' has fabricated its idea of 'the Orient'; and he demonstrates that such a process of fabrication produces a relationship between Orient and Occident that is constitutive of 'power, of domination, of various degrees of a complex hegemony' (5). In recent decades a number of intellectual figures have emerged with cultural and political projects directed towards interpreting complex hegemonic and textual relations between the so-called First and Third Worlds. Along with Said, Homi Bhabha, Abdul JanMohamed, and Gayatri Chakravorty Spivak focus on a critique of the symbolic, figural, and discursive aspects of an imperializing 'Western' epistemology – an epistemology responsible for forging the 'Third Worlding' of countries in Africa, the Middle East, Latin America, and Asia in order to legitimate the continued economic exploitation of these countries. The readership or constituency of this critical discourse is, for the most part, North American and British; and this body of work circulates as a consuming virus, feeding off the ills perpetuated by the epistemic violence (to borrow Spivak's phrase) of imperialism in an effort to heal the dislocation and alienation that has ruptured the ties between a 'homeland' and academic privilege. Taken as a body of knowledge, this critical work maps out the terrain of *postcolonialism*. As a process of changing the oppressive ideological relations between imperial powers and their knowledges, these literary and cultural critics chart a specified course through the exigencies of postcolonization.[1]

The familiar term 'postcolonialism' resonates with other contemporary critical -isms, particularly post-structuralism and the writings of Michel Foucault, Jacques Derrida, Gilles Deleuze, and Felix Guattari. Colonization as a formal political structure is no longer dominant; neocolonialism represents an economic form in which colonization is no longer reducible to its political parameters; but postcolonialism is neither another stage in the developmental logic of colonial history nor part of an evolutionary model signalling the demise of the historical effects of colonialism. Postcolonialism is a contemporary configuration which implies a new direction in the analysis of ideological relations which constitute the 'First World's' symbolic debt to the so-called Third World. Significations of the 'Third World,' since modernism, have served as a vessel of 'otherness,' intrigue, curiosity, and exotica to the depleting resources of a First Worldist subjectivity. Demeaning as well as idealistic representations of the people who occupied the territories imperialized during European empire-building and capitalist expansion in the 'Age of Imperialism' (1880s to 1914) became in themselves a material force, forging in the concrete practices of imperial expansion a modern version of the ideology of civilization. This ideology of civilization, illustrated so well in the American context in Roy Harvey Pearce's seminal book, *Savagism and Civilization: A Study of the*

*Indian and the American Mind*, justified a mission of imperial expansion and colonial controls, so that the ruling nation could set about to dominate indigenous peoples, economically, politically, culturally, religiously, and legally. The subject-position allotted to the indigenous populations by the imperial nations was that of 'colonial other.' Cultural and educational inferiority as well as narrow economic specialization constituted a mode of epistemological enforcement used to maintain domination and exploitation as well as severely damage, if not destroy, indigenous social formations.

The process of decolonization which followed the Second World War dissolved the former British Empire into the Commonwealth of independent states, among other states, and the French Empire into the Communauté française. Although the process of decolonization implied that the metropolitan country paternalistically gave up its political authority over its dependent territories, foreign national intervention and economic controls remained. The term 'neocolonialism' describes the false sense of autonomy the previously dependent colonial territories are said to have achieved. The notion of a Third World sovereignty, as that ideological construct is perpetuated by a First Worldist projection of its own desire for a new world order, a new totality of globalization, contradicts the overdetermined ideological mixings that already exist because of Western First World imperialism; and it is important to emphasize that this ideological mixing and crossing-over constitutes a mode of hybridity which has also become a site of resistance on the part of indigenous peoples to an imperial division of geopolitical space.

Postcolonialism has shifted the critique of colonialism from strictly economic and political determinations to ideological ones. Louis Althusser's conception of ideology is useful to an understanding of the material forces which shape subjectivity in the specific relations to the dominant social formations of late capitalism. As Althusser argues in his essay 'Ideology and Ideological State Apparatuses (Notes towards an Investigation),' 'ideology represents the imaginary relationship of individuals to their real conditions of existence' (162). Its material force appears in the concrete embodiment of what Althusser calls 'ideological State apparatuses': educational, religious, political, legal, trade union, communications, and cultural apparatuses, and the family. The importance of Althusser's re-configuration of ideology lies in its view of revolutionary practice in late-capitalist social formations; it is not enough that structures be overthrown but that a change in ideology must also accompany other structural changes because the ideology of late capitalism is also capable of reproducing the relations of production and positioning individuals as subjects within those relations. In Althusser's terms, the individual-as-subject is interpellated through this process of being and becoming ideologically overdetermined. For a theory of the subject in transformation Althusser turns to the work of Jacques Lacan and the psychoanalytical investigation into the 'split subject,' a subject who lives both 'real' and 'imaginary' relations to the social, a de-centred subject who lives in and through contradictory positions.[2] In the relations between colonizer and colonized, ideology functions in support of economic and political institutions to maintain the relations of domination and exploitation between those subjects positioned as 'colonizer' and 'colonized.'

If, in the previous process of decolonization, the metropolitan country severed its official relationship with the colonized countries, in its most recent transformation that process has become for indigenous people one of 'self-determination,' a mode of decolonization by which the indigenous population reclaims its collective right to the process of achieving autonomy. Along with this shift in the process of 'decolonization,' the subject of investigation has also changed to include not only the duality of colonizer/colonized but an examination of the relations among indigenous peoples.

In *Orientalism* Said outlines the material effects produced by the ideology of the Orient and the Oriental, in which the order of subordination produced between Orient and Occident supported a 'positional superiority'(7) of the West over the East; as a result of its monopolistic control over the discourse on and of the Orient, the following relationship emerged: 'the [Orientalist] writes about, whereas the Oriental is written about. For the latter passivity is the presumed role; for the former, the power to observe, study and so forth' (308). The process of 'othering' which takes place within the colonial epistemic formation of Orientalist knowledge, is not, however, without a certain gender specificity. For Said, I would argue, the construction of a de-centred colonial subject is based largely on Western or European standards of masculinity, masquerading as transparent and universal representations of the colonial experience.

The first chapter of the present work, 'Gender and the Discourses of Orientalism,' examines the gender construction of 'woman' in Edward Said's writings, principally *Orientalism* and *After the Last Sky: Palestinian Lives*. The initial foundation of this critique is a discussion of Said's notion of *exteriority*, a concept which discloses contradictions between Said's use of Michel Foucault's discourse analysis and Said's desire to hold onto some remnants of humanism. It is this residual humanism in Said's analysis of power and knowledge which, in part, opens the way for a feminist critique. The articulations between the social forma-tion of colonialism and women as subjects within this particular social formation are already present in Said's work; however, Said frames the issue of gender construction in terms of sexual difference, thereby assigning particularly phallocentric values and meanings to the figure of Woman. Woman, as an ideological construct and as a living Pales-tinian subject, is rarely, if at all, figured as a maker or unmaker of her own historical representation or, indeed, as an agent of signification.

In order to situate this critique of Said's analysis of Orientalist discourse it is necessary first of all to clarify the feminist position from which that critique emerges.

## Materialist Feminism

The feminist position taken up in this book draws on a variety of other critical positions, such as marxism[3] and post-structuralism. The phrase 'materialist feminism' has, in some respects, come to signal this com-plex combination of critical discourses. However, the history of the contemporary Anglo-American feminist movement, its critical practice and theoretical development in the human sciences, cannot be reduced to a single, continuous metanarrative. Even to describe the cultural politics of feminism as a heterogeneous play of forces produces a totalizing representation of feminist practice; an incorporated diversity of autonomous positions, including, for example, liberal-democratic, radical-separatist, and materialist socialist, which masks 'difference' behind an impenetrable shield of metaphysical equalities. While the boundaries or limits among, within, various feminist critical practices may remain irreducibly fluid, mobile, and historically constituted, the positing of a unified feminist collectivity constructed on the metaphys-ics of 'plurality' can do little more than reinscribe the anxiety of the bourgeois individual. The imperial sovereignty of the Lone Ranger as intellectual superhero is re-established.[4] The consensual feminist man-date, 'the personal is political,' has, at times, lead to a 'self-centring' of the subject-as-intellectual. When such forms of individualism become disguised as a pluralism of differences, 'the generalizable result' writes Gayatri Chakravorty Spivak, is, 'lack of any conceivable interest in a collective practice toward social justice' (48). From this same essay, 'Revolutions That As Yet Have No Model: Derrida's *Limited Inc*,' Spivak outlines the possibility of a deconstructive theoretical practice 'that would fix its glance upon the itinerary of the ethico-political in authoritarian fictions; call into question the complacent apathy of self-centralization; undermine the bigoted elitism (theoretical or practical) conversely possible in collective practice; while disclosing in such gestures the condition of possibility of the positive' (49).

A deconstructive methodology not only enables this critical investigation but as a way of reading informs the process of situating feminism and marxism *deconstructively*; as Gerald MacLean further explains this relationship in 'Citing the Subject,' this involves 'privileging neither term, but seeking rather to make possible their mutual, though discontinuous, articulation' (144). A feminist marxist critical strategy seeks to create resistance: resistance to the hegemonic interests of state and capital, and to their discriminatory mechanisms of control and oppressive modes of regulation in the forms of (hetero) sexism,[5] racism, colonialism, and class exploitation; resistance to the dominant institutional structures of a late-capitalist and phallocentric social formation which maintains a privileged elitism. Feminist practice in the United States and Britain has recently included a new stance on the feminist/marxist articulation, deploying the denomination 'materialist feminism' as its innovative critical lever. Judith Newton and Deborah Rosenfelt's introductory essay to their edited collection *Feminist Criticism and Social Change: Sex, Class and Race in Literature and Culture* addresses some of the philosophical and critical bases of this position. Their approach to historical interpretation is a useful introduction to feminist critical practice. Newton and Rosenfelt argue that the essays in their collection

interpret history not as an assortment of facts in a linear arrangement, not as a static tale of the unrelieved oppression of women or of their unalleviated triumphs, but as a process of transformation. They read the act or artifact of cultural production as an intervention in that process – usually with contradictory implications of its own. This dialectical approach enables us to view ideological struggle and social change as possible, for through it we may examine and understand the tensions and contradictions within both ideology and society. (xxiii)

As Newton and Rosenfelt outline the materialist feminist approach to history, questions concerning the interpretation or reading of history are foremost. The assumption of what constitutes 'history' and the textual implications of the practice of historiography have recently been called into question by cultural critics such as Dominick LaCapra

and Gayatri Chakravorty Spivak. Historiography as a radical alternative to the logocentrism of history ('an assortment of facts in a linear
arrangement') deals with a series of related concerns: the ethico-political or ideological implications of textual practices; the relationship
between subjectivity and textuality; and the representation of socio-
symbolic contexts derived through textual production. Newton and
Rosenfelt, however, take a different position on 'textuality' as a privileged materialist site of struggle: 'Materialist-feminist criticism ... while
acknowledging the importance of language as a site of political activity, is sceptical of the isolation of language and ideas from other realms
of struggle' (xxi). The separation between language and 'other realms
of struggle,' between language and a world 'outside,' presupposes, to
paraphrase Christopher Norris in the context of his discussion of
Jacques Derrida, a naïve or pre-critical idea of reference which makes
possible just such an idealist conception of the isolation of language
from 'the real,' thereby producing a fetishized notion of both the 'text'
and 'reality.'[6] Historiography's engagement with contemporary critical
thought in the disciplines of literary criticism and philosophy is largely
based on their debates with, and their appropriations and applications
of, Derrida's deconstructive philosophy. In order to avoid the establishment of materialist feminism as yet another choice in the marketability of feminist practices, in order to avoid adding a new check-out
counter in the supra-marketability of subjectivities, feminism must
question its own metaphysical presuppositions. This involves a
rigorous critique of textuality as a material practice to which feminist
practices are also ideologically accountable. A deconstructive methodology at least makes this mode of critique possible. The encoding of
an anti-post-structural investigation into language by Newton and
Rosenfelt is in danger of furthering the production of yet another
authorial fiction, another discourse refusing to acknowledge its own
specific relationship to the production of meanings and values, in
short, truth.

Newton and Rosenfelt's position on marxism raises a second problem concerning the ideological agenda of their materialist feminism:
'Materialist-feminist criticism differs from most Marxist criticism in
emphasizing difference between women and men and in foreground-
ing the extent to which cultural discourse is gender-specific' (xxv). The
antagonistic relations between feminism and marxism have been well
documented by Heidi Hartmann in her influential essay 'The Unhappy
Marriage of Marxism and Feminism: Towards a More Progressive
Union.'[7] In response to the privileging of class, feminism argues for

the equal importance of gender as a determination in the relations and forces of production. An emphasis on the issue of gender alone in feminism, however, as Hartmann notes, 'is inadequate because it has been blind to history and insufficiently materialist' (2). Although materialist feminism attempts to correct these problems, its position on materialism also remains insufficiently theorized, particularly in relation to the study of ideology in discursive and textual practices.

In 'Architecture and the Critique of Ideology' Fredric Jameson criticizes the current use of the term *materialism* as a facile and dishonest reconciliation of the tensions between feminism and marxism. He writes that 'the slogan also seems to be extraordinarily misleading as a synonym for "historical materialism" itself, since the very concept of "materialism" is a bourgeois Enlightenment (later positivist) one and fatally conveys the impression of a "determination of the body" rather than, as a genuine dialectical Marxism, a "determination by the mode of production"' (42). In distinguishing between materialist feminism and 'socialist feminism,' Newton and Rosenfelt write: 'We do so because the former term is more inclusive and because it reminds us that materialist analysis appears, however unevenly, in the work of many feminist critics who do not consider themselves socialists (especially in the United States where Marxism and socialism are so marginalized and negatively viewed by the culture as a whole)' (xviii). The 'materialist analysis' that appears in the work of many feminist critics, to which Newton and Rosenfelt refer, is, as Jameson anticipates, centred on questions of sexuality and the body. Jameson is right to be concerned about a positivist emphasis on 'the body' in many analyses of women's sexuality; however, his dismissal of the possibility of an analysis of the body which takes into account how sexuality is organized and how gender divisions are set in competing and conflicting relations within different modes of production, only serves to perpetuate a needless, if not unproductive, tension between feminism and marxism. It is also the case that Newton and Rosenfelt's notion of materialist feminism does not provide an adequate theoretical model for dealing with this problem. For Newton and Rosenfelt the notion of class would appear to mean little more than an economic category in terms of which women can be identified as working-class or middle-class. That the notion of class must be apprehended relationally is central to marxism. It is important, then, to view the antagonistic relations between dominant and labouring classes, between those who control the means of their production and those who do not, in terms of their dialectical relationship. On the one hand, to separate out classes and the women who occupy those classes represses the inevitable antagonistic relations between working-class and bourgeois women. On the other hand, to represent the struggle over ideology between the principal dichotomous classes as gender-neutral, and hence masculinized, masks the mutual complicity of working-class and bourgeois men in phallocracy and the domination of women.

Two further problems arise in the position Newton and Rosenfelt take on marxism and socialism: (1) If a materialist-feminist approach is to remain true to the mandate that all the social categories of race, class, colonialism, sexual identity, and gender are critical terms in the investigation of a First Worldist, Western, patriarchal, white, late-capitalist social formation, then privileging gender over these other categories will miss the complexities of how these modes of social relations interconnect with one another. Feminists such as Gloria Anzaldúa, Teresa de Lauretis, bell hooks (Gloria Watkins), Audre Lorde, Lee Maracle, Barbara Smith, Dorothy Smith, and many more have challenged feminism to confront its own 'race-blindness' so as to develop a theoretical practice which can articulate the complexity of race and gender in social relations. However much marxism has been incapable of de-privileging its own gender bias, to abandon the marxist critical narrative *a priori* is to ignore a useful critical discourse for analysing the specificity of class, race and gender in the relations of production. (2) The parenthetical comment in the above quotation reveals perhaps the main reason for Newton and Rosenfelt's 'anti-marxism': the interdiction against marxism in America is so forceful as to become an acceptable justification for dismissing its critical value.[8] Should not this censoring of marxism indicate precisely an important site of ideological struggle to be addressed rather than ignored?

The notion of a materialist feminism need not conflate the tensions between marxism and feminism; however, as it now stands in its particularly Americanist version, materialist feminism merely profits from liberal feminist arguments about the necessary 'plurality' of social relations and a heterogeneity of critical positions. Without an analysis of gender and race in relation to class, materialist feminism can do little more than deliver up a set of determined choices or subject-positions which will inevitably cohere under the paradigm of a gyno-centric feminism. The spectrum of choice in feminist positions circumscribes a set of definitive relations; even as Newton and Rosenfelt are at pains to define the parameters of materialist feminism, it is an already presumed critical paradigm with no history of its own: 'Materialist-feminist criticism differs from ...' In spite of these criticisms, the term, 'materialist feminism' remains useful, although feminism's grounding in a materialist analysis can only be adequately theorized in relation to class as a constitutive product of productive and repro- ductive relations, which would include gender and race analyses. Under late capitalism, ideology critique, discourse analysis, and the relationship between these and subjectivity are necessary to this mode of analysis.

The failure of feminism to inscribe its historical significance through a totalizing 'master' narrative for socio-economic transformation, which would subsume the diversity of 'women's experiences' in its regional and cross-global contexts into its constituency, has become a produc- tive as well as debilitating force for feminist critical practice. The desire on the part of feminist practice to obtain 'redemption,'[9] in the form of an ideal liberating force, continues to fuel, in part, its critical stance, at the expense, however, of levelling the antagonisms and contradictions among women. Liberal feminism is concerned with emphasizing the plurality of experience and the differences in class and race that inform critical practice: the once neutral face of the humanist subject, exposed as a unity constructed on white male privi- lege, has been transformed into a multiplicity of humanist subjectivi- ties. The struggle for equal rights which characterized the first wave of liberal feminism has, as Julia Kristeva noted in her essay "Women's Time," given way to a second phase based on a radicalizing of sexual difference. The emphasis on difference, which came to include not only sexual but also race and class difference, has not, however, dis- pelled the liberal ideology of feminism; it has, if anything, fetishized a conception of 'difference' as a plurality of rights, all separate and autonomous in their interests, yet united, on the basis of gender.

The critique of humanist subjectivity in post-structuralism has also been enlisted in support of liberal feminism. In Chris Weedon's *Femi- nist Practice and Poststructural Theory*, for example, the heterogeneity of subjectivity is viewed as a site for struggle, a battlefield of contesting and competing voices in the social text (124). This analysis, however, is unable to retain an understanding of the contradictions which emerge in the relations between and among dichotomous antagonisms, such as those between the working and bourgeois classes, between women and men, between 'white' and 'black,' engaged in a constant process of ideological struggle and transformation. In attempting to produce a coherent narrative of a post-structural feminism, Weedon also reduces the tensions and contradictions between these articula- tions.[10]

While liberal feminism has sought to bring about *alignments* between various politico-cultural struggles, many people involved in those struggles argue that autonomy must come first, before any real dialogue can emerge. In her introduction to *Home Girls: A Black Feminist Anthology* Barbara Smith makes this point in response to the antagonism that emerged between many sympathetic leftist and feminist groups and the African-American women's movement during the 1970s. She argues for the important distinction between an autonomous and separatist politics of difference:

... separatism as a strategy often takes a 'to hell with it' stance as opposed to a directly confrontational one. Instead of working to challenge the system and to transform it, many separatists wash their hands of it and the system continues on its merry way ... Autonomy and separatism are fundamentally different. Whereas autonomy comes from a position of strength, separatism comes from a position of fear. When we're truly autonomous we can deal with other kinds of people, a multiplicity of issues, and with difference, because we have formed a solid base of strength with those with whom we share identity and\or political commitment. (xl–xli)

Smith's analysis suggests that 'autonomy' is a necessary move in the political struggles of liberal democracy. However, this strategic pause in the violence of radical autonomy with a view to working with other political struggles in the future still retains the utopianism of a liberal nostalgia for a solid and coherent identity. Smith's analysis poses a major area of struggle within contemporary feminist practice: the conflict between establishing autonomous difference, on the one hand, and the desire, on the other, for an identity which surpasses the neutral face of a humanist ideology of subjectivity.

The de-centring of subjectivity, the breakdown of a coherent and unified subject, has given way to a notion of subjective heterogeneity from which subjects may be reconstituted in a process of alignment, articulated through a process of negotiating and constructing autonomous differences. The subject in negotiation is the subject in contradiction, centring and de-centring its identity and difference in order to substantiate a place and position within the dominant social formation. This process, which for Julia Kristeva in *Desire in Language* is the subject-in-process [*sujet en procès*] (135), can be found in those cultural productions when moments of excess or subversion disclose ideological sites of struggle.

The realm of possible subject-positions, determined by the separate classifications of race, class, sexual identity, gender, and colonialism, realign in a multiplicity of ways. The political significance of heterogeneous subjectivity is located in the alignments made between or among subjects hitherto disconnected and hierarchically separated by the totalizing logic of humanism; in its utopian expression, then, society is transformed by negotiating a non-hierarchical alignment of differences. The problem with this position is the autonomy permitted individual differences. The relations between or among differences, the contradictions and clashes at work in the production of difference, are effaced, and subjectivity is no longer theorizable in terms of contradiction but as a series of substitutable fragments or individuated units.

Gayatri Chakravorty Spivak, in her *In Other Worlds: Essays in Cultural Politics* and other essays, examines the relations between feminism and marxism with a deconstructive methodology. Her work provides a complex mapping of these critical positions onto the terrain of postmodern neocolonialism. Spivak's work raises the general problematic of what it means to be a 'Third World Woman' writing within the United States. This contradictory configuration, which Spivak herself reminds her readership of, can serve as a useful 'representation' for interpreting the postcolonial position of Native women. Spivak's work speaks to the situation of indigenous people in Canada, who are also 'other-ed' as 'Third World' figures within the dominant social formation. The historical and material specificities of those contradictions are, however, very different. Spivak's work is useful; but to appropriate her theoretical terrain wholesale does an injustice to her own work on East Indian women writers and the history of colonialism and neocolonialism in an Indian nation-state. To expect her work to grapple fully with the contradictions of neocolonialism in Canada also occludes the specific history of Canadian colonialism. Nevertheless, her work is important in the context of this study of gender formation within the postmodern discourses of neocolonialism for elaborating the articulations of indigenous cultural practices in Canada, post-structural theory, and feminist criticism.

While Said overturns the East/West duality in *Orientalism*, Spivak directs her critical practice towards the 'Third Worlding' of the Indian subcontinent by European and Anglo-American epistemologies. Both postcolonialist theorists – Spivak, through her translations and interpretations of the fiction writer Mahasweta Devi, and Said, through his discussion of Palestinian films, writings, and artistic productions in *After the Last Sky* – deconstruct the imperial signifieds of an elite formation of knowledge by reading these various cultural productions as interventionary forces which contest and destabilize the metaphysical assumptions of that knowledge. Unlike Said, Spivak examines the metaphorical displacement of the woman's body in the construction of sexual difference within the imperial, discursive assemblages of the West. Similarly, Chandra Talpade Mohanty notes the pervasive use of the ideology of sexual difference as an underlying assumption and organizing principle in the reception and construction of a Third World feminism.

Chapter 2 of this book, 'Engendering Textual Violence,' examines work that has been done in the fields of feminism and the critique of colonialism. Negotiating contextual and textual differences between the geopolitical, cultural, and social domains of the 'West' and 'East' has become the recent focus of feminist and postcolonial theorists such as Teresa de Lauretis, Chandra Talpade Mohanty, Nawal el Saadawi and Gayatri Chakravorty Spivak. Chapter 2 traces the theoretical trajectories of de Lauretis and Spivak and the emergence of a feminism of decolonization through a reading of Nawal el Saadawi's writings on Arab women. El Saadawi's work occupies a unique place in cross-cultural feminist work, mostly because she has staged an intervention into the elitist assumptions of First Worldist feminism. Her critical practice has become doubly directed, both towards the Egyptian state and its collusion with the medical profession in supporting the practices of female circumcision and towards a critique of the Third Worlding assumptions of European and North American feminist criticism. El Saadawi argues that European and American feminisms contribute to the ideological fabrication of Arab countries as 'uncivilized' when the practices of clitoridectomy and infibulation are decontextualized from a historical and politically informed analysis. Furthermore, by concentrating on the question of clitoridectomy and infibulation, First World feminist debate across the First/Third World axis continues to reproduce the ideology of sexual difference. One of the effects of this focus has been to unify many Arab women, from different class positions, within a system of exclusively sexual exploitation.

The first two chapters of this book represent studies in the general problematics of feminism and postcolonial criticism through the writings of several key figures. The work of de Lauretis, el Saadawi, Mohanty, Spivak, and Said are clearly directed towards an understanding of the Third Worlding of subjects within the discourse of the so-called 'West.' What happens, however, when we turn our gaze towards the Third Worlding of subjects within the already existing geopolitical borders of the 'West'? Part 2, 'Native Women and Anglo-

American Feminism,' addresses the situation of Native peoples within Canada, a situation which is not too far off the Third World map, although the geographic configuration of Canada, its proximity to the United States, and its own well-developed capitalist economic base might suggest otherwise. Internal colonialism, however, exists in Canada, and an analysis of subject formation and North American discourse on Native peoples has much to find useful in postcolonial critique. Such an analysis both challenges the limits of a First World discourse on 'the Third World,' which is one way of saying that First World discourse should come home to meet its more local forms of 'othering,' and suggests further the necessity of a critical approach to the issues of colonialism as those issues are specifically tied to Canada and the United States.

### Ethnic Diversity or Internal Colonization?

The situation of Canada's indigenous peoples differs both geopolitical-ly and ideologically from that of the indigenous peoples of the so-called Third World. Although postcolonial theory is relevant to under-standing the relations of cultural imperialism between dominant En-glish-/French-Canadian society and Native peoples' self-determination to achieve a land base and self-government, it is not always represen-tative of the conflicts which currently exist in this specific historical formation of colonialism. Unlike 'Third World' countries Native people living within the geopolitical designation known as Canada do not occupy this country as an inscription of their band territories, although those territories have never ceased to exist for Native history. The official cartographic imagination of Canada does not recognize the same inscriptions of the earth which a Native conceptual epistemology does. Reserves (a state-imposed containment of land mass for Native peoples) are not the same thing as self-determined band territories. All of which is to say, without the recognition of Native entitlement to the land, including self-government, Native peoples do not have a place or space to return to in the event of cultural, spiritual, and social genocide. 'The vanishing race' proclaimed by Edward S. Curtis's photograph of the same name carries a double burden of meaning: the projection of a genocidal wish-fullfilment on the part of the colonial culture and a projected outcome of real effects based on continuing state policies of assimilation. The term 'internal colonialism' has been used to express this particular effect of imperial domination whereby indigenous First Nations have been systematically pushed to the oceanic frontiers of the Canadian imaginary to the point of a virtual denial of their existence except as self-serving symbols in the Canadian-history enterprise. Current sea-changes in postcolonial critical thinking are engaged in resuscitating for the all too typical Canadian 'identity crisis' an at least provisionally identifiable history in the struggle of Native peoples living and coping with five hundred years of British, French, American, English- and French-Canadian cultural imperialism.

Two concepts generally used in the literatures of the human sciences to represent the situation of Native peoples in Canada are ethnicity and internal colonialism.[11] Peter Kulchyski criticizes the 'ethnicity' approach for, among other things, assimilating Native people into another colourful fragment of Canada's multicultural fabric, thereby reducing the historical specificity of Native peoples' claims to original occupancy of the land. The result: 'Native culture becomes reduced to the status of closet costumes, brought out to impress tourists and severed from any meaningful lived experience' ('Towards a Theory of Dispossession,' 251). Unlike the term 'ethnicity,' 'internal colonialism' has the advantage of signalling the historically particular situation of Native peoples. However, writers such as J. Rick Ponting and James Frideres, according to Kulchyski, equate Native peoples in relation to colonialism with other colonized groups in Canada, namely the Québécois. This equation is produced on the basis of an economic approach and a proto-class analysis. Menno Boldt and J. Anthony Long, in *Pathways to Self-Determination*, take a different approach to the concept of internal colonialism, arguing, along with Leroy Little Bear, that the notion of internal colonialism is paradigmatically a political issue: '... this paradigm can best be described as internal colonialism, whereby the greater part of Canada's Indians have been given separate legal status by virtue of an Indian Act, have been subject to special legislative programs, and have been settled on specific land areas known as reserves' (70). The major difficulty with both the ethnic and internal colonial approaches, Kulchyski concludes, is that neither can account sufficiently for the continuing marginalization of Native peoples and what constitutes the specificity of their 'cultural difference' (276–7). Kulchyski argues that an analysis of the relations between the state and Native peoples provides a better understanding of what he calls, after Jean-Paul Sartre, their 'dispossession' produced by the state's totalizing powers. In struggle with the state Native peoples have produced alternative subject-positions based on what has come to be called a gatherer/hunter social formation. Kulchyski views Native people in a dynamic of negotiating their subject-position as gatherer/ hunters with the state.

The entry of Native storytelling into print culture, in particular during the last twenty years, is part of this process of negotiation in which Native artists and writers are demanding the incorporation of Native cultural productions into industrial media, which also include film. Such demands and subsequent actions exemplify the notion of hybridity so much in use in current cultural criticism. But this form of hybrid – integrative knowledge – is not merely part of the utopian projection of an unprecedented overlay of 'traditions' as James Clifford would have it; it is a struggle to overcome the violence of epistemological enforcement that has ignored, yet 'freely' appropriated, the cultural contributions of those people whose history and culture have been relegated to a wasteland of stereotypical by-products. As Homi Bhabha writes in his essay 'DissemiNation: Time, Narrative, and the Margins of the Modern Nation,' 'hybridity is the perplexity of the living as it interrupts the representation of the fullness of life; it is an instance of iteration, in the minority discourse, of the time of the arbitrary sign ... through which all forms of cultural meaning are open to translation because their enunciation resists totalization' (314). It is this resistance to totalization that can be read in the discursive praxis of Native literatures.

### Literature, Politics, and Representation

The use of the label 'Native Women' or 'Indian Women' writers contains, on the one hand, a political and historical inscription of subjectivity that delimits 'authenticity' and, on the other hand, delimits a cultural politics of autonomy in which Native women writers engage in a critique of dominant ideological representations of 'the' Native Woman, remaking subjectivity through the very act of writing. Native women's literature can be read, then, for a critique of sexism, racism, colonialism, and economic exploitation as well as for its mark of cultural, and not essential, differences. It is in reading such literature that feminist scholarship has the most to learn about the complexity and difficulties involved in addressing the political demands to reformulate a critical methodology that does not circumscribe cultural autonomy within a liberal pluralist program of so-called 'diversity' disguising 'choices' or categories with which to facilitate assimilation. Nor is it possible to produce an interpretation of an absolute figure of Native cultural autonomy. The feminist critic must read for the contradictions and clashes that emerge in clearing a subject space from which to speak (and write) and must read against the grain of representations engendered in the textual violence of colonial discourse.

Chapter 3, '(De)constructing Affinities,' contains a discussion of some of the issues and debates with which Native women have confronted feminism in Canada during the 1980s. I have focused in this chapter on a series of conferences in which Native women intervened, established their autonomy, and clarified the diversity of experiences, concerns, and issues, not only in relation to feminism, but, more importantly, in relation to each other. In an effort to understand the differences between the struggles of Native women and those of Anglo-Canadian feminists, this chapter also traces the historical effects of the Indian Act on Native women, which have been well documented by Kathleen Jamieson, and the passing of Bill C-31 in 1985, designed to eliminate those sections of the Indian Act which discriminated against Native women. A tracing of the specific historical struggle on the part of Native women to resist imperial patriarchy will make clear, I hope, their need also to resist the totalizing tendencies of feminist theories and practices, and provide a better understanding as to why feminists must seek new possibilities for respecting the autonomy of Native women's issues while still learning from their struggle how to braid their respective differences in such a way that all can benefit from each other's mutual support. It is from this contemporary context of Native women's struggle that chapter 4 rereads Native women's subject-positioning in an archival document.

Central to the analysis in chapter 4 is Gayatri Chakravorty Spivak's notion of 'epistemic violence,' developed in her essay 'Subaltern Studies: Deconstructing Historiography' and used to refer, in part, to the discursive violence committed by First Worldist dominant discursive formations in the images, stereotypes, and representations of the 'subaltern' or indigenous woman. In this chapter, entitled '"A Gift for Languages": Native Women and the Textual Economy of the Colonial Archive,' I have taken a well-known Canadian archival document and read it against the grain of current historical and sociological readings in order to demonstrate the ways in which those readings have produced a particularly circumscribed representation of Native women's subjectivity. By rereading the historical archive with attention to its aberrant textual moments, it is possible to produce readings of Native women's subjectivity in colonial texts that construct the figure of 'Native Woman' as neither an idealized victor in the face of irrevocable oppression nor as a passive victim of some inevitable force of exploitation, as Newton and Rosenfelt suggest, but as a contradictory subject involved in alternative strategies of resistance.

Barbara Harlow's *Resistance Literature* is a useful study for any attempt to correct the textual violence in literary interpretation, especially that of American New Criticism. Harlow demonstrates that the political affectivity of cultural production is a constitutive part of the network of forces that comprise resistance movements to colonial and neocolonial practices in Africa, the Middle East, and South America. Political events inform the production of resistance narratives, poetry, and testimonials, written by men and women of the geopolitical colonial designation known as the 'Third World,' often living in exile, under occupation, or in prison. This writing 'calls attention to itself, and to literature in general, as a political and politicized activity' (28). The 'literary' text, then, is not a supplement to political events but a constitutive element in the political process. Unfortunately, Harlow does not question the concept of 'literature,' a keyword in the ideology of cultural hegemony. Although she may be using the term in order to overturn an elitist First Worlding of texts, the reversal still begs the question: what does not come under this category in Harlow's estimation? The term need not be delimited by a bourgeois or hegemonic ideology; nor, however, can its use be taken for granted, as Michel Foucault has made clear in *The Order of Things* where he examines the relatively recent use of the term 'literature' in the nineteenth-century French tradition as a bourgeois phenomenon that sought to ensure ontological closure (300).

Harlow's study raises the theoretical problematic of Anglo-American literary criticism's interpretation of the texts of decolonization. Harlow's study can be read as a critique of the American school of New Criticism and its exclusive principles of the formalist ideal of the poem as self-enclosed 'verbal icon,' exemplified by such well-known studies as W.K. Wimsatt's, *The Verbal Icon: Studies in the Meaning of Poetry*. Extrinsic sources, such as political events, historical contexts, social and economic factors, are dismissed by New Critics as irrelevant to the interpretation of 'literature.' Harlow's notion of 'resistance literature' would appear to challenge the New Critical blindness to extraneous historical processes by insisting that knowledge of colonial and neocolonial political and economic events is necessary to read or interpret politicized fiction. This critical intervention responds, in part, to what Spivak calls in 'Subaltern Studies' the 'sanctioned ignorance' of the history of imperialism exhibited by 'Western' intellectuals, even those who 'express genuine concern about the ravages of contemporary neocolonialism in their own nation-states' (209). As a corrective to New Critical principles of exclusion, which reproduce sanctioned ignorance, Harlow's generic formulation of 'resistance literature' and her close attention to political themes make important interventions. The representation of writings of decolonization as 'resistance literature,' which 'calls attention to itself, and *to literature in general*, as a political and politicized activity' (emphasis added), can also be read as an implicit call to recognize that 'literatures' written within North America are also ideological and political.

In reading Harlow's text as a call to decolonize Anglo-American epistemology, the limits can be traced in the reformulation of Anglo-American criticism to meet the political demands to interpret colonial and neocolonial writings within North America. Harlow's study remains symptomatic of this reformation. Her study provides a critical point of departure for questioning the representation and containment of 'Third World' texts within 'First World' traditions of interpretation. All modes of textual production are, to some extent, intertextual in that they dialogue with dominant discourses through a variety of strategies: subversive, parodic, polemic, and otherwise. Harlow's study, however, suggests the possibility of autonomous readings of this literature disconnected from the relations of power and knowledge between the Third and First Worlds. The idealism of an Archimedean point which allows the critic to stand back and observe from the outside is implied by the presupposition of autonomous readings.

As an intervention into New Critical principles of exclusion, 'resistance literature' figures as a generic trope, masquerading as a new-found site of truth which will redeem the 'West' from its desires for epistemological conquest. This new literary paradigm functions, in Harlow's study, as an object of resistance to exclusions and silences within Western canon formation. On the one hand, writings of resistance lay claim to a political authenticity that works to correct 'the exploitation of knowledge by the interests of power to create a distorted historical record' (116); on the other hand, this writing occupies a contentious space within geopolitical and cultural borders containing injunctions, demands, and interests discontinuous from power and knowledge relations within North America. The opposition between Western and non-Western knowledge and power masks a system of valuation; the 'distorted truth' of official histories, however much they are corrected through a critique of their politics of representation, is still endowed initially with a privileged narrative of 'truth' over the historical 'fictions' produced by resistance writings. Resistance literature, then, is valued as a corrective to the distorted truth of the 'West,' in order to bring about the 'truth' of the West. To fulfil this function, the narrative of truth in resistance literature must be represented as unambiguously and reducibly transparent.

The problems in Harlow's study, the way in which her opposition between 'West' and 'East,' for example, deconstructs to disclose the intertextual relations between the United States as a dominant imperial power since the Second World War and those countries affected by its imperialism – from which Harlow derives her literary sources – make her work useful to an analysis of Native women's writing within Canada.

Part 3, 'The Cultural Politics of Representation,' contains two chapters which analyse several Native women's texts, including Okanogan, Métis, and Inuit writers. Chapter 5, 'History Lies in Fiction's Making and Unmaking,' focuses on Jeannette Armstrong's *Slash*, its theme of Native politics in the 1960s, and the inscription of a Native political subjectivity through textual strategies which incorporate Native oral traditions. Chapter 6, 'Occupied Space: Métis and Inuit writings and Feminist Critique,' discusses aspects of Maria Campbell's *Halfbreed*, Beatrice Culleton's *In Search of April Raintree*, and Minnie Aodla Freeman's *Life among the Qallunaat*. While the figure of the Métis poses a challenge to the delimitations of 'difference' and indeed stands at the threshold of difference between the critical morphologies of poststructural theory and indigenous practices of self-determination, Minnie Aodla Freeman's Inuit feminist anthropological study of colonial culture challenges the figure of the ab/original in feminist theory. These two theoretical problematics are elaborated through readings of a selection of essays by Elaine Showalter, Teresa de Lauretis, Julia Kristeva, and Jacques Derrida.

### Confronting Racism: A 'Personal' Polemic

Don't look at me with guilt   Don't apologize   Don't struggle with the problem of racism like algebra
Don't write a paper on it for me to read or hold a meeting in which you discuss what to do to get us to come to your
time & your place
We're not your problems to understand & trivialize
We don't line up in your filing cabinets under 'R' for rights
Don't make the racist assumption that the issue of racism
between us

is yours     at me
Bitter boiling I can't see you

Chrystos, from 'Maybe We Shouldn't Meet If There Are No Third
World Women Here'

To ignore the recent proliferation and emergence of the literature of
the 'dispossessed' is to deny a vital history of our times. In the context
of 'making sense' of our times, of bringing about greater understanding and awareness of the gendered and race-oriented meanings and
values attributed to aesthetic production, writings by Native women
stand at a significant place in cultural history. There were many times
when I doubted the possibility and validity of this project, a sense of
its impossibility that led me to the following reflection: a historical
figuration of a white middle-class liberal-humanist feminist subjectivity
formed and deformed by the history of a racist and elitist colonialist
socialization. It would seem all too obvious that racism constitutes the
very metaphorical and conceptual apparatus on which feminist knowledge turns. If we take this position as a point of departure, the inscription of a critical consciousness resisting that learned racism – to unlearn the hatred, contempt, fear, superiority, and other poisons that
racism injects into our emotional and intellectual well-being – would
awaken an understanding that the forces of socio-symbolic regulation
imposed on what we receive to be 'human' are ironically, terribly, and
tragically, 'inhuman.' However benevolent or well-intentioned this
rhetorical gesture may be, the humanization of 'inhumanity' can lead
to all sorts of perverse forms of colonial legitimacy. Advertisements for
the Foster Parents Plan of Canada in *Maclean's* magazine (see, for
example, the issues of 2 January 1989, page 49, and 16 January 1989,
page 11) work on the basis of producing 'inhumanity' in their Third
Worlding of countries in order to produce a new order of humanity
for those who would become the Foster Parents Plan of Canada's First
World participants and supporters. If women are human beings inasmuch as they are *like* men, and Native women are human beings
inasmuch as they are *like* white women, then whether it is possible to
revitalize the metaphor of 'humanity' as a critical term becomes ques-
tionable. What this problematic traces, I think, is the limit of the decolonization of feminism as the colonizer's redemptive dream of self-
criticism and self-correction.

Racism is as much an institutional and discursive form of social
violence as it is an individual concern. When Valerie Amos and

Pratibha Parmar write in 'Challenging Imperial Feminism' that 'feminist theories which examine our cultural practices as "feudal residues" or label us "traditional," also portray us as politically immature women who need to be versed and schooled in the ethos of Western Feminism'(7), they are challenging the 'white chauvanism' (8) inscribed in Western feminist institutions and textual practices. To adopt an anti-racist position is not only a matter of advocating a liberal ideal of the moral wrongness of racism, it also, and perhaps more importantly, means taking a political position from which to argue that Native women's writings constitute a significant thread in the weaving and unweaving of our worlds.

A historical materialist theory of language is one that must read in the fabric of textuality a violent collision of sign systems symptomatic of the contradictory values constitutive to competing and conflicting relations between gatherer/hunter and capitalist modes of production. A materialist feminist deconstructive reading of gender, then, will examine the contradictions among various women's struggles for how they inform a theoretical understanding of oppositional productivities, and, under a capitalist mode of production in particular, the hierarchical constitution of power relations between men and women and among women themselves. That such a system of hierarchical values does not exist for gatherer/hunter societies provides, I would suggest, a different cognitive mapping of gender relations from which feminists might retrace the meaning of women's trans-global movements for social change as we continue to resist the reality of imperial oppressions in an increasingly dominant late-capitalist social and economic 'new world' order.

PART ONE

A FEMINIST/NEOCOLONIAL ENCOUNTER

# 1 Gender and the Discourses of Orientalism

... her picture seems like a map pulling us all together even down to her hair net, her ribbed sweater, the unattractive glasses, the balanced smile and strong hand. But all the connections only came to light, so to speak, some time after I had seen the photograph, after we had decided to use it, after I had placed it in sequence. As soon as I recognized Mrs. Farraj, the suggested intimacy of the photograph's surface gave way to an explicitness with few secrets. She is a real person – Palestinian – with a real history at the interior of ours. But I do not know whether the photograph can, or does, say things as they really are. Something has been lost. But the representation is all we have.

Edward W. Said, with photographs by Jean Mohr, *After the Last Sky: Palestinian Lives*, 84

## Disorient(aliz)ing the Reader

Edward Said's text *Orientalism* is a landmark in postcolonial critical theory. Influenced by the work of the French post-structuralist Michel Foucault and his elaboration of the relationship between knowledge, power, and discourse, Said's text sets out to track the discursive manoeuvres of a European 'geographical imagination.' Said not only stakes out the historical and intellectual terrain of Orientalism, the textual and disciplinary circumscription of 'the Orient' as a discursive formation, he also formulates an epistemological ground in support of the Palestinian project of decolonization. Said's commitment to the political project of the Palestinian struggle has emerged in his intellectual work in such books as *After the Last Sky: Palestinian Lives*, with photographs by Jean Mohr, which I will be addressing later in this chapter. The following discussion focuses on some aspects of both Said's contribution to the field of cultural politics in his literary theory and his writing on the Palestinian question. In particular, this chapter explores the possibilities and limitations in Said's work, initially in *Orientalism* and then in *After the Last Sky*, for an articulation between feminist and postcolonialist theories of interpretation. A feminist intervention into Said's work on colonial discourse runs the risk of reclaiming a privileged space, particularly as a 'First Worldist' feminist discursive formation, already situated in an unequal relationship to work done by activists, academics, and cultural workers in the so-called 'Third World.' I am interested, then, not only in a feminist intervention into Said's textual criticism but also in a critique of the limits of a 'First Worldist' construction of Third World women. More often than not, First World feminisms minimize the contribution of a diversity of women addressing their immediate and geopolitically specific situations within the so-called 'East' or 'Third World.'

### The Geography of 'Man'

Before examining the construction of gender in *Orientalism*, it is necessary to consider some aspects of the metaphysical assumptions at work in this text, in particular Said's humanist assumptions about the 'author' as an investigating subject in the discourse of Orientalism. Although Said has made extensive use of Michel Foucault's method of discourse analysis, he qualifies his use of Foucault's work with its trenchant 'anti-humanism' in the following terms: 'unlike Michel Foucault, to whose work I am greatly indebted, I do believe in the determining imprint of individual writers upon the otherwise anonymous collective body of texts constituting a discursive formation like Orientalism' (23). While Said finds discourse analysis a useful methodology for investigating the power which adheres to knowledge constructions, he is unwilling to let go of the figure in which that power is conventionally centred: the author. There are implications in preserving the individual author for Said's own position as an investigating subject in the critique of the discursive formation of Orientalism. In maintaining the 'imprint of individual writers,' Said suggests that a critique of the investigating subject is necessary to the study of Orientalism, and yet his own position as critic and author would seem to be transparent. Such a disinterested stance on the part of the investigating subject contradicts the spirit of Said's project; namely, a rigorous critique of the production of an Orientalist discursive formation, to which he wishes to hold accountable the writer as well as the structural overdeterminations of time and space responsible for producing an Orientalist body of knowledge to begin with.

Said's lack of self-reflexivity in *Orientalism*, his disinterest towards the epistemic violence that informs or deforms postcolonial investigated and investigating subjects, is symptomatic of a residual humanism: a residual humanism which sustains a fully coherent and unified conception of 'self' and 'language,' even as this unitary figure of non-contradiction differs radically from the fragmentary experience of postcolonial subjectivity Said will later articulate in *After the Last Sky: Palestinian Lives*. This residual humanism in *Orientalism* brings to crisis the necessity for a theory of gender constitution in postcolonialist discourse, for the humanist subject is constructed on the assumption that masculinity is the central axis from which all other modes of subjectivity can be determined. As Toril Moi describes traditional humanism in *Sexual/Textual Politics*, it 'is in effect part of patriarchal ideology. At its centre is the seemingly unified self – either individual or collective – which is commonly called man ... this integrated self is in fact a phallic self, constructed on the model of the self-contained, powerful phallus. Gloriously autonomous, it banishes from itself all conflict, contradiction, and ambiguity' (8). Such a position of centrality, although capable of producing sensitivity to the oppression of other men (centrality extended to other centralities), inevitably excludes the play of autonomy and difference among those subjects de-centred from the epistemic relations of power and knowledge, such as women.

Said's use of the concept of exteriority and its relevance to what he calls 'a geographical imagination' is also important to understanding the contradictions of gender specificity in *Orientalism*. Said's working of this concept is applicable to a later discussion in this chapter on the territorialization of women's bodies as a key figure in neocolonialist discourse when that discourse attempts to circumscribe the value and meaning of a 'homeland.' Said sets out some of the underlying assumptions of a geographical imagination in the following passage:

It is perfectly possible to argue that some distinctive objects are made by the mind, and that these objects, while appearing to exist objectively, have only a fictional reality. A group of people living on a few acres of land will set up boundaries between their land and its immediate surroundings and the territory beyond, which they call 'the land of the barbarians.' In other words, this universal practice of designating in one's mind a familiar space which is 'ours' and an unfamiliar space beyond 'ours' which is 'theirs' is a way of making geographical distinctions that *can be* entirely arbitrary. I use the word 'arbitrary' here because imaginative geography of the 'our land – barbarian land' variety does not require that the barbarians acknowledge the distinction. It is enough for 'us' to set up these boundaries in our own minds; 'they' become 'they' accordingly, and both their territory and their mentality are designated as different from 'ours.' (54)

Said's notion of a geographical imagination maps an arbitrary and figurative play of forces that circumscribe, contain, represent, exteriorize, territorialize an area of study, a tradition and disciplinary field known as 'the Orient.' According to Said, 'Orientalism is premised upon exteriority, that is, on the fact that the Orientalist, poet or scholar, makes the Orient speak, describes the Orient, renders its mysteries plain for and to the West' (20–1). And further, Said writes, 'the principal product of this exteriority is of course representation: as early as Aeschylus's play *The Persians* the Orient is transformed from a very far distant and often threatening Otherness into figures that are relatively familiar (in Aeschylus's case, grieving Asiatic women)' (21). The individual author, who shapes the contours of a geographical imagination (although perhaps does not embody that geodetic consciousness) exists, or rather positions 'his' existence, as an 'outsider' beyond the confines of discursive borders.

Said's use of the notion of exteriority leads to a double-edged confusion. There are at least two arguments that can be made. On the one hand, *Orientalism*, as text(s), reproduces the mechanisms of exteriority as a symptomatic response to an originary textual violence that has already constituted 'exteriority' as its principal mode of discursive production; on the other hand, Said's reproduction of the universal mechanisms of exteriority in his representation of the drawing of boundaries of the 'us' and 'them,' the familiar and the unfamiliar, is an ironic critique and parodic re-presentation of the omniscient author who stands over this imaginary terrain, determining its limits and positing a verifiable reality of the Orient. This contradictory tension operates in a text like *Orientalism* where an ideological struggle of symptomatic reproduction and resistance is at work: in order to produce a critique of the literature of Orientalism, Said reads this vast body of material; in order to engage in a critical debate with the disciplinary forefathers of Oriental studies, Said submits himself to their imperial significations; in order to do battle with these books, Said knows his enemies better than they know themselves. This mode of critical writing has as part of its motivation a strategic intervention into the field of Orientalism as well as a subversion of its epistemological assumptions. Said explains his critical approach in the following terms:

My principal methodological devices for studying authority here are what can be called *strategic location*, which is a way of describing the author's position in a text with regard to the Oriental material he writes about, and *strategic formation*, which is a way of analyzing the relationship between texts and the way in which groups of texts, types of texts, even textual genres, acquire mass, density, and referential power among themselves and thereafter in the culture at large. (20)

This sympto-critical mode of analysis embodies a dialectic of negative, regeneration; it reproduces a set of derogatory, negative and demeaning representations of an 'Oriental reality' at the same time as it sets out to expose the hierarchical binary oppositions within which it operates, in order to critique or supplant that 'reality' with alternative possibilities:

My analysis of the Orientalist text ... places emphasis on the evidence, which is by no means invisible, for such representations *as representations*, not as 'natural' depictions of the Orient ... The things to look at are style, figures of speech, setting, narrative devices, historical and social circumstances, *not* the correctness of the representation nor its fidelity to some great original. The exteriority of the representation is always governed by some version of the truism that if the Orient could represent itself, it would; since it cannot, the representation does the job, for the West, and *faute de mieux*, for the poor Orient. (21)

An alternative realm of representation is suggested by Said's study of Orientalism, although it is not formulated, largely because Said does not hold to the possibility of an authentic or faithful representation of the Orient within 'Western' discourse. Said is interested in the way 'texts can *create* not only knowledge but also the very reality they appear to describe' (94): in describing the state of Orientalism after Napoleon, Said writes, '[Orientalism's] descriptive realism was upgraded and became not merely a style of representation but a language, indeed a means of *creation* ... the Orient was reconstructed, reassembled, crafted, in short, *born* out of the Orientalists' efforts' (87, Said's emphasis).

Said's emphatic use of such metaphors as creation and birth suggests that his concept of exteriority is constructed along a particular chain of gender-specific and humanist significations. The (male) author may no longer be the creator of culture, the producer of '"natural" depictions of the Orient,' for example, even though Said wishes to hold to his 'imprint' (i.e., his 'printability'), yet the 'text' has now become a displaced figure of male author/ity, and male author/ship. Now the text can 'create,' give birth as it were, to naturalizing representations.

'It seems a common human failing to prefer the schematic authority of a text to the disorientations of direct encounters with the human' (93). It is this residual humanist element in Said's text, which also implies the exteriority of a reality and subject formation *outside* a 'Western' discursive formation in opposition to the radically internalized textual construction of the Orient within the 'West,' that produces an irreducible contradiction in Said's textual attempt to disorient(alize) the 'Western reader.' When, for example, is an encounter 'direct' or unmediated? It is a contradiction that registers the radical difference and discontinuity produced by the discourse of the 'West' to contain the space of 'the Orient' through its 'radical realism' (72). One of the most amusing examples of an excessive rupture in Said's text that delimits the latent presence of a residual humanism is to be found, appropriately enough, in a scatological reference to the representation of Mohammed in Dante's *Inferno*, of which Said is critical: 'Mohammed's punishment, which is also his eternal fate, is a peculiarly disgusting one: he is endlessly being cleft in two from his chin to his anus like, Dante says, a cask whose staves are ripped apart. Dante's verse at this point spares the reader none of the eschatological [sic] detail that so vivid a punishment entails: Mohammed's entrails and his excrement are described with unflinching accuracy' (68). One wonders, even as we understand the structuring of Oriental discourse that positions the figure of Mohammed in this other, profane way, how Said 'knows' Dante's text to be 'unflinchingly accurate'?

The 'exteriority,' or the 'reality,' of Orientalism is a decidedly masculine gender construction. Said's disinterest in alternative constructions of the Orientalist reality is, in part, a result of the overwhelming male gender specificity of the Orientalist discourse he is investigating. As Said writes, 'Orientalism encouraged a peculiarly ... male conception of the world ... The Oriental male was considered in isolation from the total community in which he lived and which many Orientalists ...

have viewed with something resembling contempt and fear. Orientalism itself, furthermore, was an exclusively male province; like so many
professional guilds during the modern period, it viewed itself and its
subject matter with sexist blinders' (207). However aware Said is of the
patriarchal limits of Orientalist discourse, his own analysis remains
complicitous with the masculine gender specificity of the discourse of
Orientalism, caught within the interior/exterior opposition; an opposition constructed on the silent mediation of another universal gender
construction: the Woman/Body.

## A Feminization of the Orient

Said's residual humanism, based as it is on a male gender-specific
notion of exteriority, reconstructs and maintains the assumptions of
phallic supremacy. In his essay 'Orientalism Reconsidered,' Said claims
that the praxis of Orientalism is not unlike that of male gender dominance or patriarchy in Western societies. Said locates this gender bias
in the metaphors which frame a representation of the Orient 'as feminine, its riches as fertile, its main symbols the sensual woman, the
harem and the despotic – but curiously attractive – ruler.' Said goes on
to say that

much of this material is manifestly connected to the configurations of sexual,
racial and political asymmetry underlying mainstream modern western culture, as illuminated respectively by feminists, by black studies critics and by
anti-imperialist activists. To read, for example, Sandra Gilbert's brilliant recent
study of Rider Haggard's *She* is to perceive the narrow correspondence between suppressed Victorian sexuality at home, its fantasies abroad and the
tightening hold on the nineteenth-century male imagination of imperialist
ideology. (12)

Although Said recognizes that the feminization of the Orient in the
discourse of Orientalism lends itself to a feminist critique, he sets his
own critique of this particular discourse of knowledge and power
apart from those of feminists, African-American critics, and even anti-
imperialist activists. Said's work has done a great deal to carve out the
specificity of a critique of colonial and neocolonial discursive practices.
In *Orientalism* Said locates within the disciplinary formation of knowledge of the Orient a tributary of power which uses representations of
the Orient and the Oriental as an aid to ideological containment.
Whereas Said perceives obvious links between his project and other

modes of intellectual and political resistance, it is in the form of an analogy that the claim to common links among these various threads of resistance is made: lines of struggle would appear to be parallel, but that is also to say they never cross each other's path.

Said views crossing of disciplinary boundaries in the academy as a progressive methodology for dismantling hierarchical assumptions in disciplinary formation; however, I would argue that the analogical method of producing parallel associations between critical concerns is insufficient to interrupt these borders of thought. On the contrary, critical orthodoxies emerge to stake out territories, partition off constituencies, and interpellate the subjects of their constituencies in a struggle for individuating rights based on the legitimation of essential and authentic differences. The socio-symbolic constructions of race, gender, sexuality, class, and colonialism, when deployed as critical tools and wedged between the comfortable conclusions of humanist epistemology, rupture the sort of disciplinary confidence that takes a singular aspect of political struggle to be a sufficient indicator of the climate of global aggressions. Said's cultural critique in *Orientalism* and his critical investigations into a series of problematics in literary theory contained in the essays included in *The World, the Text, and the Critic* lack a self-reflexive awareness on the figural use of women's bodies, the metaphoric and metonymic anatomy which, while being used to represent a universal and hegemonic Woman subject-position, displaces the historical and material specificity of women, such as those living in Arab countries. In his more recent text, *After the Last Sky: Palestinian Lives* (with photographs by Jean Mohr), Said recognizes a crucial absence of women, not within his own textual practice necessarily but within his perception of Palestinian society: 'And yet, I recognize in all this [vague pronoun] a fundamental problem – the crucial absence of women. With few exceptions, women seem [caution!] to have played little more than the role of hyphen, connective, transition, mere incident' (77). Said's recognition of the way in which women 'seem' to function as silent or silenced figures of mediation in the geopolitical specificity of Palestinian life strikes me as an excellent illustration of a First Worldist feminist critique of Said's own discursive practice: (dis)similar for example, to the work of French feminist Luce Irigaray, who, in her critical rereading of Plato's parable of the cave, entitled 'Plato's *Hystera*,' folds back the primacy of the signifying phallus as bio-graphical origin in a series of coded metonymies for the unspeakable, non-signifying vagina:

Of the 'go-between' path that links two 'worlds,' two modes, two methods ...
Of the passage that is neither outside nor inside, that is between the way out
and the way in, between access and egress ... But what has been forgotten in
all these oppositions, and with good reason, is how to pass through the passage, how to negotiate it – the forgotten transition. The corridor, the narrow
pass, the neck. (246–7)

The metonymic value attributed to the body of woman is to be found
in her capacity for mediation and negotiation between, for example,
the male critic and his phallocentric discourse, in the imitative and
forged repetition of the act of birth in the act of writing. Compare this
to Said's criticism in *Orientalism* of the sexual figures in a twentieth-
century Orientalist text, Raphael Patai's *Golden River to Golden Road*:

Yet in each case the relation between the Middle East and the West is really
defined as sexual: as I said earlier in discussing Flaubert, the association
between the Orient and sex is remarkably persistent. The Middle East is
resistant, as any virgin would be, but the male scholar wins the prize by
bursting open, penetrating through the Gordian knot despite 'the taxing task.'
'Harmony' is the result of the conquest of maidenly coyness; it is not by any
means the coexistence of equals. (309)

In reference to a nineteenth-century French Orientalist, Leroy-Beaulieu,
Said notes a metaphorical play in his discourse that links self-repro-
duction with colonization. Said concludes that Leroy-Beaulieu's stylis-
tic nuances suggest that 'the space of weaker or underdeveloped
regions like the Orient was viewed as something inviting French
interest, penetration, insemination – in short, colonization' (219). Said
attends to the sexual/textual politics at work in the discourse of these
Orientalists; however, the oppressive representation of women as
victims, weak and passive, and the focus on penetration and virginity
function for Said's purposes as rhetorically ironic gestures, useful
analogies that drive home his point about the discursive machinations
of colonial conquest.

The biological and sexual constitution of women's subjectivity under
patriarchy is precisely what Irigaray criticizes by reclaiming biological
and biographical reductionism – a historical agent of women's oppression – and exploiting their metonymic (virginity/hymen) or metaphoric (reproduction/mother) value as a subversive strategy for under-
mining the naturalization of biological concepts. Irigaray reawakens in

a contemporary currency an essentialist biological discourse, thus providing a historical dimension to the production of meaning of these terms. In other words, there is nothing essential about the meaning of essentialism except that which is historically produced as a fixed and natural definition of the word. Although Irigaray does not flesh out the implications of her reference to the 'path that links two "worlds," I would suggest that this image carries with it an oblique reference to colonialism. Irigaray could be said, then, to be making an uncritical analogy between the women of these two worlds, and in so doing, confirming First Worldist feminism's sanctioned ignorance of the historical and material specificity of the construction of sexuality and gender in Arab countries. Her work, of course, is directed towards the constituency of a First Worldist feminism; and though useful to a study of the pervasive power invested in the production of a signifying-Woman, based on bio- and ana-logical metaphors and metonymies, it still remains at the level of sexual difference. As I will discuss in the following chapter, the discourse of sexual difference, in both its feminist and non-feminist usages, is limiting and limited when confronted by the discourses on clitoridectomy and infibulation in the Arab countries.

In Said's work the problem of referentiality in discourse is twofold. Although the patriarchal aspects of epistemology, used to frame a representation of the Orient and the Oriental, invite a feminist critique, Said's use of female sexuality as an analogy for explicating the violence of colonialism fails to address the specificity of both Arab and non-Arab modes of patriarchal oppression and effaces a critique of the way Arab women are contained and represented by the discourses of Orientalism. When Said does address the way in which the production of 'Western' knowledge frames the subjectivity of women, he turns to Flaubert's construction of the typically Oriental woman. Said cites a comment made by Flaubert in a letter to Louise Colet: 'the oriental woman is no more than a machine' (187). Any mode of 'expression' by the Oriental Woman as she is depicted in the travel literature and novels of the late nineteenth century took the form of fulfilling male fantasies: '[Oriental women] express unlimited sensuality, they are more or less stupid, and above all they are willing' (207). In both his discussion of the feminization of the Orient and the almost uniform association of the Orient and sex, the figure of a woman is constructed on the basis of sexual difference. As such she remains useful as a metaphorical and metonymic device for mediating between 'two "worlds."' Neither in Said's critique of colonial discourse nor in Irigaray's critique of patriarchal discourse, do the Arab women of Palestine or the diverse classes of women generally thrown together under the homogenizing colonial figure known as the 'Third World Woman' achieve any textual agency as makers and unmakers of their own worlds.

### 'Her Picture Seems like a Map'

In *After the Last Sky* Said describes how the process of history affects a nation of people he has come to know as living subjects. This revelatory text contrasts with Said's absorption in the discourses of power and knowledge in *Orientalism*, in which he admits his study has very little to contribute to the 'fact' of those 'cultures and nations whose location is in the East, and their lives, histories, and customs [having] a brute reality obviously greater than anything that could be said about them in the West' (5). *After the Last Sky* is emblematic of Said's return to that which the rhetorical violence of knowledge has silenced for him. Said shifts from an engagement with discourses that attempt to contain and represent 'the Orient and the Oriental' to a mode of 'self-representation' in *After the Last Sky*: 'As I wrote, I found myself switching pronouns, from "we" to "you" to "they," to designate Palestinians. As abrupt as these shifts are, I feel they reproduce the way "we" experience ourselves, the way "you" sense that others look at you, the way, in your solitude, you feel the distance between where "you" are and where "they" are' (6). This shift expresses itself in Said's textual praxis through a questioning of what it means to read, the choices that are made as to what texts, social as well as literary, are read and valorized. *After the Last Sky*, Said insists, also 'reads the reader':

We are also looking at our observers. We Palestinians sometimes forget that – as in country after country, the surveillance, confinement, and study of Palestinians is part of the political process of reducing our status and preventing our national fulfillment except as the Other who is opposite and unequal, always on the defensive – we too are looking, we too are scrutinizing, assessing, judging. We are more than someone's object. We do more than stand passively in front of whoever, for whatever reason, has wanted to look at us. If you cannot finally see this about us, we will not allow ourselves to believe that the failure has been entirely ours. Not any more. (166)

When Said turns to the question of Palestinian women, he recalls a memory of his mother after she had been stripped of her passport following marriage: 'I ... interpreted her trauma as the sign that she passed from full immediacy of being – the fullness of being that comes from her person as a young Palestinian woman – to a mediated and perhaps subsidiary person, the wife and the mother' (78). Woman, as wife and mother, figures in Said's discourse as a slight, vacuous mediation, a silenced go-between that links two worlds. These two spheres of enclosure are represented by the 'fullness of being' embodied in a 'young Palestinian woman' and the world of men, in which that fullness of being, which includes, implicitly, the denotation of virginity, has been lost. Upon marriage she is now a 'hyphen, connective, transition, mere incident'; a figure of mediation who lies, somewhat (il)literally, between man and himself.[1] As the discussion of Nawal el Saadawi's critique of the value attributed to the hymen, elaborated in Chapter 2, suggests, the hymen's figural significance lies in its metonymic value for textual mediation, or hyphen-ation: an image which implicitly represents a loss of fullness, of a coherent female subject, regaining an imaginary closure through the intervention of the symbolic phallus.

Said's discussion of Palestinian women also deals with a film entitled *The Fertile Memory*. The film centres on an old woman's refusal to sell a piece of land to the Israelis, who have already dispossessed her of it but want to 'legalize her dispossession by giving her money in return for final entitlement' (80). For Said this woman represents the predicament of all women in an Islamic society and, specifically, Palestinian women. She is a 'potent symbol' of what Said terms '*internal exile*' (80). Said does not elaborate a definition of internal exile, but it appears to mean something other than physical and material dispossession, more perhaps a psychoanalytical effect than a socio-economic one. We should also note here Said's use of the phrase 'internal exile' in reference to Palestinian women in comparison to his concept of 'exteriority,' which works as a phallocentric re-presentation of the primacy of the male-authored text. 'Internal exile' would appear then to be something of a natural and familiar phenomenon.

In *Orientalism* Said produces special categories of 'marginals': 'delinquents, the insane, women, the poor' (207). Ann Curthoys, writing in a collection entitled *A Double Colonization: Colonial and Post-Colonial Women's Writing*, criticizes the production of special categories of marginals which effaces a material specificity and fails 'to see that many of the so-called marginals are in fact working class, whether they are employed or not. It fails to see also that some people within these special categories – such as middle class women ... have considerable resources with which to combat the specific discriminations and inequalities they experience' (15). Curthoys's marxist analysis, however, cannot account for territorial dispossession brought on by colonial practices. A materialist feminist approach might allow for a reading of Said's notion of internal exile as an effect of the women's dispossession and dis-enfranchisement from a property-owning class, to which her association is conditional upon her husband's, as Said points out (82). Said can then be held accountable for effacing questions of class in his psychoanalytic and symbolic figure of Palestinian women as potent symbols of internal exile. The complicity between metaphysical oppositions such as criminal and judge, working class and property-owning class, in their respective and hierarchical sites of (il)legitimacy, denies, by the metaphysics of enclosure, the dispossessed figure of mediation which connects, acts as a hyphen, a transition, between these two 'wor(l)ds.'

That class association permits the possibility of transforming a dispossessed figure of mediation into a figure of negotiation is made apparent in Said's reference to his aunt, 'the Mother of Palestine.' Said describes this privileged negotiator as follows:

My aunt, like my father, had little faith in officialdom. In the years since I came to New York, I have continued to meet people who worked for organizations like UNRWA or CARE, and who knew and admired my aunt. She bandied about the initials – CMS, ICRC, WHO, UNRWA, CARE – as well as the names of the personnel, though she knew in her inarticulately tough way that they weren't at bottom to be relied on. And this is the point she grasped: that the Palestinian must work within the system as well as against it – since every society is going to oppose Palestinians as if by heavenly edict – and be able in some way to create a parallel, or alternative, system that would respond to Palestinian needs. (119)

Neither inside nor outside, this figure of the mother of resistance, or the negotiator, bridges the difference between the internal colonizer and colonized. She works both within and without the system, in order to produce a 'parallel' system. In the image of Said's aunt, unlike the mother of the film, the silent hyphen or invisible passage has become a vocal mediator, albeit her articulatory abilities would seem to be muted by Said's descriptive reference to 'her inarticulately tough way.' The move from the crucial absence of women to their presence in Said's text suggests that there are class as well as gender issues at work in the production of a Palestinian ruling body. Furthermore, the desire to produce a 'parallel' system separate from the present system of rule, the desire for which Said has his aunt 'speak' as it were, further suggests that Said is not interested in investigating the production and reproduction of colonialism as a systemic result of national ideologies. The figure of the mother of Palestine becomes a trope for figuratively bearing or creating this alternative nation and staking out its territorial boundaries. What is displaced in Said's metaphor of the mother of Palestine and Palestinian women as figures of mediation is the material and historical specificity of colonial and neocolonial practices.

Why is the figure of the mother so significant here? In a collection of interviews and essays entitled *Third World: Second Sex*, Soraya Antonius, in her piece, 'Fighting on Two Fronts: Conversations with Palestinian Women,' records the words of May Sayigh, a Palestinian poet and a member of the General Union of Palestinian Women, discussing recent representations of women in Palestinian literature:

In Palestinian literature the mother has always been the symbol, and played the role, of the land: strong, protective. The son leaves and returns, she is there, the recurring protection ... But the younger writers and poets, like Knalid abu-Khalid, Yahia Badaw and others, now depict two faces of woman: the strong mother, the home and the land, who encourages her son to fight, and the young woman, the beloved, who is herself a fighter and active in the struggle. These are new depictions of woman: to be loved she has to fight actively for her country; the mother is no longer just generous, making coffee and baking bread, but has become the strong one who celebrates her son's death in battle in songs and who goes side by side with him through the nights of terror. In my own poems I try and emphasize that I am a woman, although I don't feel a second-class citizen at all. I feel the Palestinian cause is mine and the work is mine. (67–8)

This account, recorded and documented through the agency of First World feminists, publishers, and translators, attempts to provide an 'authentic' representation of the views of Palestinian women, with little critical commentary or dialogue. The above declaration indicates that the figure of the mother predominates as an important symbol linked to seemingly benign notions of 'land' and 'home,' and, by extension, 'homeland.' On the one hand, this appropriation of the figure of motherhood could be said to reinscribe an essentialist view of women; and further, this process of reinscription has been supported by the textual context of May Sayigh's remarks in a First Worldist feminist book that provides little room for discussion or critical dialogue. On the other hand, another interpretation is possible, and I take this possibility for reinterpretation from Michael Taussig's commentary on the struggle of mothers in another imperial context. In his essay 'Violence and Resistance in the Americas: The Legacy of Conquest' Taussig turns to 'the mothers of the disappeared,' whose open resistance as a collectivity in various Latin American countries he interprets as a recuperation of collective memory:

I see the way by which an essentialist view of woman has been radically refunctioned by women in relation to the State ... Such refunctioning of assumed essences is part of the struggle for the definition of the past, as it flashes forth involuntarily in an image at a moment of danger. As I understand this refunctioning with reference to the mothers of the disappeared and current State terror in Latin America, these women are wresting from the State its use of woman to not only embody the nation and the people in a moment of intense political crisis, but the embodiment of memory itself at that precise moment when it is the aim of the State to bury collective memory in the frightened fastness of the individual soul. (49)

Taussig's reinterpretation of the mothers of the disappeared in terms of an emancipatory refunctioning of motherhood as an essential category offers the possibility for a reinterpretation of May Sayigh's and other writers' use of the figure of the mother in recent Palestinian literature as one that also reclaims that 'essentialist' figure for an emancipatory purpose. What this interpretation cannot account for, however, is that the figure of motherhood, although an essential one, is not only a sign, it is also a representation of the reality of lived experience for many women. There is a difference, then, between May Sayigh's appropriation of mothering, which can contain the real and imaginary contradictions of 'motherhood,' and Said's discussion of the film *A Fertile Memory* and the renaming of an individual, his aunt, as the mother of Palestine. I would still argue that in Said's work an essentially symbolic value is being invested in the figure of the Palestinian mother as the embodiment of the limits of territorial possession. Winifred Woodhull comes to similar conclusions in her insightful study of the figure of the veil in Algerian nationalist struggle. In her essay 'Unveiling Algeria' Woodhull notes, 'For though women are indeed underrepresented in political institutions, silenced in public debates, and denounced as anarchists whenever they make themselves heard, they are, at the same time, the *embodiment* of Algerian national life, whether in its "progressive" or repressive guise' (116). So, too, the

figure of Woman in Palestinian nationalist discourse, limited to a
biological and reproductive framing, represents a paradigmatic subject
of the current configuration of neocolonial nationalist struggles for a
land base; hence, Said's commentary on Jean Mohr's photograph of
Mrs Farraj (85): '.... her picture seems like a map pulling us all
together,' as quoted in the epigraph to this chapter. As the figure of
mediation, whether it be the silent hyphen of discursive predications
or the vocal negotiator and promoter of a nationalistic neocolonialism,
women connect the First and Third Worlds. To extend Simone de
Beauvoir's category, the second sex, and its usage in the title *Third
World: Second Sex*, which includes the cultural and ideological implications of neocolonialism, it is, perhaps, more telling to say that women
have become a figural 'second world.' As mother earth or homeland,
women bear the metaphorical force of their 'labouring' (reproductive)
bodies, while the reality of their physical labour has been lost or disconnected from this metaphorical transformation. Said (and to some
extent Taussig) resolves the uneasy contradictions of the ideology of
sexual difference in both Western and Eastern or Latin American
epistemologies by using the figure of a woman's body as a metaphorical and metonymic tool that will carry, like an empty vessel, the disturbing signs of imperial conquest. In so doing, Said continues to
subject women in an international frame to a position of deprivation
in which he assumes that women, as mothers and lovers, too, do not
'scrutinize, assess, and judge' for themselves.

A deconstructive feminist approach to Said's *Orientalism* reveals that
certain biological and reproductive metaphors function within his
discourse as devices for centring a critique of East/West colonialism
around an ideology of sexual difference. As a critical lever or hyphen,
the metaphorical and metonymic figural use of woman's biological
body mediates the internal conflicts and contradictions of neocolonialism. The ideology of sexual difference provides Said with an imaginary resolution to the contradictions of a (anti-)nationalistic discourse,
in which the desire to preserve the purity of metaphysical enclosures
is contested by the reality of imperial violence. In his critique of Orientalist discourse Said discloses the hierarchical forces contained in the
binary opposition between East and West. In the process, names, such
as East/West, become things; nations and cultures become internally
homogeneous structures, objects bounded by their uncontaminated
difference from an Other. If any 'thing' were to bear the burden of
cultural diversity, generic mixing, hybridization, such a dirty and
profane job appears in Said's imaginary resolutions to be the work of

women, the work of an ideology of women's bodies. In order to preserve a clear and undifferentiated cultural lineage, Said manages the
potential crisis of contamination through a metaphorical displacement;
women's bodies become the means by which to reproduce a colonial
metaphysics of hierarchical opposition. Said deploys, then, a metaphoric displacement in which the materiality of Arab and non-Arab labouring women is exploited for their symbolic value as textual modes of
mediation. The axes of textual antagonism are limited in Said's *Orientalism* to a nationalized and 'naturalized' politics of representation.

## (De)naturalizing Af/filiations

Said's essay 'On Repetition,' in *The World, the Text, and the Critic*, lends
itself to a feminist intervention because of its naturalized politics of
representation which deploy a figural displacement of a generic woman's body as a mediating force in the narratives of eighteenth- and
nineteenth-century 'natural history' and modern, secularized literary
theory. As in *Orientalism*, Said's attempt to overturn binary oppositions
facilitates a deconstructive feminist approach. Precisely at the moment
his text displaces the silent value of a bio-logical mediation, it offers
the possibility of a feminist critique.

In this essay Said sets up a binary opposition between filiation and
affiliation in order to explore the contradiction between 'natural' bonds
of association, such as those of the family or clan, and 'cultural' modes
of socio-economic affiliations, such as those brought about by political
commitment, ideological boundaries, or institutionalized determinations. In an imaginary secular European society which has no recourse
to divine resolutions the point of contact between filiation and affiliation becomes a discontinuous, irreconcilable site of struggle. In reference to Vico's metaphorical and conceptual representation of human
history as a 'series of genealogical repetitive cycles' Said frames this
struggle in the following terms: 'For intentionally, in an unmediated
and wholly natural way, filiation gives rise not only to conflict but is
driven by a desire to exterminate what has been engendered, the
abandonment of offspring. Unintentionally, however, the opposite
takes place: marriage as an institution is established, offspring and
parents become bound by it' (118). By way of analogy Said transposes
this contradiction onto the production of literary theory: 'My interest
is in maintaining that for literary theory, for Vico's gentile history, for
natural history up to and including Darwin, it is natural to see the
passing of time as *repeating* the very reproductive, and repetitive,

course by which man engenders and reengenders himself or his off-spring' (117). The example Said inserts into his discussion in order to demonstrate this generalized, if not generic, tendency is Flaubert's contribution to the birth of modern realist fiction, *Madame Bovary*: 'In Emma Bovary's refusal to be the same kind of wife that her class and the French provinces require of her, the filiative bonds of society are challenged. She is a woman about whom it was possible for Flaubert to write because repetition, her feeling of boring, prosaic sameness, gives birth to difference, her desire to live romantically, and difference produces novelty, which is at once her distinction and affliction' (117).

In order to break the filiative/affiliative metaphor at work in Vico's 'gentile history' Said turns to Marx's 'The Eighteenth Brumaire of Louis Bonaparte,' recapitulating the now famous statement: 'Hegel remarks somewhere that all the great events and characters of world history occur, so to speak, twice. He forgot to add: the first time as tragedy, the second as farce' (146). Said begins his discursive intervention into the reproductive, repetitive motor of history by disclosing Vico's privileging of a filiative over an affiliative cycle of repetition, and then deploys Marx's critical overturning of repetition as farce rather than reproductive simulation, in order to displace the opposition. Said concludes with Marx's example: 'Repetition shows nature being brought down from the level of natural fact to the level of counterfeit imitation ... Marx's is neither a natural feat nor a miraculous assertion: it is an affiliative repetition made possible by critical consciousness' (124). Said is at pains in this essay to overturn the oedipalization of the plot of poetic history, to take to task the use of generative and procreative metaphors as central tropes used to repeat the paternal and familial sequences of a gentile history. With Marx's help Said turns the mimetic fantasy of humanistic and bourgeois reproduction into a parodic scene; natural history becomes a history of naturalizing and neutralizing the forces and events of dramatic change. Bourgeois representation generates images of past abuse in the clothes of a fool or clown.

Said has done a great deal to unravel the underlying class issues at stake in a familial writing of history; however, he takes for granted the discursive production of a male-dominated mode of filiation. Said would have us believe that reproduction is the equal fate of both men and women – 'Men and women give birth to; human beings are born' (118) – thereby continuing to perpetuate an assumed ruse of male dominance: even as the codes of filiation begin to emerge as a form of paternal and patriarchal oppression, the move to an affiliative order, to a recognition of the construction of 'nature' as a counterfeit imitation, wilfully forgets just what that counterfeit imitation of a patriarchal construction of 'nature' is predicated upon. Both filiative and affiliative constructions of history partake of a complicity in the metaphorical appropriation of women's reproductive labour.[2] A materialist predication of women's subjectivity can only be produced if these idealist notions of Woman as the mother, a mother viewed as an empty-headed body of ontological production who carries and bears the Word of imperialism, are deconstructed to disclose the way in which the metaphorical appropriation of women's bodies maintains an ideology of sexual difference in which the mind of one gender of human being is seen as superior or inferior to the sex of another. Said preserves, then, a gender construction of women's sexuality as 'natural' and finally reproductive, and naturalizes a gender construction of male intellectual superiority as productive, cultural, and affiliative.

### The Power of Connection

By turning towards the centrality of Palestinian experience, Said effectively breaks the degree of exteriority produced in *Orientalism* between a radical and yet complicit opposition of East and West. Said is careful, though, in *After the Last Sky*, to mark the limits of this politically charged venture into the 'fact' of those 'cultures and nations whose location is in the East.' He reminds the reader that any attempt to produce an 'authentic' representation of Palestinian life is a paradoxical project since the dominant condition of Palestinian life is one of exile, estrangement, de-centred subjectivity, and a fragmentary, incoherent, hybridized sense of time, place, and self. If we can speak of 'Saidian desire' at this point, that desire extends towards a unified counter-narrative and coherent re-representation of self and nation, where boundaries remain secure, stable, and fixed by inscribing the earth and the body with territorial borders and (af)filiations. In *Orientalism* the anatomy of women's bodies becomes a displaced site on which to map out those territorial affiliations.

Teresa de Lauretis's psychoanalytic and semiotic investigation into the material effects of desire offers grounds for another feminist intervention into Said's metaphysical nostalgia for structural totalities of being and world. Saidian desire is at least partially dependent on the predication of sexual difference, or woman's reproductive bio-body, as a metaphoric or metonymic mediation within his critical discourse. This metaphysical construction of sexual difference determines its symbolic power as a valuable asset in the discursive economy of Said's texts. Without the figure of Woman the discursive cohesion of Said's text would lose its mediating value. Without the hegemonic figure of Woman the reproductive capacity of Said's text to generate itself would be lost. And yet, as valuable as the figuration of women is, as a key to the productive operations of phallogocentric-critical discourse, women never appear as subjects who also produce culture. This paradoxical formulation I take to be a version of what de Lauretis notes in *Alice Doesn't: Feminism, Semiotics, Cinema* as 'the confusion, the double status of women as bearer of economic, positive value, and women as bearer of semiotic, negative value, of difference' (19).

It is women's biological body as a semiotic, negative value of difference that allows Said to use that bio-body as a metaphor for Palestinian oppression. In this metaphysics of women's body women bear the economic and positive value of Said's neocolonial nationalism; hence the mother of Palestine becomes a valorized figure of mediation, a hyphen with the power of connection. I would suggest that the articulations between various political struggles is necessary in order to dismantle a parallelism that effaces the ways in which certain metaphorical sites become the silent figures of mediation. Women, as silent figures of mediation, are displaced and turned into reified objects. Whereas Said will grant Palestinians the power to assess, judge, and scrutinize, Palestinian women are not necessarily included. Said textually positions women, in terms of refusing to acknowledge their contributions to cultural production, in the same way he criticizes 'Western' authors for writing the 'reality' of the 'Orient.' A feminist/ postcolonial articulation is necessary in order to force to a crisis the contradictions and clashes that emerge between discontinuous political struggles. As much as feminism needs a theory of decolonization, so too does postcolonialism need a theory of gender. To ignore the history of patriarchy, its effects as an ideological force in colonial discursive formations, is to maintain, paradoxically, a conservative position masquerading as radical politics.

As 'feminism(s)' deconstructs the binary closures in Said's textual practice, such as the exterior/interior opposition, feminism, too, can be deconstructed on the basis of its own oppositional dualism between the hegemonic constructions of a 'First World'/'Third World' Woman. The following chapter looks at the writings of Nawal el Saadawi, and of the critical theorists Teresa de Lauretis, Chandra Talpade Mohanty, and Gayatri Chakravorty Spivak, as their work intervenes in the privileged textual spaces of a First/Third Worlding of feminism.

# 2  Engendering Textual Violence

The very notion of a 'rhetoric of violence' ... presupposes that some order of language, some kind of discursive representation is at work not only in the concept 'violence' but in the social practices of violence as well. The (semiotic) relation of the social to the discursive is thus posed from the start ... the representation of violence is inseparable from the notion of gender, even when the latter is explicitly 'deconstructed' or, more exactly, indicted as 'ideology.' I contend, in short, that violence is engendered in representation.

Teresa de Lauretis, 'The Violence of Rhetoric: Considerations on Representation and Gender,' in *Technologies of Gender*, 32–3

Although some of these Western intellectuals express genuine concern about the ravages of contemporary neo-colonialism in their own nation-states, they are not knowledgeable in the history of imperialism, in the epistemic violence that constituted/effaced a subject that was obliged to cathect (occupy in response to a desire) the space of the Imperialists' self-consolidating other. It is almost as if the force generated by their crisis is separated from its appropriate field by a sanctioned ignorance of that history.

Gayatri Chakravorty Spivak, 'Subaltern Studies: Deconstructing Historiography,' in *In Others Worlds*, 209

There are many modes of representation, whether authentic, experiential, symbolic, semiotic, resistant, and/or subversive, through which to explore the relationship between knowledge and violence. De Lauretis's feminist position on the problem of violence and representation, and Spivak's anti-colonialist one, themselves represent two different approaches as to how textual violence is engendered in academic practices. The first section of this chapter discusses how their respective work on violence, in relation to gender and colonialism, can lead to some understanding of the way women's bodies – both literally and figuratively – are often the central site on which and through which social violence is produced and reproduced. One of the most important contributions to an understanding of this phenomenon is to be found in the critical and fictional writings of the Egyptian feminist Nawal el Saadawi, on which subsequent sections in this chapter will focus. El Saadawi's writings, as do Spivak's and de Lauretis's, raise important questions about feminist scholarship and the modes of representation that scholarship deploys in its effort to both describe and analyse women's oppression. Although el Saadawi's critical writings represent the violent oppression of the women she studies in an Egyptian context, her fictional modes of representation, while attempting to imaginatively surpass the oppression of women by offering images of resistance, tend more towards a reinscription of textual violence than to alleviating the pain of that violence. I argue that this textual violence is the result of an intellectual elitism which does not consider, as an informed representation of their experience, the actual writings and activities of the Arab women she describes. I am not suggesting a naïve or uncritical approach to the 'voices of the oppressed'; I am, however, insisting that feminist scholarship cannot deny that its work, whether explicitly acknowledged or not, is often in dialogue with the political, intellectual, and creative contributions of women for whom it, somewhat ironically, purports to speak. This chapter's concluding section addresses the crisis of the feminist investigating subject and her own difficult relationship to the textual violence of academic scholarship, in particular, scholarship that is interested in that homogeneous fiction Chandra Talpade Mohanty has taught imperial feminists to recognize as the 'Third World Woman.'

### (En)gendering Textual Violence

De Lauretis's critique of the gender sur-text of rhetorical violence in her essay 'The Violence of Rhetoric: Considerations on Representation and Gender' and Spivak's elaboration of neocolonial epistemic violence in her essay 'Subaltern Studies: Deconstructing Historiography' articulate similar interventions into critical theory.[1] Both de Lauretis and Spivak focus on the *feminization of knowledge* as the basis for a critique of the gender specificity of theoretical discourse. However, their considerations of the relationships among violence, language, representation, and subject-constitution differ in their respective sites of resistance and struggle. For de Lauretis the violence that is engendered in representation is the violence of patriarchal modes of oppression. Spivak's critique of the epistemic violence of 'Western' apparatuses of knowledge focuses on the exploited figure of the subaltern woman and the feminization of the figure of the subaltern, man or woman, in the texts of colonialism.

Two distinct critical positions on the problem of violence and representation result from articulating de Lauretis's feminist position and Spivak's anti-colonialist one. Following Spivak, feminism, too, must question the colonial assumptions which have shaped its critical discourse. This internally directed critical process would involve a historically based study of imperialism, or more accurately, a study of the textual inscriptions of the history of imperialism. De Lauretis's critique of the gendered character of representation suggests that a feminist analysis of postcolonial theory is also necessary to a more comprehensive understanding of the history of imperialism as a 'text' written through the lens of the patriarchal eye. A further position, that of a feminism of decolonization, would involve what de Lauretis calls 'the positivity of political action' (36). Against the contradictory move in the 'negativity of critical theory' de Lauretis situates a dialectical confrontation between the desire to supplant colonial, sexist, and racist ideologies of containment with an alternative scene of representation and the effort to transform the material force of ideology so that an alternative field of representation can be put into play. With reference to Michel Foucault's 'radical politics' de Lauretis elaborates the effects of this irreducibly contradictory moment: 'the positivity of political action, on the one front, and the negativity of critical theory, on the other' (36). She charges Foucault with a 'paradoxical conservatism,' which she explains 'is a very appropriate phrase for a major theoretician of social history who writes of power and resistance, bodies and pleasures and sexuality as if the ideological structures and effects of patriarchy had nothing to do with history, as if they had no discursive status or political implications' (49). Edward Said's incorporation of Foucault's method of discourse analysis results in similar crimes of subject exclusion. Although there is nothing inherent in Foucault's approach to the discursive relations of power and knowledge that should lead him to ignore the specificity of male dominance and limit a dialogue with feminist theories of culture, history, representation, and subjectivity, it is the case that Said's texts contain a similar limitation. Said's attention to the 'feminization of the Orient and the Oriental' also fails to address the ideological effects of phallocentrism on those discursive structures which have circumscribed the domains of 'East' and 'West.'

The difference within Said's work from *Orientalism* to *After the Last Sky* dramatizes the contradiction between the negativity of critical theory and the positivity of political practice. In *After the Last Sky*, a text that directly engages with the political situation between Israel and the Palestinian struggle, Said is finally able to recognize the implications of patriarchal domination in his selective discussion of Palestinian women. That the construction of Palestinian women's subjectivity becomes an issue in the context of this 'positive' project confirms de Lauretis's observation that the dynamic tension between critical theory and political practice is constitutive of, although not exclusive to, the specificity of feminist thought. Said's inability to articulate feminist and postcolonial theory in *Orientalism* reproduces patriarchal ideologies of containment in which women's bodies serve as a silent mediation through which Humanist Man (re)possesses his relationships among his body, pleasures, and work. This anatomical frame of mediation represents a vessel of containment, a postmodern figure which embodies the violent processes of gendering, ideology, and representation.

The process of syntaxing figural metonymies and metaphors represented by a Woman/Body constitutes a feminization of knowledge – an anatomical frame which permits the possibility of *reproducing*, in another form, heterosexist and racist colonial ideologies. In a rereading of Lévi-Strauss's essay 'The Effectiveness of Symbols' de Lauretis turns the discussion of 'a Cuna incantation performed to facilitate difficult childbirth' into an *exemplum* of the use of woman's 'body' as a generative textual site of mediation: 'The effectiveness of symbols, the work of the symbolic function in the unconscious, would thus effect a splitting of the female subject's identification into the two mythical positions of hero (the human subject) and boundary (spatially fixed object or personified obstacle – her body). The doubt that the apprehension of one's body or oneself as obstacle, landscape, or battlefield may not "provide the ... woman with a language" does not cross the text' (45).

In de Lauretis's critique of Lévi-Strauss the body of woman, the reductive gendering of women to biological, sexual difference, has been territorialized into a boundary, a borderline and demarcation of the frontier of anthropological discourse. In the context of her critique of Derrida and Lévi-Strauss, Spivak situates, in her essay 'Displacement and the Discourse of Woman,' 'a "feminization" of the practice of [deconstructive] philosophy' (173) taking place within the global transaction of the spectacle of 'the Third World Woman' under the economic regime of late capitalism. The relationship between the gendering and colonizing of subjectivity Spivak explains as follows:

> If the peasant insurgent was the victim and the unsung hero of the first wave of resistance against territorial imperialism in India, it is well known that, for reasons of collusion between pre-existing structures of patriarchy and trans-national capitalism, it is the urban sub-proletarian female who is the paradigmatic subject of the current configuration of the International Division of Labor. (218)

> ... through all of these heterogenous examples of territoriality and the communal mode of power, the figure of the woman, moving from clan to clan, and family to family as daughter/sister and wife/mother, syntaxes patriarchal continuity even as she is herself drained of proper identity. In this particular area, the continuity of community or history, for subaltern and historian alike, is produced on (I intend the copulative metaphor – philosophically and sexually) the dissimulation of her discontinuity, on the repeated emptying of her meaning as instrument. (220)

What remains a gap in de Lauretis's analysis – the feminization of knowledge in postcolonial critical theory – becomes in the epistemological frame of Spivak's investigation the subject-positioning of the gendered subaltern.[2]

Said's inattention to a theory of gender in relation to colonialism in *Orientalism* reproduces, in his separate discussion of Palestinian women in *After the Last Sky*, the continued marginalization and dispossession of Palestinian women as subjects who also produce Palestinian culture and history. It is only as a special category, as an added feature in political and cultural struggle, that Palestinian women can be discussed in Said's work, not as constitutive subjects always already involved in a struggle of decolonization. Said's work, then, although 'positive' in its production of images of the Palestinian people as subjects of their own historical making, does not radically transform the ideologies of containment that engender the violence of representation. Palestinian women become untheorized remainders in a limited representation of political practice. This limited representation in Said's work is contested by such institutions as the General Union of Palestinian Women (al-Ittihad al-'Am lil-Mara al-Filastiniva) founded in 1969.[3]

As more information becomes translated, published, and made available to Anglo-American audiences, the specificity of the construction of the patriarchal oppression in relation to Palestinian women becomes clearer. Although de Lauretis and Spivak provide a basis for a feminist critique of postcolonial theory, without the knowledge of the political practice Arab women are engaged in, the formulation of a feminism of decolonization, which can only be produced in the dialectic of a theoretical and practical contradiction, would be insufficient.

The decolonizing of feminism, a critique of the imperialist assumptions in feminist theory, involves an investigation into feminist scholarship produced in the 'First World,' particularly those works which reproduce imperialist relations of domination by circumscribing a homogeneous representation of the 'Third World Woman.' This homogeneous representation of the 'Third World Woman' often functions as an instrument of consolidation for liberal feminism. Liberal feminism situates the problem of Arab women's oppression in terms of the plurality of cultural differences. Without recognizing the complicity of Anglo-American epistemology in enforcing a violent representation of Arab women, First World feminists maintain an elitist view of themselves as superior to a homogeneous group of presumedly non-educated, non-civilized Arab women.

### Min(d)ing the Field: Nawal el Saadawi

There is no doubt that to write about women in Arab society, especially if the author is herself a woman, is to tread on difficult and sensitive areas. It is like picking your way through territory heavy with visible and hidden mines.

Nawal el Saadawi, *The Hidden Face of Eve: Women in the Arab World*, 3

Nawal el Saadawi has become an important figure in the dialogue between 'First' and 'Third' World feminists. She is herself an intellectual, a feminist, and a political activist. Her personal history, recorded in such texts as *The Hidden Face of Eve* and *Memoirs from the Women's Prison*, reveals the extent of her political commitment and the controversy with which her work has been received, not only by Anglo-American feminists but, importantly, by the Egyptian state. El Saadawi is a medical doctor, who became a director within the Ministry of Health Education and editor-in-chief of the magazine *Health*. The publication in 1972 of her first non-fiction work, *Women and Sex*, provoked an antagonistic response from both religious and political authorities and lead to her removal from her professional positions as editor and director. El Saadawi continued to produce and publish four more books dealing with similar issues in the treatment of Arab women: *Female Is the Origin, Women and Neurosis, Man and Sex*, and *The Naked Face of Women in the Arab World*. *The Hidden Face of Eve* (1980) was her first work to be published in English, a text written, according to el Saadawi, to inform European and American women of the political issues affecting Arab women. On 5 September 1981 el Saadawi, along with 1,035 other leading Egyptian intellectuals, was arrested and imprisoned under a decree issued by Sadat. Because of Egyptian censorship her recent work has been published in Beirut, whereas her earlier books were published in Cairo.

### Symbolic Clitoridectomy

El Saadawi rightly criticizes 'First World' feminists for exploiting their knowledge of clitoridectomy as an excuse for labelling Arab countries barbaric and therefore in need of First Worldist feminist development. This position of First Worldist feminist superiority belittles the feminist activism already at work in Arab countries. El Saadawi has forced Anglo-American feminists, among others, to dialogue with feminist intellectuals and activists within Arab countries. The hierarchical relationship between the North American feminist intellectual and the peasant Arab women, a relationship that exploits peasant Arab women as objects of investigation, is destabilized by el Saadawi's presence as a 'representative' Arab woman knowledgable and grounded in the oppression and the exploitation of Arab women within Arab countries.

In her preface to *The Hidden Face of Eve* el Saadawi criticizes American and European feminism for reproducing a spectacle of 'female circumcision' and thereby restricting analysis to questions of sexuality removed from the specificity of geopolitical, economic, and religious contexts:

But I disagree with those women in America and Europe who concentrate on issues such as female circumcision and depict them as proof of the unusual and barbaric oppression to which women are exposed only in African and Arab countries. I oppose all attempts to deal with such problems in isolation, or to sever their links with the general economic and social pressures to which women everywhere are exposed, and with the oppression which is the daily bread fed to the female sex in developed and developing countries, in both of which a patriarchal class system still prevails. (xiv)

In her discussion of the Zed Press / Women in the Third World publication series (which originally published *The Hidden Face of Eve*), Chandra Talpade Mohanty criticizes the problematic of sexual difference as a basis for cross-cultural feminist practice: 'An analysis of "sexual difference" in the form of a cross-culturally singular, monolithic notion of patriarchy or male dominance leads to the construction of a similarly reductive and homogeneous notion of what I call the "Third World Difference" – that stable, ahistorical something that apparently oppresses most if not all the women in these countries' ('Under Western Eyes,' 335). Although Mohanty directs her criticism towards 'First World feminism,' her criticism could equally apply to *The Hidden Face of Eve*. El Saadawi insists on economic and social analyses, but her text fails to provide such a discussion: the use of a progressive idiom does not deflect el Saadawi's own focus on sexuality and patriarchy. In the above quote from *The Hidden Face of Eve* the notion of a 'patriarchal class system' is universally applied to 'developed and developing countries.' El Saadawi does not link questions of patriarchy and class to colonial and neocolonial relations of exploitation. Her use of the terms 'developed and developing,' terms which have been used to produce the Third Worlding of Arab countries as 'underdeveloped' precisely in order to be 'developed' for exploitation by transnational corporations, is one indication of this failure to connect the internal structures of oppression in Egypt with external forces of economic imperialism.

The conflation of differences between and among non-Arab and Arab women is further produced in el Saadawi's text when the physical operation of clitoridectomy is paralleled with a psychological notion of clitoridectomy projected onto the experience of European and American women: 'Women in Europe and America may not be exposed to surgical removal of the clitoris. Nevertheless, they are victims of cultural and psychological clitoridectomy ... No doubt, the physical ablation of the clitoris appears a much more savage and cruel procedure than its psychological removal. Nevertheless, the consequences can be exactly the same, since the end result is the abolition of its functions so that its presence or absence amount to the same thing' (xiv–xv). In response to First Worldist feminist decontextualization of clitoridectomy from its historical and social specificity, el Saadawi, in turn, produces a spectacle of symbolic victimage in the figure of 'cultural and psychological clitoridectomy' among American and European women. The figure of cultural and psychological clitoridectomy as a symbolic sign of women's oppression allows el Saadawi to incorporate First World feminisms into the realm of Arab women's oppression in the form of a symbolic clitoridectomy. Clitoridectomy, in both its figural and material forms, takes on symbolic value as an example of women's presumed 'universal oppression.' Through the symbolic transaction of making clitoridectomy a sign of Arab and non-Arab women's universal oppression, the possibility of a trans-geographical, national, and economic connection is established. In the process of creating a trans-cultural feminism, however, the material specificity of clitoridectomy remains unformulated.

In Gayatri Chakravorty Spivak's essay 'French Feminism in an International Frame' the symbolic valorization of clitoridectomy plays an important role in Spivak's own formation of the notion of 'ideological victimage.' Spivak begins her essay with reference to a discussion she had with a 'young Sudanese woman in the Faculty of Sociology at the Saudi Arabian university,' who announced that she had 'written a structural functionalist dissertation on female circumcision in the Sudan.' Spivak writes: 'I was ready to forgive the sexist term "female circumcision." We have learned to say "clitoridectomy" because others more acute than we have pointed out our mistake' (154). For the (Western) feminist versed in the critical morphologies of post-Freudianism, the metaphor 'female circumcision' reinscribes a representation of woman's body within a phallocentric discourse. Although el Saadawi is critical of Freudian theories in *The Hidden Face of Eve*, she retains both terms, 'female circumcision' and 'clitoridectomy.' Spivak does not acknowledge those 'others more acute than we,' and, although her discussion of clitoridectomy demonstrates solidarity with el Saadawi, the gesture suggests that the 'correction' is also implicitly directed towards el Saadawi's text.

Spivak criticizes the philosophical bases of the 'structural functionalist approach' as a *disinterested* stance which valorizes forms of social phenomena on the basis of their ability to function. Spivak then cites a passage from *The Hidden Face of Eve* in order to demonstrate, implicitly, the severity of her Sudanese woman's disembodied approach to what Spivak assumes to have been the Sudanese woman's experience.

Spivak depends upon the following quote from el Saadawi to produce the horrific spectacle of the practice of clitoridectomy, and it is, without doubt, an effective passage. El Saadawi writes:

In Egypt it is only the clitoris which is amputated, and usually not completely. But in the Sudan, the operation consists in the complete removal of all the external genital organs. They cut off the clitoris, the two major outer lips (*labia majora*) and the two minor lips (*labia minora*). Then the wound is repaired. The outer opening of the vagina is the only portion left intact, not however without having ensured that, during the process of repairing, some narrowing of the opening is carried out with a few extra stitches. The result is that on the marriage night it is necessary to widen the external opening by slitting one or both ends with a sharp scalpel or razor so that the male organ can be introduced. (9)

Immediately following this description el Saadawi writes: 'My feeling of anger and rebellion used to mount up as I listened to these women explaining to me what happens during the circumcision of a Sudanese girl. My anger grew tenfold when in 1969 I paid a visit to the Sudan only to discover that the practice of circumcision was unabated, whether in rural areas, or even in the cities and towns' (9). Spivak follows el Saadawi's description with: 'In my Sudanese colleague's research I found an allegory of my own ideological victimage' (155). Spivak elaborates the notion of ideological victimage as an expression of her experience as a feminist academic, who, coming from 'an upper-class' remains 'caught and held by Structural Functionalism, in a web of information retrieval inspired at best by: "what can I do *for* them?"' (155). Spivak specifies her 'ideological victimage' as the result of a class position which has placed her in the role of 'spokeswoman,' a subject-position the allegory of the Sudanese woman's academic work has led Spivak to 'unlearn'; to unlearn, that is, her collusion in reinscribing an elitist relationship to Arab women because of her social and economic status. In a further self-reflexive gesture Spivak questions the ways in which her 'knowing,' like that of the Sudanese woman, has also been ideologically determined. It is as if Spivak assumes the subject-position of the 'American Feminist' el Saadawi situates as the 'victim of cultural and psychological clitoridectomy.'

The material specificity of clitoridectomy has become for Spivak, and in her interpretation of the Sudanese woman's academic work, a symbolic register of women's oppression or ideological victimage within the production of knowledge. It is through this symbolic transaction that Spivak can see herself also as a similar victim of the disembodying and dispossessing power of (elite) knowledge. The sign of the clitoris, however, has once again been *excised* from the material context of Arab women in Egypt and the Sudan. It is as if the symbolic valorization of clitoridectomy has been returned to Arab women as a doubly monstrous displacement, reproducing their victimage as symbolic rather than as a result of economic and material exploitation:

The clitoris escapes reproductive framing. In legally defining woman as objects of exchange, passage, or possession in terms of reproduction, it is not only the womb that is literally 'appropriated'; it is the clitoris as the signifier of the sexed subject that is effaced. All historical and theoretical investigation into the definition of woman as legal *object* – in or out of marriage; or as politico-economic passageway for property and legitimacy would fall within the investigation of the varieties of the effacement of the clitoris ... since an at least symbolic clitoridectomy has always been the 'normal' accession to womanhood and the unacknowledged name of motherhood, it might be necessary to plot out the entire geography of female sexuality in terms of the imagined possibility of the dismemberment of the phallus. (151)

Spivak appropriates the symbolic value of cultural clitoridectomy in order to challenge the sexual/textual politics of a French feminist *écriture féminine* which valorizes female orgasmic *jouissance* without investigating the implications of this position in relation to Arab women. Given French imperialist practices in Arab countries such as Algeria, this is an important point. However, Spivak, in her universalization of the 'geography of sexuality' from a position of symbolic clitoridectomy, reproduces on an intellectual level, along with el Saadawi (however much Spivak fails to acknowledge her critical engagement with *The Hidden Face of Eve*) what she criticizes on a politico-economic one. She takes the material specificity of clitoridectomy, as it is practised in Arab countries, as the occasion to enlighten so-called First World feminism of its symbolic clitoridectomy.

Both Spivak and el Saadawi deploy a strategic critique against the West and First World feminism, using the notion of psychological or symbolic clitoridectomy to remind European and American women that they too are subject to forms of oppression which are often veiled by their imperializing and exploitive gaze towards the women of Arab countries. As a strategic gesture, turning the binary opposition of East/West on its head, it is an effective critical move; however, failing to displace the opposition prematurely closes off analysis of the differ-

ence in class positions which affects women within these respective geopolitical domains. Spivak's remark about those 'others more acute than we' and el Saadawi's 'horror' at the knowledge that rural Sudanese women are still subjected to the practice of clitoridectomy reveal their collusion in producing an othering of peasant (in el Saadawi's case) and (in Spivak's) middle-class educated Arab women. Spivak is at least aware of her participation in the elitism of Western knowledge, albeit the crisis of being an investigating subject has been managed through a symbolic displacement of the material effects of female clitoridectomy. El Saadawi does not question her (liberal) representative position as a spokeswoman for all Arab women and manages this particularly contradictory position in a series of imaginary resolutions, both in her fiction and in her critical writings.

Whatever the advantages of el Saadawi's position *vis-à-vis* the First Worlding of feminism in North America, her work raises questions about the possibility of producing alignments between feminist scholarship and activism in an international frame. The homogenizing tendencies within feminist scholarship often permit articulations on the basis of sexuality and a trans-cultural analysis of gender construction, but they ultimately efface the tensions produced between different classes of women and by the institutionalization of racism, which is also part of maintaining the international division of labour. El Saadawi engages in a proto-class critique, deploying the vocabulary of a class analysis in her insistence that the issue of clitoridectomy cannot be separated from other social, economic, and political factors; however, her method of investigation and discussion, for which she relies mostly on personal experience and information acquired in her position as a doctor, does not accomplish the analysis she lays claim to performing. Although el Saadawi is adept at criticizing relations of domination between Arab feminism and the feminism of non-Arab countries, she remains uncritical of her own vanguardist relationship within Egypt and in relationship to peasant Arab women.

### Class and Colonialism

Through the use of a progressive and socialist idiom el Saadawi represents herself as a vanguard leader of Arab women. In an interview with the journal *Race and Class*, entitled 'Arab Women and Western Feminism: An Interview with Nawal el Sadaawi [*sic*],' a form of *socialist idealism* leads to the following sort of paternalist analysis on el Saadawi's part: '... the majority of Arab women don't as yet know how to fight back politically. But if they really organized they could do so much, not only against patriarchy but against the class system too' (176). In the following reflection, in the same interview, on 'middle-class educated urban women, even those with roots in the village' (of which el Saadawi is one), el Saadawi consolidates and legitimizes her positions as a political vanguard:

That is the problem of middle-class educated urban women, even those with roots in the village – they may know nothing about the majority. Most ordinary people are still deeply religious, though not necessarily hidebound by it, for in an economic crisis they can leave religion to attend to their basic needs. So any revolutionary person must start from this reality – not ignore it – accept it and go step by step to cure it and raise the consciousness of the people so that they themselves will do the fighting. It's no good patronising or talking down to them, you must bring them along. (182)

The question of already existing peasant political organizations is left unexamined by el Saadawi; nor does she assume that Arab women have any understanding of this economic exploitation, and of political and sexual oppression, the kind of experience that, presumably, once understood – and here is the supplementary role for the intellectual – becomes the knowledge that is the basis of political praxis. One of the difficulties the women's movement faces is the limitations of a feminist practice produced on the basis of 'self-identification,' and yet this is the place out of which political feminist subjectivity, with its emphasis on consciousness-raising and the consensual mandate, 'the personal is political,' has historically emerged. When self-identification remains on the level of narcissism,[4] however, the differences of 'particular experience' become reintegrated into the individual's realm of self-referentiality. The constitution of a global and not universal feminist practice will involve, then, critical reflection on the flight into interiorization, self-consciousness, and subjectivism, on the one hand, and, on the other, resistance to the functionalism of dominant capitalist social formations that would have women and men act as interchangeable human units.

El Saadawi's work demonstrates this flight into interiorization, self-consciousness, and subjectivism, as in her account of a representative Arab woman writer in 'Creative Women in Changing Societies: A Personal Reflection':

Lucky is the woman who is able to learn how to read and write and is not fully taken up with a constant striving for her livelihood and endless household work in the service of family, husband and children ... This fortunate woman represents a small minority in Arab countries ... where the vast majority of men, women and children are left crushed and breathless in the continuous struggle for existence.

The creative woman occasionally allows herself to step back and forget her true self – she practices what men practice ... She loses her identity, even though she may continue to work and produce. Her creative work declines steadily, even though her bank account and her fame might be mounting rapidly.

But she is sometimes saved from this state of futility by a distressing incident in her public or private life, or a tragedy within the home or in society ... *Circumstances might drag her down to the company of the sick, the poor, the rejected, the prisoners, the divorcees or the prostitutes, thus allowing her to get acquainted with the ugly face of this system and to realise that she is not part of it. She begins to struggle to recover her self and her truthfulness, and recovers creative ability side by side with those whose life she is now partly sharing. Her creative work rings with the authenticity that comes with truth.* (164, emphasis added)

El Saadawi produces in this passage a displaced narrative of her own life. Her search for the 'true self' strangely precludes her use of the first-person pronoun; instead el Saadawi produces a third-person narrative of a seemingly universal figure of the 'Arab Woman Writer.' The marginalized figures of the 'sick, the poor, the rejected, the prisoners, the divorcees or the prostitutes' are made to cathect, to borrow Spivak's words – to occupy in response to a desire – the space of the imperialists' self-consolidating Other. El Saadawi resolves the class differences between herself and these women through her 'creativity.' Indeed, these figures become the substance of el Saadawi's fiction. The 'circumstances [which] drag[ged] her down to the company' of the women she marginalizes as Other legitimate for el Saadawi her 'authenticity' as author of their lives – politically, artistically, and philosophically.

The recuperation of the authenticity of subjugated gender and class experiences into el Saadawi's critical and literary realism represents an instance of an abstracted disembodied knowledge of ruling, to paraphrase Dorothy Smith. In her book *The Everyday World as Problematic: A Feminist Sociology* Smith writes:

A standpoint in the everyday world is the fundamental grounding of modes of knowing developed in a ruling apparatus. The ruling apparatus is that familiar complex of management, government administration, professions, and intelligentsia, as well as the textually mediated discourses that coordinate and interpenetrate it. Its special capacity is the organization of particular actual places, persons, and events into generalized and abstracted modes vested in categorical systems, rules, laws, and conceptual practices. The former thereby become subject to an abstracted and universalized system of ruling mediated by texts. A mode of ruling has been created that transcends local particularities but at the same time exists only in them. (108)

Smith locates the analytical value of the everyday-world problematic 'at the juncture of particular experience, with generalizing and abstracted forms of social relations organizing a division of labour in society at large' (157). In Smith's analysis 'particular experience' translates into embodied (self-)knowledge of concrete experience. The translation or dislocation of 'naïve' particular experience into the analytical morphologies of a social science discourse alters or re-configures the knowledge of experience. Smith privileges the notion of everyday concrete experience as the single most important phenomenon on which to base a feminist methodology. If feminist practice is to be capable of producing alignments between women with different narratives of particular experience, then feminist methodology must resist assimilating the range of different textual formations of concrete experiences into universal categories and surpass the threshold of 'identity' Julia Kristeva 'imagines' in her essay 'Women's Time' when she asks: 'What can "identity," even "sexual identity," mean in a new theoretical and scientific space where the very notion of identity is challenged?' (51–2). To do so would involve confronting the self-identifying and at times inclusive practices of feminism.

In el Saadawi's account of the Arab Woman Writer the use of a third-person narrative, the grammatical positioning of peasant women as other-ed and marginalized figures, and the imperializing references to 'people of the Third World' and 'developing countries' are examples of metaphorical modes of disembodied abstraction. The universal figure of the Arab Woman Writer produces a subjective identification with the 'other' women in order to mis-recognize her collusion in 'the ugly face of the system.' In the final analysis, however, 'she is not part of it' – the 'it' here being the inevitable victimization, exploitation, and oppression that Arab peasant women are, supposedly, powerless to change. The Arab Woman Writer, however, is able to walk away from the scene.

Throughout *The Hidden Face of Eve* anecdotes describing events appear, in episodic fashion, to demonstrate or exemplify the oppressive nature of 'the patriarchal class system.' The anecdotes inform el Saadawi's critical realism, destabilizing genre boundaries between critical analysis, autobiography, and storytelling. The following is a lengthy example of one such anecdote:

Numerous were the nights which I spent by the side of a young girl in a small country house or mud hut during my years in rural Egypt, treating a haemorrhage that had resulted from the long dirty finger nail of a *daya* cutting through the soft tissues during the process of defloration. For in many villages this ritual ceremony in honour of virginity is performed by an ugly old crone, the *daya* who earns her living by amputating the clitoris of children, and tearing open the vagina of young brides ... On one occasion the *daya* embedded her long nail in the hymen, but only a few drops of scanty blood were forth-coming. To my horror, she pushed her finger up the vagina and the blood welled out in a steady stream ... I realized that she had cut through the wall of the vagina. At the end of the night, in answer to my questions, she explained to me that on marriage nights she was very much in demand. Her fame, built up on her capacity for bringing forth a vigorous flow of blood in the process of defloration, had earned her an unusual popularity and a steady income from such auspicious occasions ... When the finger of a rural husband replaces that of the *daya*, then defloration becomes even more brutal. His only experience in the use of his hands is related to gripping the thick handle of the plough or the harrow. The *daya* at least has some notion of the female body. And nothing can be more brutal than a thick coarse finger plunging mercilessly into the external opening of the vagina, and boring up in an unknown direction. Thus it was that, on a cold winter's night, a young girl was carried into my clinic bleeding profusely between her thighs, only for me to discover that the husband's finger had perforated the interior vaginal wall into the urinary bladder. (29)

El Saadawi does not analyse the anecdote for what it reveals about the socio-symbolic forces that produce the conditions of possibility for such abuses. The event becomes another spectacle. Failing analysis, a contradiction is produced in the privileging of the *daya*, with its socially constituted status for women, over the rural husband, a singular man deconstituted as a universal figure of contempt because of his working-class position. This contradiction permits el Saadawi to say, 'The *daya* at least has some notion of the female body,' without recognizing that such knowledge is at least as lethal as ignorance.

### Disembodied Fictions

El Saadawi's fictional realism theorizes her concern for a psychological, rather than socio-economic, approach to feminist analysis. The divisions between consciousness and unconsciousness, reality and dream worlds, freedom and imprisonment, constitute the major metaphors of her fiction. Characters are represented by a split consciousness separated from an embodied experience of a meaningful and accessible 'reality.' The threshold of entry into this presumed 'reality' is often barred or impassable; outside the door events repeat themselves, characters re-enact the scenes of others, phrases re-echo the discursive containment of previous representations. The climax, or final rupture from the seriality of an oppressive everyday world for women, consists of an act of murder in *God Dies by the Nile*, execution in *Woman at Point Zero* and *The Fall of the Imam*, and imprisonment in *Two Women in One*. In these texts a psychological state of internalized incarceration characterizes the consciousness of a peasant woman (*God Dies by the Nile*), a young student (*Two Women in One*), a prostitute (*Woman at Point Zero*), and the allegorical figure of Bint Allah (*The Fall of the Imam*).

In *God Dies by the Nile* the female characters Zakeya, her bother's daughters, Nefissa and Zeinab, and the wife of Sheikh Zahran, Fatheya, appear as substitutable figures in a series of similarly abusive situations. Fatheya refuses in silence to marry Sheikh Zahran but is forced by her impoverished father to comply after pressure has been placed on him: 'But there was no answer, so he climbed up on to the top of the oven, pulled her out by her hair, and beat her several times until she came down. Then he handed her over to Haj Ismail and the same day she married the pious old Sheikh' (31). Nefissa also refuses to be sent to the mayor's house to become his servant and mistress. She is eventually coerced into obedience by her father, whom Sheikh Zahran intimidates into compliance: 'But Nefissa showed no signs of doing what he told her, so he clambered to the top of the oven, struck her several times, and tugged at her hair until she was obliged to come down. He handed her over to Sheikh Zahran in silence' (21).

The textual seriality of these scenes of abuse dramatizes Arab peasant women as subjects of mundane and repetitious acts of violence. Figures of authority, such as Sheikh Zahran, also reappear, whether as direct causes of the abuse or as indirect mediators, in substitutable representations as oppressors of peasant women. The resolute resistance on the part of the women is also reproduced in passages that echo one another:

The two shadows disappeared into the darkness to emerge out of it again over the river bank. Zakeya's face stood out in the pale light of dawn, gaunt, severe, bloodless. The lips were tightly closed, resolute, as though no word could ever pass through them. The large, wide-open eyes fixed on the horizon expressed an angry defiance. Behind her, the head of the buffalo nodded up and down, its face gaunt and bloodless, but not unkind, its wide-open eyes humble, broken, resigned to whatever lay ahead. (1)

This opening passage is reinscribed following the death of Elwau, Nefissa and Zeinab's brother, who is framed and murdered by the mayor in order to cover up Nefissa's pregnancy. This time Zakeya walks with Zeinab, who is also forced to go to work in the mayor's house:

Two shadows slipped out, their heads and shoulders draped in long black shawls. Zeinab's face was drawn and pale under the first rays of dawn. She looked up at the sky with an expression of angry defiance. Moving alongside her could be seen the thin, emaciated, lined face of Zakeya, her black eyes gleaming in the half-light. (81)

The cycle of repeated abuses breaks when Zakeya murders the mayor. In the closing scene of the novel Zakeya is in prison. El Saadawi re-echoes the opening description of Zakeya: 'She stared into the dark with open eyes but her lips were always tightly closed' (138). Following this repetition, however, Zakeya's silence also breaks:

But one of the prisoners heard her mutter in a low voice, 'I know who it is.' And the woman asked her curiously, 'Who is it, my dear?'
    And Zakeya answered, 'I know it's Allah, my child.'
    'Where is He?' sighed her companion. 'If He were here, we could pray Him to have mercy on women like us.'
    'He's over there, my child. I buried him there on the bank of the Nile.' (138)

Zakeya's violence, an act of political negation, breaks the silence of her voice and the silence of criticism directed towards Islamic religion. El Saadawi has insisted elsewhere that 'Islam is not the enemy of women, but it has been and is being used by patriarchal systems so that its most repressive and reactionary aspects are emphasized.'[5] In *God Dies by the Nile* the manipulation of the Islamic religion by political forces in the village in order to oppress women is represented in the image of women memorizing the Koran without understanding the words

(33). The novel also narrates Zakeya and Zeinab's journey to the mosque, Sayeda Zeinab,[6] a journey that is suggested to them by the local religious powers in order to alleviate Zakeya's possession by the devil. The authorities require Zakeya to collect a certain sum of money (money she does not have but must borrow from neighbours and friends), then to travel to the mosque and give the money to a particular figure so as to receive religious absolution. The figure, unknown to Zakeya and Zeinab because he is disguised, turns out to be the same village authority who recommends the absolution. The figures who produce Zakeya's initial insanity and despair are also the figures whom she trusts, because of their religious devotion, to cure her misery. It is in the context of this contradiction and cycle of abuse that Zakeya's violent act of murder, a nihilistic politics of negation, must be placed. In killing the mayor, a representative of political and patriarchal oppression – along with the other male village authorities – figured in the end by Allah, Zakeya negates the Islam of abuse in order to affirm the emancipatory Islam el Saadawi locates in her historical account of a revolutionary Islam that, as she says in her interview 'defended women and slaves' (176).

Georges Tarabishi criticizes what he calls el Saadawi's 'nihilistic asceticism' in *Woman at Point Zero*: 'This nihilistic asceticism may be one way of rejecting reality, but it is not the only way to change it. Firdaus's story is undoubtedly worth telling. However, presenting it as an individual, isolated case is one thing; and elevating it to the level of a theoretical issue is quite another' (32–3). Tarabishi rejects el Saadawi's nihilism, or what I would prefer to call her negationist politics, as a meaningful way of transforming the oppressive reality some women face in Arab countries. However, his own difficulty in accepting the politics of el Saadawi's position closes the possibility of understanding the relationship between the choice of political action and the degree of exploitation and oppression to which women are subjected. It may be that el Saadawi's literary representation of peasant Arab women suffers from a problem similar to her experience in a vanguard position: the force with which she silences peasant Arab women can only be broken with an equally forceful degree of violence. El Saadawi clears a space for Zakeya to speak, as it were, against her oppression; but el Saadawi also produces an intolerable representation of her silence to begin with. Whether this intolerable silence is a representative account of peasant Arab women's lives or the result of el Saadawi's elitist silencing of peasant Arab women in order that she may 'speak for them' is an irreducible problem.

To criticize el Saadawi's work with the use of a critical epistemology produced within the so-called West raises at least two problems: firstly, a homogeneous representation of Western epistemology as always already complicit in the abstracted and disembodied knowledge of imperial ruling; and secondly, a homogeneous representation of knowledge produced within the East as exempt from the violence of imperial epistemological enforcement. In other words, while it is possible to deconstruct the class bias in el Saadawi's work, because her work is produced, in part, on the basis of a dominant European epistemological tradition, concrete historical and political analysis can only be forged in an understanding of the relations between the local or particular context in which her writings take place and the effects of European epistemic imperialism. El Saadawi's writings are important to the practice of an Arab feminist critique; however, they also contribute to masking the relations between the violence of imperial epistemic enforcement and the specific experience of peasant Arab women. It is this contradiction that destabilizes the spatial homologies between geopolitical designations of epistemological traditions such as Eastern and Western. Horizontal planes of encounter between spatially defined bodies of knowledge, are, at present, the dominant figure on which international feminist alignments are built. The vertical axis of investigation remains invisible, as do, then, domestic modes of exploitation and oppression, within both Western/Eastern elite (feminist) theory. Bourgeois feminists render labouring women or women who are economically dispossessed invisible by claiming their (bourgeois) victimage and interests as 'all' women's under a class-blind notion of patriarchy.

### The Investigating Subject and the Spivakian Paradox

El Saadawi and Spivak have taken on the position of political representatives in their respective institutions of power, the medical profession in el Saadawi's case, the academic institution in Spivak's. To take on a position as a representative of the 'voices of the oppressed' is not without its own problems. Spivak elaborates some of the problems that arise for the investigating subject in her essay 'Can the Subaltern Speak?'

In this essay Spivak distinguishes between two modes of 'representation' – representation as proxy or substitution and re-presentation as reflection or staging – in order to demonstrate that the conflation of this double session of representations by post-structural critics, particularly Foucault, Deleuze, and Guattari, continues to reproduce epistemic violence in the constitution and effacement of the colonial subject as Other. Her argument is relevant to the academic interpretation of el Saadawi's writings as well as those by Native, Métis, and Inuit women discussed in chapters 5 and 6. Texts such as *Slash, Halfbreed, In Search of April Raintree*, and *Life among the Qallunaat*, in making use of realist and autobiographical genres, implicitly produce a confrontation between their re-presentations of a mode of life and the readings of the intellectual, who, by proxy, claims an institutional responsibility in representing their political interests.

Spivak elaborates the irreducible and discontinuous distinction between 'representation as "speaking for," as in politics, and representation as "re-representation," as in art or philosophy' (275), in the context of Marx's play between *'vertreten'* (represent in the former sense) and *'darstellen'* (re-present in the latter sense) in 'The Eighteenth Brumaire of Louis Bonaparte.' For Spivak the difference between these metaphors of 're(-)presentation' hinges on a difference between their descriptive and transformative powers. This distinction is necessary, Spivak argues, for displacing an 'essentialist, utopian politics' in intellectual production. Foucault, Deleuze, and Guattari, according to Spivak, disclaim their function as political representatives, insisting, rather, that 'oppressed subjects, speak, act and know *for themselves'* (276). While fetishizing 'concrete experience' as somewhere out there (in the factory, the school, the barracks, the prison, or, we might add, the reserve), a positivist empiricism is reinscribed, paradoxically so, in a post-structural enterprise that claims the heterogeneity of subjectivity, a heterogeneity which allows for the transformation of subjectivity, as a condition that makes impossible the fixing of a sovereign, unified subject, necessary to the positivist episteme. Such a 'brandishing of concrete experience,' Spivak argues, 'help[s] [to] consolidate the international division of labour' (275). In so doing, Spivak concludes that the intellectual represents her/himself as transparent (275), masking her or his role as an investigating subject, and denying the complicity of the intellectual, as fractured subject, in her or his own class interests, even as she or he is attempting to transform, or, in Spivak's term, 'unlearn'[7] class consciousness.[8] The intellectual reclaims her/himself as a sovereign subject, subject to the totalizing logic of power and desire.

The following lists outline a set of contingent oppositions essential to Spivak's elaboration of the differences between representation and re-presentation:

| | |
|---|---|
| representation | re-presentation |
| politics | art/philosophy |
| political | economic |
| the state | the subject |
| the law | subject-predication |
| proxy | portrait |
| *vertreten* | *darstellen* |
| rhetoric-as-persuasion | rhetoric-as-trope |
| transformative | descriptive |
| the law of the father | the hero |
| subject of power and desire | the subject of the oppressed |
| community (assembly) | staging |
| speaking *for* | speaking *for themselves* |
| orator | actor |
| speech | writing |

Although this set of distinctions graphically displays the difference between political and 'literary' modes of representation, the distinctions are, as Spivak notes, difficult to fix; representation and re-presentation slide into each other, and hence their conflation in the work of Deleuze and Guattari. For Spivak a 'radical practice' of cultural politics 'should attend to this double session of representations, rather than reintroduce the individual subject through totalizing concepts of power and desire.' Spivak consolidates her critique in the following:

... the relationship between global capitalism (exploitation in economics) and nation-state alliances (domination in geopolitics) is so macrological that it cannot account for the micrological texture of power. To move toward such an accounting one must move toward theories of ideology – of subject formations that micrologically and often erratically operate the interests that congeal the macrologies. Such theories cannot afford to overlook the category of representation in its two senses. They must note how the staging of the world in representation – its scene of writing, its *Darstellung* – dissimulates the choice of and need for 'heroes,' paternal proxies, agents of power – *Vertretung*. (279)

When Spivak asks the question(s) Can the subaltern speak? and Can the subaltern (as woman) speak? she is also asking, 'What must the elite do to watch out for the continuing construction of the subaltern?' (294). Although Spivak recognizes the importance of an articulation between the First and Third Worlds in the area of anti-sexist work, she is critical of the assumptions and constructions of a monolithic 'Third

World Woman' consciousness or subject: 'such work ... will, in the long run, cohere with the work of imperialist subject-constitution, mingling epistemic violence with the advancement of learning and civilization. And the subaltern woman will be as mute as ever' (295). The re-presentation in Anglo-American feminist theory of a monolithic Third World Woman on the bases of notions of essentialism and authenticity, 'a search for lost origins,' reintroduces the fetishization of the concrete and a fully conscious subject. What Spivak takes from this contradictory move, between the silencing of the subaltern woman and the speaking subaltern woman as fully conscious subject, is that the notions of essentialism, consciousness, and positivism are themselves serious fictions, not practical, non-theoretical terms belonging to an innocent, uncontaminated representation of 'Reality.' To lose touch with this understanding of essentialism-as-theorizable is to lose touch with a profound and productive problematic (296).

Spivak's and el Saadawi's work on the silencing of the dispossessed begs the question What happens when the sub-proletarian women does 'speak'? And further, what are the contradictions that emerge for a deconstructive morphology which focuses on the de-centring of subjectivity and a critique of identity and self-presence in spoken language, at a time when the 'voices of the oppressed' demand a *positive* approach to representation, a self-centring of subjectivity and identity, and a claim to authenticity on the basis of the spoken word. Deconstruction is useful to a process of unmooring the humanist model of a heroine, a Jeanne d'Arc, who will fully redeem the ills of Western liberal democracy from its intolerable hierarchies of racism, gender disparity, and class exploitation. Although deconstruction overturns the centring of a unitary political agent as a redemptive model of political praxis, in its liberal and pluralist appropriation it has failed to yield a theory of autonomous heterogeneity which would benefit a popular, collective process of social change.

The need to confront feminist methodologies and morphologies with their blindness to questions of racial difference, the diversity of sexual orientations, and class-specific forms of exploitation and oppression has emerged in the last twenty-some-odd years to reveal clashes and contradictions within feminist practice. Differences of class, race, sexual orientation, and gender, which have been used to inform the silent metaphors of mediation of an elite epistemology, have been reclaimed as emancipatory signifiers, textual sites from which to elaborate the ideological forms of containment at work in the production of knowledge. In doing so, however, feminist morphologies and methodologies gamble with certain intellectual re-investments when they comply with interpretive practices in the academic institution; hence risking, as Audre Lorde's writes in her influential article 'The Master's Tools Will Never Dismantle the Master's House,' 'learning how to take our differences and make them strengths' (99). Out of this troubled space of complicity and resistance emerges the crisis of the feminist investigating subject.

When confronted with the unequal predications of 'other' in those subjects struggling for political and cultural representation, whose cultural productions are the material of her study, the figure of the investigating subject (and I include myself) finds herself occupying a duplicitous position of resistance. I say 'duplicitous' in reference to the investigating subject's position of resistance because the deployment of a rhetoric of resistance on the part of the investigating subject to the hegemonic destabilizations of colonialism often amounts to an elitist lament for the silence of the 'indigenous voices of the oppressed': already relegated to the nicely contained and sanitized laboratories of scientific experimentation, so-called 'primitive' societies, for example, are said to have disappeared or are in the process of 'vanishing.' As figures of dead matter, indigenous people do not scrutinize, judge, or assess for themselves. Over the last twenty years, however, in Canada, the entry of Native oral traditions into print culture, largely through presses owned and operated by band councils and funded through the federal Ministry of Indian and Northern Affairs, has transformed this disappearing act into the spectre of Native cultural and political autonomy, even as Native cultural politics clearly thrives in a competing mode of gatherer/hunter production not unrestricted by the real effects of postmodern neocolonialism.[9]

The position of the investigating subject in the human sciences – in particular, the disciplines of anthropology, literary theory, and history – is currently undergoing a crisis as a *historically representative subject*. As a (self-appointed) part of an intellectual vanguard, the critic is invested with power (by whom? the secretary of state?) to speak for the 'voices of the oppressed,' to represent their concerns even as the material interests of the representative subject conflicts with those she speaks of, for, or about.[10] This is the first alibi of authenticity the critic gives her/himself in the denial of agency and authenticity on the part of those voices whom s/he represents. Self-representation, agency, and authentic subjectivity are hence recuperated and displaced in the figure of the investigating subject as a historically representative subject.

This figure of the investigator as a historically representative subject

in crisis is a metaphorical displacement of its 'other,' the 'native informant.' Spivak explains the process of 'othering' in the figure of the
'native informant' in her essay 'Imperialism and Sexual Difference':

The clearing of a subject-position in order to speak or write is unavoidable.
One way to reckon with this bind is an interminable pre-occupation with the
(autobiographical) self. If we are interested in a third-worldist criticism, however, we might want to acknowledge that access to autobiography, for whole
groups of people, has only been possible through the dominant mediation of
an investigator or field-worker. The 'autobiographies' of such people have not
entered the post-Enlightenment European 'subjective' tradition of autobiography. They have gone, rather, to provide 'objective evidence' for the 'sciences'
of anthropology and ethnolinguistics. 'Oral history,' coming of age in the
sixties, tried to efface or at least minimize the role of the investigator. Much
third-worldist feminist work has taken on this task of the effacement of the
investigator in works typically entitled '— Women Speak.' This brief account
reveals the various alibis that the dominant subject-position gives itself as it
constructs the subordinate as other. The curious 'objectified' subject-position
of this other is what, following the language of anthropology and linguistics,
I call the position of the 'native informant.' In order to produce a critique of
imperialism, I suggest the invention of a reading-subject's perspective that
would occupy or cathect the representative space or blank presupposed by the
dominant text. The space will remain specific to the dominant text which
presupposes it and yet, since this is not a space of the critic's autobiography
as a marginal, it must be foregrounded as a historically representative space.
The other must always be constituted by way of consolidating the self. This
method will at least make the problems visible, and the efforts at hedging the
problems provisionally accessible to the reader. (229)

The space of the marginal consolidated subject as autobiographical self
has indeed been occupied by the investigating subject producing
innovative alibis of authenticity which further enforce the lack of a
space from which indigenous subjects are able to give 'voice.' Though
I use 'voice' here in its colloquial sense, this usage does not discount
or reduce 'voice' to a non-written form. The entry of Native oral traditions into print culture is one example of how various technologies of
cultural production are adaptable, even in the commodity form, to
serving as a communicator of stories, from the sacred to the everyday
variety. Giving 'voice' in print culture is one way Native writers
empower themselves and claim themselves as agents of their own
cultural traditions.

The position of Native women in Canada compares to that of the third worlding of women in Arab countries: similar to sub-proletarian women in their marginalization and dispossession; but different in that this process of marginality takes place in a country which is not simply dominated by a representation of itself as constitutive of the 'First World,' but which is a major First World consumer and producer. Although Canada is officially a Commonwealth country, reminded of its colonial heritage by the occasional media spectacle of visiting royals, twentieth-century state policies of development in the North, the institutionalization of the Indian Act in the late nineteenth century, and the current impoverishment of Native people living in urban areas are only some of the signs of the internal structure of colonialism that is pervasive throughout English- and French-speaking Canada. To speak, then, of a Third Worlding of Native, Métis, and Inuit women in Canada is to disclose a contradictory position. It is these two sites of contradictions – the positioning of Native women writers in Canada as both 'Third' and 'First' World subjects and the importance of the speaking voice in aboriginal women's literature at odds with post-structural theory – which, together, have brought to a new level of crisis the processes of ideological containment in postmodernism.

The decolonization of feminist theory and a supplementary reading of postcolonial theory from a feminist perspective might be said to have critical value only inasmuch as it is possible to recognize the colonizer's own self-critique. This is to mark a limit, a boundary which draws a line over its ideology of mediation: the indigenous woman. In which case, the space of the semiotic difference of indigenous women, speaking, desiring, and producing meaning for themselves remains foreclosed. In other words, a critique of the epistemological assumptions in feminism, which continue to contain indigenous or subaltern women as marginalized, can do no more than call attention to the problem of their 'silencing.' And this is the Spivakian paradox: to affirm the silence of the dispossessed does not necessarily address the voices of the dispossessed. A theory of interpretation based on a notion of subjective authenticity, read in the literature of the dispossessed, makes it possible to see within that writing an act of agential critical praxis, resistant to the totalizing tendencies of feminist critique. Although Spivak and el Saadawi may lament the cultural and symbolic forms of clitoridectomy which constitute First World feminism's 'ideological victimage,' such a critical position does not acknowledge the degree to which so-called Third World women make their own place within the circumstances with which history has confronted them.

### A Fourth Worlding

The following chapter looks at the history of conflict and alliance-making that emerged between feminism and Native women's struggle for self-determination in Canada during the 1980s. The boundaries of Canadian academic discourse do not function through the figures of so-called First and Third Worlds. An abstracted medium of differentiation emerges in the use of the notion of a 'Fourth World'; on the one hand, the phrase signals the collective resistance of indigenous peoples of North and South America, as used by George Manuel and Michael Poslums in their book *The Fourth World: An Indian Reality*; on the other hand, the phrase also circumscribes another form of ideological containment, the Fourth Worlding of indigenous cultures. Land claims, entitlement, self-government, and self-determination constitute the ground of struggle for Native decolonization in general. Within Canada the discourse of boundaries, of 'multiculturalism' (which is a ruling ideology supported by state policy), displaces the material specificity of 'reserves,' the structural contradictions of internal colonialism. Unlike the global distancing of the Third World from the First, the forms of ideological containment under internal colonialism are in the backyards of our suburban paradises.

Spivak's, Mohanty's, and de Lauretis's critical reflections on the making of the Third World Woman in Anglo-American feminism are important, not simply by way of analogy, to an elaboration of the contradictions that exist between Anglo-American feminism and Native, Métis, and Inuit women's specifically decolonial mode of feminist critique. Postcolonial feminist discourse, however, does not always come 'home,' as it were, to examine some of the internal contradictions of its own agency within a North American context that has its own history of imperialism. It is to this history, particularly in the Canadian context, that I will now turn.

PART TWO

NATIVE WOMEN AND ANGLO-AMERICAN
FEMINISM

# 3   (De)constructing Affinities

We are reclaiming our pride and traditions. We are asking for opportunities to practice our culture. To transmit the braiding of our past, present and future into terms others can understand and respect.

Osennontion (Marlyn Kane) and Skonaganleh:rá (Sylvia Maracle), 'Our World,' 5

Let us then say that we can reinterpret ideologies of difference only because we do so from an awareness of the supervening actuality of 'mixing,' of crossing over, of stepping beyond boundaries, which are more creative human activities than staying inside rigidly policed borders. That awareness is the achieved product of a political process responding to the travail and expense of separation imposed upon – and, to some extent, creating – a national community, the Palestinian Arabs. Perhaps more important, we develop in the process a heightened critical consciousness not only of what difference can do but of where its politics can lead.

Edward Said, 'Ideology of Difference,' 43

## Discerning Politics

The Third International Feminist Book Fair / Troisième Foire internationale du livre féministe, held in Montreal during June 1988, has become a watershed in Canadian feminist cultural politics. Of the interventions staged at this mainstream feminist conference, it was Native and Métis women activists, poets, critics, and writers who were to pose the most significant challenge to previously held assumptions in feminist theory, in particular, concerning the relationship between patriarchal formations deriving from a Western European epistemology and the effects of Western European imperialism on the specificity of gendered relations within gatherer/hunter societies.[1] The theoretical consequences of this intervention are far-reaching for the project of a feminist postmodernity. Feminists are called upon to rethink the concept of gender through competing historiographic narratives and diverse cultural experiences. For a pluralist feminist vision indigenous women's discourse challenges the metaphysics of difference and diversity. Under this epistemological rubric feminism expands its frontiers of inclusion in order to circumscribe a global feminist project. Such an ideological resolution to the current contradictions of colonialism and nationalism within Canada not only subsumes the historical and cultural particularity of indigenous women's experience under a universal representation of Woman, but a site of exclusion remains firmly entrenched in the image of Man as the main enemy. This position, as I argue in more detail below, structures feminist debates on a heterosocial model. Cultural and political debate centres around male/female relations to the detriment of any discussion about the constitution of social relations among women, including the relationship of feminist theory to the women about whom it purports to speak. To posit a feminism of decolonization, as I would wish to do here, involves examining the contradictions and clashes between indigenous women's struggle for decolonization and Anglo-American feminist theory. There is a productive tension in this relationship. By examining some of the internal contradictions in feminist theory, I hope to keep alive that 'essence' of the triangle Teresa de Lauretis elaborates as central to the shaping of feminist discourse. In her essay 'The Essence of the Triangle or, Taking the Risk of Essentialism Seriously: Feminist Theory in Italy, the U.S. and Britain' de Lauretis reclaims the notion of essence:

... it is the specific properties (e.g., a female-sexed body), qualities (a disposition to nurturance, a certain relation to the body, etc.), or necessary attributes (e.g., the experience of femaleness, of living in the world as female) that women have developed or have been bound to historically, in their differently patriarchal sociocultural contexts, which make them women, and not men. One may prefer one triangle, one definition of women and/or feminism, to another and, within her particular conditions and possibilities of existence, struggle to define the triangle she wants or wants to be – feminists do want differently. And in these very struggles, I suggest, consist the historical development and the specific difference of feminist theory, the essence of the triangle. (5–6)

De Lauretis's argument stems from a critique of heterosexism: the essence of the triangle containing an implicit reference to the Pink Triangle of lesbian theory. Heterosexist assumptions underlie and reify aspects of our theoretical analysis of gendered social relations; therefore lesbian theory is vital to any examination of the socially constituted textual as well as sexual relations among women. This chapter examines those discursive and textually differentiated relations in the emergent articulation between the discourses of Anglo-American feminism and the indigenous women's movement for self-determination in Canada. In order to meet some of the demands brought about by Native and Métis women's interventions at the feminist book fair in 1988, I shall focus here on indigenous women's concerns as they have been articulated within the 'local' context of Canadian cultural politics. And although drawing on a range of American, British, and Canadian feminist theories (the ABC's as it were), I hope to carry that irreducible tension which the ambivalence of the name 'feminism' has itself come to insist on, encourage, and sustain.

### Secretaries of State

Anglo-American feminism refers to an institutional configuration, the practices and activities of which engage women in the project of furthering their access to 'higher' education, their empowerment through knowledge, and their entry into a professional managerial class.

To walk into any women's bookstore in a thriving First World metropolis is to encounter a world of women writers' concerns as diverse as the social structures will allow. This diversity is constructed for us, of course, and therefore it is susceptible to political and economic forms of privilege and limitation: from government funding agencies for research and publication, such as the federal ministry of the Secretary of State in Canada, to publishing corporations with their editorial cartels, marketing informants, technocratic specialists, and so forth. The architectural frame of a women's bookstore may provide a strong sense of its permanence and solidity, the walls lined with shelves of books, an image of plenty – the market-place a site of liberal and tolerant consumers. Women have achieved democratic access to the technologies of print culture: free, free at last; 'free,' that is, to exchange our cultural value under late capitalism. And yet, within the academic institution, women's scholarship and feminist writings remain marginal to conventional disciplinary intervention; just as women's bookstores remain a false representation of women's collective impact on market forces. Although we may celebrate the existence of women's studies programs and women's bookstores, in the wake of a post-sixties proliferation of new social movements, the separate and marginal status of women's intellectual work can only contribute, in the long run, to shaping and continually reshaping the marketability of feminism's marginal value. In *Materialist Feminisms: An Introduction* Donna Landry and Gerald MacLean, argue: 'It is, however, within feminism's emancipatory potential as a social and political movement, working against patriarchal exchange, that the use-value, rather than the exchange-value, of feminism as a commodity is to be found. But to the extent that feminists happen to be or identify themselves as women, the exchange of feminisms in the academic market place is overdetermined by the traffic in women, or capitalist-patriarchal business-as-usual' (forthcoming). The political, economic, and social consequences of this marketing venture into what Landry and MacLean have aptly called 'commodity feminism' are devastating, particularly for feminism's theoretical assumptions about its relationship to the women for whom and about whom it speaks.

The answer to the persistent question Who speaks for whom? cannot be answered without recourse to a theorizable notion of essentialism. Teresa de Lauretis rethinks the notion of essentialism through a conventional and dualist definition of 'essence,' based on the difference between a conceptual entity and a real entity. The distinction between a 'real entity' and a 'conceptual entity' is like the difference between an inside and outside. A real entity represents 'intrinsic nature as a "thing-in-itself,"' while a conceptual entity represents 'the totality of the properties, constituent elements, etc., without which it would cease to be the same thing.'[2] De Lauretis cites Locke's statement in the *Essay on Human Understanding* – 'The Essence of the Triangle, lies in a very little compass ... three lines meeting at three Angles, make up that Essence' (5) – as an example used to illustrate a conceptual entity. Locke's example of the triangle provides de Lauretis with a metaphor with which to understand the essential difference of feminist theory and practice, a difference of *re*-vision (per Adrienne Rich), a term which already foregrounds historical specificity and not a God-given belief in the essential or 'immutable nature of woman' (5).

The struggle to address the diversity of women's political and personal histories constitutes feminism as an *epistemology* of difference. Taking the risk of this historically specific definition of the essential difference of feminism from other social movements will enable a political project unfettered by 'male-dominant and heterosexist ideologies of liberal pluralism, conservative humanism, or, goddess forbid, religious fundamentalism' (32). For de Lauretis, to take up this position involves 'challenging directly the social-symbolic institution of heterosexuality' (32).

One way to challenge the institutionalization of heterosexuality within critical feminist debate would be to turn our attention towards an examination of the socio-symbolic relations among women as well as analysing the more traditional women/men coupling. Let me elaborate this point by considering the metaphysics of inclusion/exclusion in current cultural political debate.

### Autonomy/Auto-critique

The sign of Woman and the political signature of feminism contain their own universal strategies for broadening the field of inclusion as well as shifting the frontiers of exclusion. No one likes to be excluded, or is it that no one likes to give up their power? (If the latter, then we have the basis of an argument for legislating gender and racial parity.) Paul Smith responds to the feminist exclusion of men in *Discerning the Subject* in the following terms:

The 'enemy' for feminism, therefore, is more the institutions, logics, and discourses of the patriarchy than the real people who inhabit it. Thus feminism's allies are not perforce women only – nor to be sure, *all* women. But another component and instructive feature of feminism's difference, and a consequence of its heterogeneity and fluid constitution, is that at its best moments it need not be *exclusive* ... There is thus a possible and productive disparity between the 'subject' and objects of feminism, between its self-constitution and its other. (153)

If for de Lauretis feminism's difference lies in its capacity to sustain heated debate and a willingness to accept the necessary conflict which diversity inevitably brings, for Smith feminism's difference is constituted by way of a heterogeneity and fluidity which suppresses conflict. Smith conceives of a heterogeneous diversity as non-contradictory, continuous, and fluid, ever-expansive and elastic in its ability to contain 'otherness.' And yet, like de Lauretis, he acknowledges a 'productive disparity' between the subjects and objects of feminism. It could also be said that Smith's notion of 'heterogeneity,' though it implies diversity, is more accurately a form of heterosexism in which the binary opposition of man/woman no longer constitutes a basis for deconstructing their order of subordination, but rather represents a subsuming of the opposition into an abstracted unity of one.

Smith's position is a contradictory one because he conflates mythic modes of exclusion with the realities of exclusion. The contradiction stems from the initial relationship Smith poses between patriarchal institutions, logics, and discourses and the real people, namely, men, who inhabit them – a slippery difference not unlike the one between the phallus and the penis. At the same time as Smith wants to retain the referential power of the metaphors of man/woman, he would have us abstract the problem of patriarchy into unspecified zones such as institutions, logics, and discourses. At this level of abstraction the categories of woman and of man begin to reify and homogenize groups of real people. This level of abstraction works, ideologically, to resolve the unequal relations that really do exist for women. Hence, the problem of exclusion has also become abstracted. This mythic mode of the exclusion of men from feminist practice displaces the reality of exclusion for women and their lack of access to ideological apparatuses. What this means is that women are barred from criticizing problems of representation in the area of cultural production, making decisions which would alter the social relations of those productions, and participating in the very production of culture.

We have already noted the privilege that Anglo-American feminists enjoy in determining the field of feminist inquiry; some women have more access to means of representation than others. In particular, the problem of exclusion on the basis of racism remains considerable, as Michelle Wallace notes in her book *Invisibility Blues: From Pop to Theory*:

... people of color – perhaps especially black people – have very little input in decisions concerning the representation of their problems and their capacity for self-definition and self-direction. Not only are we barred from participation by racist exclusion, we have also barred ourselves from Afro-American culture by minimizing its importance. Yet it seems to me that as the social level at which representation occurs (the omnipresence of global TV, the computer program and the national and international wire news services) becomes more and more all-encompassing and indistinguishable from the problems themselves, it is increasingly important for people of color to address issues of representation directly, to become actively engaged in criticizing the politics of the production of culture. I consider it a cultural crisis of the first order that so few people of color, especially women, are in positions of power and authority in the production of newspapers, books, magazines, television, films, radio, music, movies, academic journals and conferences, and university faculty and curricula. (6)

To be excluded from the means of representation is not necessarily to be excluded from changing the modes of representation and the gendered, race, and class relations that give shape to the particular modes of representation in competition under late capitalism. It is exclusion from the existing means of representation that, as Michelle Wallace implies, brings to crisis the whole question of exclusion in the field of representation. Not only must we ask, Who represents whom? but also, Who controls the means by which representations are made and disseminated?

The myth of male exclusion emerged, I think, once feminism enabled some women to constitute autonomous political and cultural decision-making bodies. The effects of this move towards autonomy not only produced a false sense of feminism's overt exclusion of men, in which the historical forces that initially produced the demands for autonomy have been suppressed, it also produced a form of auto-critique on the part of those men who wished to take up an anti-patri-archal position. This position involved the movement of men in / with influenced by feminism in which they began to question the patriar-chal assumptions of their own political subjectivity, that of their male peers and male critical contemporaries. While I see this as a progres-sive move, the self-critical mode of reflection often manifests the worst attributes of a Christian moral imagination. A religious rhetoric of fear, guilt, redemption, and absolution emerges. A narcissistic return to self-centring lurks on the horizon. The male investigating subject, having been confronted with feminist politics, sees himself as a sacrificial son, a symbol of atonement for the original sin of patriarchy, the rule of the father.

Smith is not self-critical in this sense, nor does he see himself as an agent of change. By abstracting the problem of patriarchy in order to escape being labelled the enemy of feminism, Smith distances his own privileged, and therefore partially complicit, relationship to patriarchy. This position, while acknowledging the agency of the oppressed, denies agency to the oppressor, especially to the oppressor who wants to transform his own relationship to oppression. Smith denies his own agency as someone who, in a position of authority with access to institutional legitimation and the academic publishing industry, is responsible for bringing about change. And his engagement with feminism attempts to do this, but the myth of his own exclusion takes his critical energies in the wrong direction as, for example, when he emphasizes the fact that not all women are feminists. True enough. But, let's not forget there are even fewer men who are anti-patriarchal, and more women than men who are feminists. Smith is in danger of playing the white knight here, rescuing feminism from its internal contradictions and from those women who are not feminists. The difficult relationship between feminist textual politics and the women for whom it purports to 'speak' could easily conform to a myth of exclusion for white middle-class women similar in its abstract structure to Smith's mythic representation of white male exclusion. The problem, however, is not as simple as substituting one set of opposed binary categories for another. While feminist theorists have produced specific modes of textual abstraction and created a feminist ideology which symbolically mediates the real contradictions of many women's experiences, if only represented thus, feminism would appear to be as oppressive as its oppressors.

Feminism is about women, their structural and social relations between and among each other and between women and men. It is about how the gendered and racially inscribed character of those relations is imagined, violated, transformed, reproduced, negated, survived, lived, and reasoned. Nowhere, I think, are the contradictions between feminism and the women for whom it purports to speak made more explicit than in anti-colonial debate of the kind initiated by such cultural critics as Ifi Amadiume, Gloria Anzaldúa, Jeannette Armstrong, Nawal el Saadawi, Lee Maracle, Chandra Talpade Mohanty, Gayatri Chakravorty Spivak, Valerie Amos and Pratibha Parmar, and Maria C. Lugones and Elizabeth V. Spelman, all of whom have cleared a space from which to speak by taking to task an Anglo-American feminist tradition in which the notion of gender has been abstracted into a universal category to meet the needs of a select few women. For instance, the oppression of white middle-class women sustains a critical argument for 'equality'; however, by soliciting racial and class exploitation as the imaginary resolutions to their ideological conditions of oppression, defined exclusively as a problem of gender, class elitism and racial superiority are suppressed as the social factors which confer a relative privilege on this particular group of women. If the problem of inequalities among women is to be addressed, then we need an analysis that attends to specific historiographic narratives of resistance and the diversity of cultural experiences that informs those strategies of resistance. The following section narrates a brief history of Native women's oppression in Canada with an overview of the institutionalization of their oppression by the state, specifically through the Indian Acts. It is important to trace the colonial roots of Native women's oppression; otherwise the current struggle of Native women and their antagonism towards Euro-Canadian feminism cannot be understood properly as symptomatic of cultural imperialism and the epistemological violence involved in the solicitation of European patriarchal formations by privileged 'imperial feminists' to further the ends of a Euro-Canadian feminism.

### Indian Acts

Perhaps the most significant form of oppression to shape the lives of Native people in Canada has been the Indian Act of 1876, including its precursor, the Enfranchisement Act (1869). These pieces of federal legislation hold the lands of Native people in trust by the Crown, and they are designed to regulate many aspects of Native life, including education, politics, the administration of justice, and the family. They also define who is and is not Native through a categorical distinction between the status Indian and the non-status Indian. Métis and Inuit are not included in the Indian Acts. The institutionalization of Native women's oppression by the Canadian state occurred through a set of pointed discriminations. In the Enfranchisement Act, Native women's autonomy was subsumed under the legal jurisdiction of her husband's (if a married male Indian was enfranchised, his wife and children were automatically enfranchised). Secondly, Native women were excluded from inheriting land rights upon the death of a male spouse. They were also excluded from holding political positions within their bands: the government would recognize only an elected band council composed of and elected by adult males. And finally, under section 6, 'Provided always that any Indian woman marrying any other than an Indian, shall cease to be an Indian within the meaning of this Act, nor shall the children issue of such marriage be considered as Indians within the meaning of this Act: Provided also, that any Indian woman marrying an Indian of any other tribe, band or body shall cease to be a member of the tribe, band or body to which she formerly belonged, and become a member of the tribe, band or body of which her husband is a member, and the children issue of this marriage, shall belong to their father's tribe only.'[3]

In the Indian Act of 1876 patriarchal values were further entrenched in the service of the federal government's final solution of assimilating Native people when the definition of the term 'Indian' was altered to establish legitimacy solely through the descent of a male line. Sexual controls were also imposed on Native women: as Kathleen Jamieson points out in her important essay 'Sex Discrimination and the Indian Act,' the superintendent-general had the power 'to stop the payment of the annuity and interest money of any woman having no children who deserts her husband and lives immorally with another man' (119). Jamieson outlines further instances of discrimination, which include the passing of Bill C–79 in May 1951. This bill contributed even more restrictions to the status of Native women who married non-Natives. Section 6 of the 1876 Indian Act was overwritten in section 12(1)(b) of Bill C–79: any supplementary rights, band benefits, and marginal access to annuities women were allowed by the acts of 1869 and 1876 were now completely expropriated from her on the date of marriage. Native women with 'status' who married non-status Native men or non-Native men were stripped of their status affiliation. Correlatively, non-Native and non-status women who married status Native men accrued their spouse's status instatement (section 11[1][f]). This latter section, and, in part, the former section as well, ensured that Native women, like non-Native women, were subject to Euro-Canadian patri-archal controls over marriage, sexuality, and reproduction. Section 12(1)(b) also clearly aided the aims of a colonialist policy of assimi-lation by reducing the numbers of Native people with a claim to status and band affiliation (not only Native women were affected by this section; their children also lost their band affiliation). This legislation specified a particular colonial/patriarchal configuration of discrimina-tion directed solely towards status Native women.

The passing of Bill C–31 in June 1985 changed the position Native women occupy *vis-à-vis* Canadian law and band affiliations. Bill C–31 was designed to remove the sanctioned discrimination of those sec-tions of the 1869 post-Confederation Enfranchisement Act, the 1876 Indian Act, and the 1951 Bill C–79 (including section 12[1][b]) outlined above. Although Bill C–31 sought to reform the immediate material reality of Native women, and the Canadian state gave up some part of its jurisdiction in defining the constituency of 'Indian-ness,' the Indian Act still exists at large as the principal governing authority in defining who is and is not 'Indian.' The power to define and contain the legal subjectivity of 'Indian-ness' still rests with the state. One of the effects of Bill C–31 has been to transform the socio-symbolic inscription of Native women as legally sanctioned subjects. Although this legitimation has taken place largely through the effects of Bill C–31, it has also taken place at the constitutional level as, for example, when the Quebec Native Women's Association in 1983 resolved to amend section 35 of the 1982 Constitutional Act to include the following fourth subsection: 'Norwithstanding any other provision of this Act, the aboriginal and treaty rights referred to in subsection (1) are guaranteed equally to male and female persons.'[4] It is, in part, the legitimizing of Native women's subject-status in relation to the dominant culture that has brought political pressure to bear on the human sciences to interpret colonial archives and cultural productions such as oral narratives, films, fiction, and critical essays from this positive position.

The history behind the passing of this piece of legislative reform, its subsequent effects on Native women, and their current attempts to establish self-government, are rife with contradictions and clashes. A particular contradiction emerges between the struggle for equality for Native women based on principles of liberal feminism and the struggle for decolonization as that struggle has been, and continues to be, formulated by Native political organizations. The refusal of the Canadian state to address the complex specificity of a colonial and patriarchal configuration of discrimination has turned Bill C–31 into an unsatisfactory and ineffectual solution to the dilemma of Native women in Canada.

The history of the passing of Bill C–31 is related by Native women themselves in *Enough Is Enough: Aboriginal Women Speak Out*, as told to Janet Silman. *Enough Is Enough* makes clear the material conditions on which Native women have argued for the specificity of their oppression, as well as documenting the grass-roots political action engaged in by the Tobique women in their political and legal struggle with the state. These events, as outlined by Silman in her introduction, include the 1973 Supreme Court of Canada ruling on two women, Jeannette Lavell and Yvonne Bedard, whose complaint against section 12 (1)(b) failed because the Supreme Court ruled that the Indian Act was exempt from the Canadian Bill of Rights (13). This defeat resulted in the Tobique women taking the case of Sandra Lovelace to the United Nations. 'In 1981 the U.N. Human Rights Committee ruled in Sandra Lovelace's favour, finding Canada in breach of the International Covenant on Civil and Political rights' (14). In four more years, as a result of intense lobbying on the part of the Tobique women and with the support of women's advocacy groups, Bill C–31 was passed.

Bill C–31 was acclaimed by elements of the women's movement, a movement predicated upon a liberal critique of patriarchy and the desire for 'equality.' It is important to note here a basic epistemological difference between feminism's claims for (individual) equality and Native women's struggles for 'positive discriminations' or, worded differently, the discernment of cultural differences, in the form of collective political rights. The inscription of European patriarchal controls in the Indian Act provided the epistemological assumptions necessary for a feminist critique. The Canadian government's desire to adopt a Charter of Rights and Freedoms[5], in which sexual equality would be guaranteed (the latter achieved through a great deal of political pressure), made it possible for women's advocacy groups and equal rights proponents to place significant pressure on the government to remove section 12(1)(b) from the 1951 amendment. However, the struggle to remove the discriminatory provisions of the act was not supported by all Native political organizations. Since the instatement of Bill C–31, which made possible the reclaiming of status lost by women and children before the passing of Bill C–31, initial resistance has remained strong.

In her essay 'Sexual Equality and Indian Government: An Analysis of Bill C–31 Amendments to the Indian Act' Joyce Green analyses the contradictions that have emerged between First Nations' demands for the right to control the constitution of Native 'citizenship,' the demand for self-government and the establishment of a land base, and the demands of the women's movement on behalf of Native women for equality within this structure of self-determination. In short the Canadian government (and implicitly the women's movement) granted Native women equality within its own structure, a structure of internal colonialism, while leaving financial and land-base problems, brought about by the reinstatement of Native women and their male and female children, who had previously lost their status, to be coped with by the bands. The result, as Green notes, is that while the Canadian government has sought to correct its past sins of patriarchal control of Native women, the government is making the First Nations pay the cost of expiating those sins (93).

According to Roger Moody, indigenous women's movements throughout the world have often put 'struggles for survival, land rights, sacred places, community-controlled education, and so forth, first on the agenda' (242) before issues that are more directly gender-oriented; however, he goes on to clarify that 'there are specifically women's perspectives on all these aims, together with a growing demand for women's participation, at every level of indigenous society' (242). This observation, although affirming the difference in perspectives between indigenous women and men, does not consider the effects of the imposition of patriarchal values from the dominant colonial power. In its attempt to consider this side of the problem, and although not by design, the Anglo-American women's movement has participated in the scenario of the white-woman-feminist-saving-Native-women-from-Native-men, thereby further demonstrating how (hetero)sexism can be used as a tool of divisiveness within specific classes and subjugated groups. In this case the Euro-Canadian feminist critique of patriarchy within indigenous communities maintains a colonial ethnocentrism as the voice-of-civilized-reason that becomes the authority for helping Native women combat sexism and violence against women within Native communities. On the other hand, the oppression of Native women, the burden of poverty, violence, and dispossession they bear, is compounded because they are women and because they are Native.

What then is the place of feminism in relation to Native women's struggle? Is it another ruling ideology mediating the violence between the dispossessed and the state, and by so doing failing to resolve or clarify the origins of this violence? For those of us interested in the project of materialist feminisms, Donna Haraway provides an important place to begin when she writes, in her 'A Cyborg Manifesto: Science, Technology, and Socialist Feminism in the Late Twentieth Century,' of the 'daily responsibility of real women to *build* unities, rather than to naturalize them' (158). The current tensions between feminism and Native women's struggle for self-determination would certainly indicate that this building of affinities is difficult, however crucial.

### The Discourse of Boundaries

In an introductory dialogue between Marlyn Kane (Osennontion) and Sylvia Maracle (Skonaganleh:rá) in a special Native women theme issue of *Canadian Woman Studies/Les Cahiers de la femme*, the name of 'feminism,' for all its claims to difference and plurality (since it *allows* this special issue to be guest-edited by a collective of indigenous women), is recalled as an instrument of unification to the exclusion of indigenous women and 'women who are burdened with such labels as immigrant women, or visible minority women.' Sylvia Maracle, in conversation with Marlyn Kane, sets the terms of the debate in the following critique of feminism:

Skonaganleh:rá (Sylvia Maracle): I agree we had a hard time with this thing
called 'feminism' and writing for a 'feminist' journal ... I understand the nature
of being defined as a 'feminist,' and wanting some sense of equality, but
frankly, I don't want equality ... while I suppose equality is a nice thing and
while I suppose we can never go back all the way, I want to make an effort
at going back to at least respecting the role that women played in communities
... The 'others' have to start to think differently and they have to look in their
own mirror, at their own selves, and their own baggage that they're carrying
and where they come from. They should not look at a universal sisterhood, so
much as we should be looking at creating a situation where all people of many
colours can peacefully exist. (15)[6]

Feminist critical practice, however resistant to the universal constructions of 'Woman' in institutional discourses and cultural productions,
remains inadequate to the interests of Native, Métis, and Inuit
women's struggle for self-determination. For materialist feminists the
articulation of the relationship between a predominantly institutionalized feminist theory and aboriginal women's writings is crucial. It is
crucial because the unequal relations among women cannot be reduced
to a universal sisterhood composed of an essential plurality of differences. The philosophical question of difference needs to be mediated
through historical, geopolitical, and cultural examples if the epistem-
ologial assumptions within feminist critical practice are to be given
explanatory power.

In postcolonial feminism the dream of a global sisterhood has taken
the shape of a discourse of boundaries. Rosaura Sanchez criticizes this
theoretical move in the following way: 'The notion of pluralism, of a
multicultural society, points then to a type of heterogeneous cohesive
whole while suppressing the reality of social fragmentation. Similarly
the talk of boundaries leaves us contemplating one plane, one dimension, rather than aware of a hierarchal structure, a class system, that
establishes social constraints and creates antagonism between groups.'[7]
The discourse of boundaries relies on the referential power of 'territory' and 'homeland.' Under capitalism this referential power translates into the material determinations of land ownership, property, and
territorial nationalism. The rhetorical investment in the metaphors of
territory makes 'language' capitalism's most useful broker, trading one
figurative currency for another. Under late capitalism the fluency of
the discourse of boundaries is merely one learned textual fragment
among many in the shattered dreams of a global sisterhood.

Sanchez's comment rightly reflects the utopian aspirations of a pluralist feminism. However, the discourse of boundaries can have another sort of referential power, one which not only points to displaced questions of imperial expansion in cultural and ideological zones of containment, but works precisely to contest the boundaries and frontiers erected by a ruling power against those it would further restrict and contain. Osennontion, in the same conversation with Skonaganleh:rá mentioned above, uses the metaphor of braiding in a way that suggests the emancipatory aspects of crossing over cultural boundaries: 'One of the very small girls understands at three years old, the teaching of the sweetgrass braid – how weak one strand is, how easy it is to break it up, and it's gone. She knows, however, that many strands, braided together, cannot be torn apart' (8). In the editorial note to this aboriginal-women guest-edited issue of *Canadian Woman Studies* the following use of the metaphor of braiding also appears: 'We are reclaiming our pride and traditions. We are asking for opportunities to practice our culture. To transmit the braiding of our past, present and future into terms others can understand and respect' (5). Dismantling the walls of empire, the signs of its own defensive position, marks Skonaganleh:rá and Osennontion's call to the 'braiding' of differences – a radical dis-assemblage, on the part of Native, Métis, and Inuit storytellers, artists, film-makers, writers, and cultural critics, of the restricted access to ideological apparatuses.

The entry of Native oral traditions into print culture – of which Maracle and Kane's dialogue is a rich example of the modalities of oral instruction – represents a mode of braiding dominant technological forms with traditionally performative modes of storytelling. I agree with Sanchez that the discourse of boundaries in postmodern, neocolonial discourse can further assimilation by producing a symmetrical syntax of overlapping totalities of difference that appear to be internally homogeneous. However, given the already existing form of enclosure implied by this critique of hierarchy, the notion of braiding autonomous threads together suggests a cultural politics of difference in which fragmentation of social relations between Native and non-Native women is already a site of productive struggle; productive because it recognizes the emancipatory potential within Native oral practices to cross over the boundaries of written ideological containment.

One dramatization of Native women's subversion of this mode of ideological containment was a series of three conferences in which the clashes and contradictions between indigenous women's movements and feminism were made apparent: the Third International Feminist Book Fair (June 1988), the National Symposium on Aboriginal Women of Canada: Past, Present and Future (October 1989), and the aboriginal women's symposium 'Born Feminists – a Unique Perspective' (March 1990). Two theoretical problems inform the interpretation of these conferences: (1) the irony of a politics of difference based, as it is, on principles of specificity, particularity, and hence 'discrimination,' and yet universal in its abstract appeal to the freedom to determine one('s) identity; (2) the way in which a politics of discrimination (as difference) is caught up in the paradox of its own relationship to the 'laws' of official representation. To contest those laws is to be a 'criminal.' Along with this ambiguous process of discrimination we need then a process of de-criminalization, or dis-criminalization. To both these theoretical concerns two problems are central: that of appropriation, the theft of aboriginal cultural practices; and the access of Native artists, musicians, film-makers, and writers to the dominant ideological apparatuses of representation.

At the Third International Feminist Book Fair, Lee Maracle delivered a paper entitled 'Moving Over,' in which she addressed the productive yet debilitating discord between Native and English-Canadian women, particularly with reference to non-Native publications of Indian stories, such as Anne Cameron's *Daughters of Copper Women*. *Daughters of Copper Women* contains a collection of oral stories told to Anne Cameron by the Nuu-Chah-Nulth (Nootka) women of Vancouver Island. Although published with their permission and Cameron's public acknowledgment that proceeds from the book go to opposing the logging industry and its destruction of First Nations' lands, Cameron's book came to signify at least two contradictory moments. On the one hand, as Maracle writes in 'Moving Over,' her work contributes to 'the great turn-around – revolution – that white Canada will inevitably have to make' (11) in recognizing the material effects of imperialism in the dominant culture's ignorance of indigenous cultural practices and in their exclusion and denigration; on the other hand, Cameron's appropriation and publication of Native literatures disempowers Native writers, distorting the social relations through which the oral tradition, in its printed as well as performative and verbal forms, conveys knowledge, teachings, humour, and spirituality. Anne Cameron was asked, then, by a group of Native women writers to 'move over,' to refrain from continuing to publish for Native storytellers. In an interview with Susanne de Lotbinière-Harwood, Maracle noted, 'She agreed that she would move over, she would help promote our work' (31), though not without resistance. As Maracle writes in 'Moving Over,' 'Anne thinks that a writer has a perfect right to write about anything under the heavens. In the larger sense, this is true. But right now it is a bitter pill for me to swallow' (9).[8]

In October 1989 the National Symposium on Aboriginal Women of Canada: Past, Present and Future was held at Lethbridge University in Alberta. This conference also raised important questions about access to ideological apparatuses, in particular the publishing industry. During the discussion period following a session on Native women and literature the issue of appropriation emerged, this time in relation to an anthology of Native women's writing which was being edited by two non-Native academic women. Marie Baker's account of the conference, entitled 'Prairie Turnips: Sisters Gathering to Turn Up Our Literature and History without Using Our Digging Sticks on Each Other,' describes the session on Native women's literature in the following words:

The Panel on Literature ... began with a commentary on *Slash*, the novel of Jeannette Armstrong. The idea of decolonizing our literature was advanced by both [non-Native women on the panel]. However, when the subject of the appropriation of literature began to be discussed, Aboriginal writers were cautioned about the anthologies now being collected by non-Indian women. Suddenly we were in the real world and academics came to an anticipated stop. Yeah, while we discussed resistance literature, we also considered our control of our material. Anthologies need to have the ideas of other Aboriginal women as editors as well as contributors. Even the conference, itself, then became a target of the discussion when it seemed that the call for abstracts may have 'shut out' some potential researchers. Now this is when I thought the digging sticks would be brought out and we'd chase the obstructors to our process out – even the queasy sisters who tried to protect the non-Indians. As it turned out a stimulating dialogue determined the fate of our writing.[9]

What transpired was a discussion among the editor of an anthology of Native women's writing, who was present in the audience, and Marie Baker and several more Native women writers. The editor of an Albertan-based anthology claimed that when her associate visited Saskatchewan, no Native women writers were to be found. This came as a surprise to the Saskatchewan Native women writers present, in particular Marie Baker and Sue Deranger, who immediately offered their assistance while expressing concern that they had not been consulted previously. It was agreeed that Baker and Deranger would become part of the editorial process. The optimism which sprang from this dialogue has since been undermined by the failure of the original editorial board to follow through with its commitment to transform the social relations of its editorial practice. Why this process failed requires further analysis. But one thing still seems clear; however much the mirror has begun to crack, feminism's unexamined ethnocentric attitudes (demonstrated in part by its untheorized relationship to access to publishing) remain the principal barrier to social change for all women, including white feminist academic women, whose unacknowledged relative privilege in a racist society serves as another appetizer at the hypocrite's feast.[10]

The third event, the Native women's symposium entitled 'Born Feminists – a Unique Perspective,' was held courtesy of the Women's Studies Department, New College, University of Toronto. Whereas the National Symposium on Aboriginal Women drew on an estimated 60 per cent aboriginal input, the University of Toronto Native women's symposium was organized by Native women, supported by Dr Linda Carty, a professor in the Women's Studies Department and long-time black community activist. All the presenters – approximately fifteen in number – were Native women from a variety of aboriginal cultures, including Okanagan, Blackfoot, Algonquian, Ojibway-Odawa, Mohawk, Innu, Pottawatamie, Sioux, Ojibway-Cree, Onondaga, and Métis. Through this conference Native women asserted their autonomy to specify the issues, regarding law, prisons, education, land claims, the environment, and the arts, most pressing to achieve a Native feminism of decolonization. In effect, what this autonomy produced was a clear sense of the differences among Native women (e.g., differences between aboriginal cultures, differences between living on the reserves and in urban centres). While at the feminist book fair Native women occupied a marginal position yet made a large impact on feminist debate, and while the conference at Lethbridge was 'about' Native women, this conference effectively situated Native women as agents of their own historical and cultural experiences. And it is important to note that it was this emphasis on the diversity of Native women's cultural affiliations, even as the category of Native women was being deployed, that brought about a substantial challenge to the universal category of 'Native Women' imposed by feminists, including myself.

### Braiding the Difference

The controversy generated at the Third International Feminist Book Fair indicated, once again, that ethnocentrism and racism were still present in a predominantly white middle-class feminist critical practice, which had much to (un)learn about the difference between the tokenism of liberal pluralism and the articulation of a politics of differ-ence.[11] These two processes of discrimination are already inseparable since the reproduction of discriminatory classifications by liberal pluralism inheres (even as a symptom or remainder) in the dis-crimi-nality of oppositional complicity between the law and its illicit subjects – those who are discriminated against, rather than for, in this uncer-tain critical practice called a 'politics of difference.' Some of the stra-tegic analytical tools with which this cultural politics of difference is being built include attention to historical specificity; the recognition of a 'reality of realities' in alternative conceptions of gender and sexual differences; the constitution of social relations (the differences among Native women and between Native and non-Native [i.e., including non–English-Canadian] women) rather than individual representation (a Native woman representing all Native women); and the multivalent articulations of race discriminations and class domination with those of gender differences and imperialist border crossings.

Some Native women have responded to the continuing antagonistic and oppositional conflict with imperial feminism by claiming autono-my, not only in terms of gaining control over the publication of Native literatures and the dissemination of Native representations but also in the political sphere, by claiming an autonomous space in which to set the terms and issues of the Native women's movement.

During the last two decades the publication of poetry, fiction, auto-biographical accounts, short stories, and theatre scripts by Native, Métis, and Inuit women writers in Canada brought about a significant break in the exclusionary practices of the mainstream publishing industry, feminist or otherwise. The following is a list of some of those works: Jeannette Armstrong's *Slash*; Lee Maracle's *Bobbi Lee, Indian Rebel: Struggles of a Native Canadian Woman*, reprinted as *Bobbi Lee: Indian*, edited by Viola Thomas, with a foreword by Jeannette Arm-strong; Beth Brant's edited collection *A Gathering of Spirit*; Maria Campbell's *Halfbreed*; Linda Griffiths and Maria Campbell's, *The Book of Jessica: A Theatrical Transformation*; Beatrice Culleton's *In Search of April Raintree*; Beth Cuthand's *Voices in the Waterfall*; Minnie Aodla Freeman's *Life among the Qallunaat*; Rita Joe's *Song of Eskasoni*; Lee Maracle's *I Am Woman*; and Ruby Slipperjack's *Honour the Sun*. There have also been special-issue journal publications put out by *Fireweed* (no. 22 [1986]) and *Canadian Woman Studies / Les Cahiers de la femme* (10, nos. 2–3 [1989]). The *Magazine to Re-establish the TRICKSTER*, a Native journal publication, was also established in 1989.

In particular, writers such as Jeannette Armstrong, Lee Maracle, and Maria Campbell have resisted an articulation between Native women's struggle and feminism. An auto-critique of the colonialist assumptions in self-identified non-Native feminist (as well as other critical) practice and theory is not only important to the process of unlearning racism and ethnocentrism; it also raises the question of the possibility of collective resistance on the part of new social movements (*vide* Ernesto Laclau and Chantal Mouffe). Currently the notion of collective solidarity is taking shape in terms of articulated new social movements in which a united front of resistance is considered necessary in order to contest the antagonistic relations between new social movements such as those exemplified by Native women's struggle for self-determination and various forms of hegemonic or imperial feminism.

If the critical project of feminism is ultimately to transform the hierarchies of heterosexism, gendered and racist oppression, and class exploitation, then the prevalent form of cultural feminism in Canada must be reinvented in the historical and cultural relations of Native women's struggle for self-determination. Otherwise the unhappy sisterhood of decolonization/feminism perpetuates the failure of its critical process to braid the differences, differences that are not assembled on the basis of identifiable gender and race values, but differences that are braided together so as to overcome the intolerable hierarchies of sexual and racial differences reproduced by the consolidation of an all too self-consciously upwardly mobile feminist power. Feminism too, then, must decolonize its critical practice with a more intimate knowledge of the oppressed, without which it is left saying, they cannot be represented, let them represent themselves.

It is not surprising, then, that within the Native women's movement – a movement directed both towards decolonizing the marginal position of Native peoples generally and, for Native women, renegotiating the place of women's decision-making powers within residual gatherer/hunter and dominant neocolonial modes of production – there is antagonism directed towards the name of feminism. For 'feminism' represents a hegemonic apparatus of power, whose project of unification further induces the fragmentation of non-white, non-Anglo, non-middle-class, non-heterosexual women, who become increasingly marginalized from the name that feminism gives to the legitimate *subject of feminism*. Native women are struggling not only against the economic and cultural forces of late capitalism, but also against the totalizing tendencies in feminist theory and practice. I would not call their struggle a product of a 'double colonization,' as is fashionable nowadays, but one that is intensified by the multiple forces of capitalism. As a non-Native woman, I cannot speak to the intensity of this struggle, but I can mark it here as yet another reason why it is vital that Native women's writings are widely disseminated, published, and read if the building of affinities is truly to constitute a broadly based arena of social change.

I have argued in this chapter for historical specificity as a necessary condition of affinity-building across culturally constituted boundaries. The specificity of the history of colonialism is particularly important to understanding the formation of a postcolonial paradigm of scholarly investigation. Without some knowledge of colonial history the postcolonial rubric can be used to preserve the transparency of colonial literatures, for example, thereby continuing to ignore or deny Native peoples as active agents within the historical process. The following chapter takes an already known archival document which contains a record of British, Cree, and Chipewyan relations in the early stages of the fur trade in Canada. This archival source is particulary interesting because of the significance a Chipewyan woman comes to occupy both for the Chipewyan and the British imperialists. This rereading of an archival document is predicated, in part, on a symptomatic response to this current chapter, in which Native women's self-determined subjectivity has come to challenge not only the present condition of feminist theorization but also its conception of the past.

# 4  'A Gift for Languages': Native Women and the Textual Economy of the Colonial Archive

[Women] make their own history, but not of their own free will; not under circumstances they themselves have chosen but under the given and inherited circumstances with which they are directly confronted.

Karl Marx, 'The Eighteenth Brumaire of Louis Bonaparte'

This is the greatest gift of deconstruction: to question the authority of the investigating subject without paralysing [her], persistently transforming conditions of impossibility into possibility.

Gayatri Chakravorty Spivak, 'Subaltern Studies: Deconstructing Historiography,' 201

## The 'Slave Woman'

In the early eighteenth century Governor James Knight was stationed at York Factory in the service of the Hudson's Bay Company. In his position as captain of this trading post Knight recorded the progress of British imperialism, documenting the management of the fur trade and implementing the expansion of trade to the north into Keewatin, the territory extending westward from the shores of Hudson Bay. Contained within Knight's journal entries between September 1714 and September 1717[1] is an account of a Chipewyan woman, who, according to Knight's narrative, had a principal role in extending his trade relations to include the Chipewyan Indians. The story of 'the Slave Woman,' as Knight consistently refers to her, has become a popular signifier in the historical literature about Native women in Canada.[2] This figure of a Native woman, who functions as a 'Native informant' in Knight's text, has become for Canadian history an idealized and contradictory representation of the Native Woman as heroic proxy and sacrificial victim. How this figure of colonial textuality has been appropriated in contemporary history in order to interpret colonial confrontation is determined as much by assumptions that govern how the archive is read as by present socio-political pressures brought to bear on the historian to make use of certain interpretative strategies.

This transferential[3] relationship, the active transaction between past and present, between the object of investigation and the investigating subject, is mediated in the following discussion by two discontinuous, however supplementary, practices: the self-determined decolonization struggle of Native people living in the geopolitical territory known as Canada; and materialist feminist concerns for articulating a theory of gender subordination with a class analysis informed by an anti-racist and anti-imperialist ethico-politics. The necessity for a theory of gender subordination in postcolonial criticism cannot be insisted on too forcefully. Gayatri Chakravorty Spivak's articulation of post-structuralism, anti-colonialist critique, and feminism, as discussed in chapter 2, provides an important critique of the imperialist assumptions in self-identified – though to a large extent unacknowledged – 'First Worldist' feminist practices, as well as providing a critical space in which to recognize that the formation of a feminism of decolonization must attend to an inevitable antagonism between the (at times contradictory) values, interests, and aims of feminist and decolonialist struggle.

The historical discourse of nation-building deploys the colonial archive to establish the legitimacy of the colonizer, in the process effacing Native 'first nations' and the instrumental use to which they are put in order to facilitate colonization. Fetishizing the colonial archive as the bearer of a 'real' Canadian past occludes the imperialist moment: in Sartrean terms, the originary violence *realized* in the fundamental relation between Native and colonizer. Canada has only recently extricated itself from its symbolic metropolis although the occasional appearance of minor underemployed British royals serves as a constant reminder of Canada's colonial 'heritage.' In 1982 the latest phase in symbolic disengagement took place when Pierre Trudeau's Liberal government officially 'brought the constitution home.' No longer an official colony Canada is now a postcolonial nation-state. Focusing on the colonial and postcolonial relations between Canada and England, however, often occludes the internal colonization of Native people living within Canada. Dispossession and marginalization still characterize the cultural, economic, and political existence of both rural and urban Native people. The utopic desire on the part of the discipline of history to establish national statehood, in the history of a country such as Canada as the centre and origin of its own historical making, is carried through a reading of the colonial archive as *l'histoire totale*. But attention to the archive as a written document mediated by the antagonism of imperial conquest and colonial settlement destabilizes the narrative possibilities for historical closure. As Derrida suggests in *Writing and Difference* in his essay 'Structure, Sign and Play in the Discourse of the Human Sciences,'

if totalization no longer has any meaning, it is not because the infiniteness of a field cannot be covered by a finite glance or a finite discourse, but because the nature of the field – that is, language and a finite language – excludes totalization. This field is in effect that of *play*, that is to say, a field of infinite substitutions only because it is finite, that is to say, because instead of being an inexhaustible field, as in the classical hypothesis, instead of being too large, there is something missing from it: a centre which arrests and grounds the play of substitutions. One could say ... that this movement of play, permitted by the lack or absence of a centre or origin, is the movement of *supplementarity*. (289)

The discourse of history dramatizes the struggle between the impossibility of totalization and the possibility of a meaningful representation of totalization produced through narrative closure. Caught in the tracks of the battlefield of signification is the historical archive, a presumed centre of historical verification, an absolute proximity of the historical 'Real,' a tangible past. No such luck. The writer on the colonial scene can no more embody the unified authorial voice (with himself as the centre to which he predicates the usefulness of a particular Native women) than can the contemporary historian in attempting to master the reality effect of archival documents in order to assert the 'thing-ness' of an object of study. The disability to fully contain Native women's subjectivity can be read in the perorations of imperialist textuality, what Dominick LaCapra refers to in *History and Criticism* as 'textualized remainders' (36): a surplus of additional signs taken for waste.

## A Colonial Story Retold

24 November 1714. A Chipewyan woman arrives at Fort York, two days after the death of another northern Native woman who had been at the trading post for twenty months. Upon the death of this woman Knight writes: 'I took upon it as a Very Great Loss as to her Death in ye information I should have had of her if She had Liv'd & gave an account in Generall & in Some things particular w<sup>ch</sup> would have been much to the Companys Advantage I being fully satisfied to have a trade settled with them [the Chipewyan] would be of great Profit & it may be in Some time exceed all ye Other trade of this Country ...' (22 November 1714).[4] Both of these women are referred to in Knight's journal with the generic name 'the Slave Woman.' The Slave Woman who arrives on the 24th recently 'escaped form her [Cree] master' and had come upon a satellite encampment of British men from York Factory. She was subsequently taken to the main trading post. Knight's initial entry on the Slave Woman documents her facility with Cree and Chipewyan languages: 'she speaks but this Country Indian indifferently but will be of great Service to me in my Intention' (24 November 1714). Knight's intention, as he outlines it, was to produce a peace treaty between the warring Cree and Chipewyans in order to facilitate company trade relations with the Chipewyan and make way for the construction of another trading post further to the north at Churchill River.

30 June 1715. The Slave Woman, under Knight's orders, returns to the north, where she was originally captured by the Cree. She is accompanied by an imperial representative, William Stewart, and a group of Cree Indians. Knight delegates Stewart his official representative and charges him with specific written duties regarding the protection of the Slave Woman and overseeing her functions as translator, guide, interpreter, and peacemaker: 'I order you to take care that none of the Indians abuse or misuse the Slave Woman that goes with you or to take she has from her that is to be given amongst her countrys people & likewise to tell her to acquaint her country people that we shall settle a factory at Churchill River next fall & that we will trade with them for Beaver ...' (27 June 1715). As the centre of imperial gravity becomes further dispersed in its efforts to bring the 'outside' into its domain of socio-economic control, designated official representatives and unofficial preceptors begin to function increasingly as supplementary subjects – a surplus of substitutions whose relationship to the original centre (Governor James Knight? the Hudson's Bay

Company?) is further deferred and differentiated through the geo-political pressures of colonial expansion. It is this increasing produc-tion of *différance* that permits the play and struggle over meaning which, in turn, destabilizes this particular colonial archive and leaves it as only an interpretive fiction on the part of Governor Knight. The rhetoric of protection included in Knight's orders to Stewart not only encodes British class morality but also an instrumental necessity in that the Slave Woman must be kept alive in order to carry out Knight's imperial dream of colonial expansion. Without the Slave Woman the project might fail. But ultimately her significance extends only to the degree to which she remains useful – she is, as it will become clear, expendable and replaceable.

13 April 1716. Almost a year later, news of the expedition reaches York Factory. On 7 May the Slave Woman returns with William Stewart, accompanied by ten Chipewyan Indians. From 7 May to 9 May Knight's entries contain a description of the events that transpired during the expedition, noting in particular the role the Slave Woman played as 'Chief instrument in finishing of it what has been done ...' (7 May 1716). Praise for the Slave Woman continues when Knight describes her powers of persuasion in convincing a party of Cree Indians to continue on their journey with her and Stewart just after they had come upon nine recently killed members of their nation:

[i]t was as much as ever the Indian Woman and W$^m$ Stewart could do to persuade them to the Contrary the Woman bid them Stay where they was and Shee would follow there tracks as had made there Escape and persuaded them to Stay in the Place for Ten days and if she did not find them in the time nor comeback they might return ... on the tenth Day when they were resolv$^d$ to Stay there no Longer the Woman came and hollow$^{'d}$ and made her Signall ... and had brought with her about 160 Men the Cleverest as ever he see in his Life then came where the Indians was in the tent, but the woman had made her self so hoarse with her perpetual talking to her Country Men in persuad-ing them to come with her that shee could hardly Speak but when they were all mett then Stewart bid the Cap$^t$ tell them Indians what they was come about and when the woman had told them they had no hand in killing there Coun-try men nor did not know it twill they found them dead nor they did not come upon any there Account then but to make peace ... (7 May 1716)

Knight records that the Slave Woman dutifully carried out his orders, informing the Chipewyans of his intent to trade and build a trading post at Churchill as well as giving instructions as to how to skin and dress the furs according to European specifications (9 May 1716). In Knight's narrative the Slave Woman figures as an exemplary preceptor in the service of imperial peace and security:

Indeed she has a Divellish Spirit and I believe that if there were but 50 of her Country Men of the Same Carriage and Resolution they would drive all the Northern Indians in America out of there Country now she is here she doth Awe her Country Men they dare hardly speak to her and spares none of our Indians in telling how basely they killd 9 of there people when they had Smok$^d$ the friendly pipe to make a peace I keep all the Indians as came with her in the factory for fear of any Mischief and shall carry them on some part of there way in there return and does train them every day to use of Guns that they may know how to defend themselves with if our Indians should pursue them when they go away ... (9 May 1716)

In the guise of the devil the Slave Woman represents the power of force capable of achieving Knight's imperial, genocidal wish-fulfilment: the obliteration of 'all the Northern Indians in America.'

Knight's design to build a fort at Churchill River is delayed in the fall because a supply vessel from England fails to arrive as planned. Knight attributes the ship's failure to arrive to the incompetence of the ship's captain, a man named Davis. The inadequacy on the part of British seamanship to reach its destination, a failure of imperial dissemination, produces several hysterical outbursts in Knight's otherwise sedate discourse.

5 February 1717. The Slave Woman dies.

[T]he Northern Slave Woman departed her Life after About Seven Weeks Illness The Misfortune in loosing her will be very Prejudiciall to the Companys Interests ... I am sure the Death of her was a very considerable loss to the company for the wintering here allmost 2 years with us & going the year to make the peace & being chief promoter and acter in it w$^{ch}$ has caused respect to her & Carry'$^d$ Also a Great Sway Among the Indians and that Shee knowd well Enough Ab$^t$ 4 Days before She Died althô So Excessive Ill as She was She calld to an English Boy as I designd to Send with her up into the Country to Learn there Speech and for a Confirmation what She had told the Strange Indians She bidd the boy not to be Afraid to go Amongst their Indians for her Brother & Country People would Love him and not Lett him want for anything I am so concernd for her Deathe and for fear of the rest so Dangerously Ill as they bee that I am almost ready to break my heart to think now I be Disappointed in this undertaking wherein I had such a fair Prospect of ye business as would prove so Advantagious to the Company's Flourishing ... (5 February 1717)

6 May 1717. Three months later Knight records that another Slave Woman has been found; this time he must pay the 'dear' price for her of 'above 60 skins value':

[T]he Indian as came in brought A Northern Slave Woman w^{ch} I bought this Day haveing a Great Deal of Difficulty too gett her & Paid dear for her for she Cost me Above 60 Skins Value in Goods but have her I must let it cost me what will for there is no one Else as can Speak one Word of the Country Language and this for the Boy as is with the Capt Understands but Little of these Indians Speech here besides he is so jealous of him that he doth not care for him too come near the factory & part w^{th} I believe he would not for half the goods in the Country & it is Impossible to have brought that trade without somebody Understood us & them too and Especially as our Circumstances was with us for Else wee could not be able to give them an Account of the Misfortunes as befell their Country People Since they first Came here w^{ch} now we shall be able to give them an Account how things came to pass besides it will be a means of bringing as trade some Years Sooner than it could be done any other ways ... (6 May 1717)

Interpretations of this archival document, such as those found in 'Many Tender Ties': Women in Fur-Trade Society in Western Canada, 1670–1870, by Sylvia Van Kirk and in Ron Bourgeault's essay 'Indian, Métis and the Fur Trade: Class, Sexism and Racism in the Transition from "Communism" to Capitalism,' attempt to locate in the archival text information about the specificity of Native experience in the colonial encounter. This shift in the object of investigation from the colonizer to the colonized is constitutive to the production of post-colonial knowledge. However, the ideological crime of exclusion of Native people as subjects to and of their own historical making is not necessarily undone by a reconfiguration of the subject-position of indigenous peoples as 'colonized.' Nor can such a reconfiguration of the historical and political subjectivity of Native people take place when questions of discursive formation, textual practice, and interpretive strategy remain unexamined.

Van Kirk's and Bourgeault's texts reinscribe Knight's journal entries as transparent and unmediated representations of 'reality.' Van Kirk produces an impressionistic and sentimental historical narrative, something like an imitation of Knight's seemingly benign journals. Bourgeault reads the archival text as an unambiguous, cut and dried, tell-it-like-it-is account of quotidian history. These direct or naïve realist approaches yield, however, different and contradictory re-presentations of the Slave Woman, as victim (for Bourgeault) and heroine (for Van Kirk). In the case of this particular colonial resource the problems of the colonialist's record and its relationship to the English language as a combined measure of the universal Truth of the 'colonial encounter' emerge in Knight's text in repeated references to his anxiety and fear of violence, which only the presence of a supplicant Native translator or interpreter can relieve. The realist interpretative strategy adopted by Van Kirk and Bourgeault is overdetermined by a discursive struggle already at play in Knight's text. In other words, their textual strategies continue to work to relieve the anxiety of unassimilable differences while simultaneously working to veil the 'epistemic violence' that is inevitable in the Native/colonial confrontation.

### 'Many Tender Ties': The Feminization of Native History

During the 1970s feminist criticism challenged exclusions and silences in various disciplines of the human sciences.[5] Questions relating to the 'proper subject' of investigation led to the insertion of a universal category of Woman, defined largely by the self-identifying practices of those women (white middle-class) already engaged in academic research or affiliated with academic institutions. The inclusion of the figure of Woman initially expanded the professional field of history, filling the gap left by an absence of critical attention directed towards women as subjects to and of historical making. For example, an earlier account of Governor James Knight's journals by historian E.E. Rich describes Knight's delegate, William Stewart, as the person largely responsible for the success of the 1715–16 mission into the north. Rich describes the Slave Woman as an assistant of marginal significance. Rich writes, 'Stewart's achievement was already both great in itself and great in its promise of vital development. He had "endured great hardships in traveling to make peace amongst the northern Indians," for which he received a gratuity and a rise in salary, but despite his obvious merits and his value to the concern ... he showed no administrative skill, power of command or ability to shape a policy; and his later career is obscure.' And of the Slave Woman, Rich writes, 'she proved an admirable interpreter and an enthusiastic advocate of Knight's policy ... she died in the fort during the winter and it was with great difficulty that Knight secured another "Northern slave woman" early in 1717.'[6] The Slave Woman, who was responsible for making both Knight's policy and the mission to the north successful, receives little if any critical attention in Rich's account. And yet the man, William Stewart, who accompanied her, is considered to have made a 'great' contribution to the expansion of the Hudson's Bay Company. It is in response to such historical blindnesses and distortions of patriarchal bias that revisionary feminist historical practice has made an invaluable contribution.

Sylvia Van Kirk's *'Many Tender Ties': Women in Fur-Trade Society in Western Canada, 1670–1870* is a text that was produced during the rise of liberal feminism and its push for egalitarian relations in historical analyses. That this text registers the epistemological presuppositions of this feminist position can be seen in Van Kirk's own summary of her revisionary project:

Investigators of women's history are discovering that the view of women as 'active agents,' instead of the simplistic view of women as 'passive victims,' promises to provide the key to understanding women's motivations and actions. In this instance, it is believed that the examination of the role played by women as actors upon the fur-trade stage is essential to a full understanding of the complexities of what was an unusual society in early Western Canada. (8)

Constitutive to the epistemology of this approach is the overturning of binary oppositions. Women as 'passive victims,' a code of patriarchal discourse in which women are placed in an inferior position (passivity), is transformed into the male counterpart, the 'active agent' (activity). By positioning women as active agents, Van Kirk aims to achieve a 'full[er] understanding' of the workings of the drama of the fur trade and to include women as subjects of that dramatic representation. Van Kirk's subjects, however, occupy a position in her discursive formation that maintains their status as subjects to and not of the process of historical investigation. The metaphor of the 'fur-trade stage' in which roles previously occupied by men are allotted to women significantly alters the subject-position of Native women as dramatic subjects, but their political subjectivity as an indigenous rather than colonized subject remains unrepresented.

Implicit to the metaphor of Van Kirk's 'fur-trade stage' is the figuration of an audience removed from the action of the play. I would suggest that this implicit figure of the audience can function as a metaphorical displacement of the fieldworker, the investigator, or the historian. In which case, the relationship of the liberal feminist academic to her new colonized subject of study – Native women – does not differ significantly from an earlier benevolent view of Native/European confrontation recorded by Governor Simpson in 1857: '[Native people] hunt and fish, and live as they please. They look to us for their supplies, and we study their comfort and convenience as much as possible, we assist each other' (quoted by Van Kirk, 9–10). The representation of egalitarian relations between Native and European is based here on a correlation between material goods and the study and surveillance of Native people. The production by the state of a condition of material dependency among the First Nations permits the continued study and surveillance of Native peoples for the benefit of postcolonial knowledge. The shift in the study and surveillance of Native peoples from that of colonial object to colonized subject in postcolonial discourse maintains the condition of dependency. The material administered and exchanged in the process of subjecting Native people to colonial historization no longer exists in the form of supplies or European commodities. In postcolonial discourse it is their symbolic value as textual commodities that is being exchanged.

In postcolonial knowledge dependency is maintained by containing the subjectivity of Native peoples in the images, stereotypes, and representations deployed in colonial discourse. What is exchanged and delivered back to the Native is a representation of herself as, for instance, the civilized barbarian or the evil non-conformist, to name two sides of the same coin. Abdul R. JanMohamed explains this phenomenon in relation to colonial literature in his essay 'The Economy of Manichean Allegory: The Function of Racial Difference in Colonialist Literature.' His critique is relevant to the production of history when he observes that 'just as imperialists "administer" the resources of the conquered country, so colonialist discourse "commodifies" the Native subject into a stereotyped object and uses [her] as a "resource" for colonialist fiction ... Once reduced to [her] exchange-value in the colonialist signifying system, [she] is fed into the manichean allegory, which functions as the currency, the medium of exchange, for the entire colonialist discursive system' (64).[7]

The dominant culture still stages the production of colonialism. It is still directing the show, as it were; only this time it seeks to correct the historical error of subject exclusion by hiring a fabricated representation of Native women's marginality to play the central role of 'Native women,' a role already constructed by dominant ideological apparatuses. Postcolonial knowledge in the guise of a libertarian ethic of self-correction continues to circumscribe the field of investigation. It is only by producing parameters that a supposedly 'fuller understanding' of the colonial scene can be portrayed. The field of investigation has been delimited so that its 'new subjects' fit the conceptual order of the classifications of Euro-Canadian epistemology.

One of the ways in which Van Kirk frames the subjectivity of the Native Woman is by interpreting events on the basis of a class dialectic in a European discursive system. In framing Native women's work in the fur trade in relation to the white men they serviced, Van Kirk writes: 'Perhaps the most important domestic task performed by the [Native] women was to provide the [white] men with a steady supply of "Indian shoes" or moccasins' (54). The conceptualization of Native women's work in the category of a 'domestic task' contains a representation of that work as Eurocentric rather than specific to a Native social formation. The figuration of Native women is split between metaphysical conceptions of Native women and European women. As a metonym of Native women's displacement in this Eurocentric and phallocentric narrative, the moccasin signals her subject-position as the rawhide and stripped flesh wrapped around the white man's foot: a graphic figure of Native women's gender and race subordination both to the white man, and, implicitly, the white bourgeois woman.[8]

In a more recent essay, 'Towards a Feminist Perspective in Native History,' Van Kirk outlines her position on the articulation of feminism and Native studies. In opposition to the 'Marxist enthusiasm for the egalitarian nature of pre-contact Native societies in Canada' (379) shown by such writers as the anthropologist Eleanor Leacock and the historian Ron Bougeault, Van Kirk claims 'we' can do no better than a relativist perception of Native women: 'A convincing argument can be made that relatively-speaking pre-contact Indian societies were less oppressive with regard to women than the European societies which subsequently sought to impose their own patterns of sex roles and values on Native societies' (380). Relying for support on colonial archives and reports, Van Kirk insists, however, that male dominance existed in Native social formations and 'even though in hunting-gathering societies women contributed a good deal both in food and labour, it appears that the high status occupations were the male ones of big game hunter and warrior' (379).[9]

Van Kirk's unquestioning use of colonial archives as accurate representations of Native society, in light of her own recognition that whatever relative equality Native women sustained before colonial confrontation, European contact brought a more devastating form of male domination (381), discloses a contradiction: if European colonialists subjected Native women to a Eurocentric patriarchal system which defined women's proper 'roles,' then their reports and assessment of Native social formations presumably reflect their interest in containing Native women within a Eurocentric interpretation of women's subject-position. By way of legitimating a colonial oppression of Native women, colonialists interpellated an already existing form of European male supremacy within Native culture.

What produces a sense of 'relative equality' for Van Kirk, then, is not the accuracy with which the colonial archive disseminates the 'truth' of Native women but the colonialists' ambiguous relationship to Native women. The colonialists were keen to exploit the egalitarian tendencies of the position Native women occupied for purposes of expanding mercantile wealth, but in the process of doing so they had to reject those egalitarian social relations produced within a mode of production at odds with the introduction of European commodity production and exchange values.

For Van Kirk, economic factors are less important than other agents of 'acculturation,' such as the European church and its missionaries (383ff), the introduction of an educational system with which to 'civilize' the Natives (384ff), and the effects of the fur trade on Native child-rearing practices: 'one of the greatest traumas for Indian mothers would have been to lose control over child-rearing, a customary preserve' (384). Furthermore, Van Kirk acknowledges that the passing of the series of federal Indian Acts in the late nineteenth century contributed to the subordination of Native women. Van Kirk recognizes that the state has become since the late nineteenth century the main ideological and repressive apparatus in the historical subjection of Native peoples in Canada.[10] However, the extent to which the colonial government imposed its policy of assimilation, and the fact that the subordination of Native women was necessary to achieving that end, would seem to suggest that the degree of urgency with which the subordination of Native women was introduced was at least equal to the degree of that subordination's previous absence. In other words, Native women obviously occupied strategic positions of power; otherwise, why would the state go to such lengths to destroy those positions of power, economically, spiritually, and politically?

Van Kirk suggests that the project of a feminist Native studies, one in which she sees herself engaged, should systematically study the 'way in which the fur trade actually affected Indian women's material and social lives in the context of their tribal societies' (382). The method appropriate to this approach might involve, Van Kirk suggests, a documentation of Native women's oral history: 'We need to hear Native women's voices on this subject – what motivated individuals to make the choices they did, what have been the consequences both for them and their families. This might be the subject of a rich oral history project, if sensitively undertaken' (387). In her essay 'Imperialism and Sexual Difference' Gayatri Chakravorty Spivak addresses the documentation of 'oral histories' as a means of minimizing the presence of an investigator and as one of the 'various alibis that the dominant subject-position gives itself as it constructs the subordinate as other'; the Third World Woman is made to occupy the position of the 'native informant' (229), or in this case the 'Native informant.' Native and non-Native scholars, who take oral traditions seriously as vital to the historical, spiritual, and educational memory of indigenous knowledges, are already engaged in the process of documenting this orally disseminated knowledge and incorporating it into recent scholarship on the history of colonialism. Van Kirk's suggestion is also appropriate to feminist scholarship. However, the danger of using those traditions as an alibi of authenticity for the purposes of consolidating feminist scholarship must, as Spivak argues, be recognized and confronted; otherwise, feminist scholarship perpetuates the subjugation of Native women, who are made to occupy a space which can then be used to consolidate the colonialist 'self' as Woman.

All too often the knowledge that is constructed around Native women is used to service the needs of feminism, without acknowledging the specificity of Native women's experience and their struggle against European patriarchal controls. Take, for example, Van Kirk's description of Native women and their physical strength:

The issue of strength is particularly interesting, as it is often cited as an innate justification for male dominance over women. HBC traders were frankly astonished at the strength of Chipewyan women, who were evidently much stronger than the men. This apparently did not compromise the Chipewyan male's sense of superiority, for Chief Matonabbee informed Samuel Hearne that 'Women ... were made for labour; one of them can carry, or haul, as much as two men can do' (Van Kirk 1980:18). This should lead us to consider how the supposed natural frailty of women is culturally conditioned, and that strength is not a necessary criterion for male supremacy. (380)

Van Kirk interprets the knowledge of Native women's work for what it can substantiate for feminist knowledge, not for what it can tell feminism about Native women's work.

## The Written and the Writing of Orality

In *Many Tender Ties*, Van Kirk includes a discussion of the figure of Knight's Slave Woman, a rewriting of a piece she previously published under the title 'Thanadelthur.' Van Kirk derives the name 'Thanadelthur' from an account of Native oral history trans-cribed by the photographer Edward S. Curtis.[11] However, in making use of Edward S. Curtis's transcribed story, Van Kirk does not designate this source as a retelling of history from a Native perspective; nor does she address directly the value of this other textual source. As a corrective to the derogatory implications of the name 'the Slave Woman' Thanadelthur works well. Nevertheless, Van Kirk explains Knight's use of the term 'Slave' in the archival text as a result of antagonistic relations between the Cree and Chipewyans: 'The Crees, being the first to obtain guns from the traders, had gained the ascendancy in this tribal conflict and so devastating had their attacks been that one branch of the Chipewyans came to be known as Slaves' (41). In her repetition of the analysis of Knight's text in *Many Tender Ties* Van Kirk erases this return to historical accountability and simply states: 'Knight was immediately impressed with his new informant, whom he always referred to as "the Slave Woman"' (68). Though 'Thanadelthur' is not a proper name within Euro-

The following is Curtis's transcription of the Chipewyan oral history:

This is the Native account of the events leading up to the first contact of the Chipewyan with English traders:

The first trading post on Hudson Bay was established in Cree territory. More robust than the Slender Cree, and more reckless fighters, the Chipewyan had held their own but when they discovered that the Cree could point a stick which made a flash and a cloud of smoke and a noise of thunder and kill a man, they felt helpless. Occasionally the Cree in their raids would catch a handsome young woman and carry her away. Such a woman was Thanadelthur ('marten shake').

Her Cree husband took her on a long journey eastward, and after a time left her behind and went on. When he returned, he had supplies of articles she had never seen. She wondered where he had got them. This happened again the next season. The following year when he left her in camp she followed far behind, keeping hidden in the bush. She saw her husband and his companions disappear in the side of a rock. She crept up and found that it was a stone house. She peered through the window. The factor saw her through the glass, opened the door and called her in. She entered and he asked, 'Who are you?' She answered in Cree. He inquired if her people were numerous, and she said they were many.

pean genealogies of the vocative, which derive from lines of patriarchal descent or as marks of religious affiliation, Van Kirk's privileging of the Native name could be construed as an attempt to correct Knight's failure to record a 'proper' name. In which case, this renaming could be perceived as a 'humanizing' of the Native subject, implicitly containing her subjectivity within a Eurocentric epistemology of naming in order to produce a sense of her individuality and personalize the subject. Van Kirk establishes the original authority of the name 'Thanadelthur' in remarks such as the following: 'In the journals of York Factory, Thanadelthur is always referred to as the Slave Woman ...' (41). In the following comments the name 'Thanadelthur' is shown to be further derived from another source, as a descriptive feature of an animal: 'According to Chipewyan oral tradition, the Slave Woman's real name was Thanadelthur, which meant "marten shake" ...' (41); and Van Kirk mentions that the explorer Samuel Hearne claimed the name 'Thanadelthur' derives from 'some part or property of the Marten' (41).

'Chipewyan oral tradition' occupies the discursive space of neither history nor myth. Of Curtis's transcription in general, Van Kirk, writes, 'Although in-

'Are they good-looking people?'
'You see me. Do I look bad?'
'No, you look better than these people.'
'Well, that is how my people look.'

The man turned to the Cree, who on the woman's entrance had appeared disconcerted, and said: 'You have been telling me that the people with whom you have been fighting are bad-looking people, that they are devils; and that is why you wanted to kill them. I think you are liars.' He paid them for their furs and bought the woman.

The following winter he said to her, 'Do you think you could find your country?'

'Of course I know my country,' she replied.

So a party set out with several sleds, following the Cree trail westward for a time, then branching northward. Here the woman was sent ahead in order that her people might not be frightened. At last she met a man in the trail. She related what had happened and how she was bringing the White Flesh to trade with her people. Then she sent him home with the news and told him that the party would camp at the lake. When the people saw a great fire, the men were to come down and make a treaty. A few came to the camp, but some were fearful and hid. Those who came saw a flag flying, and they were in awe of it. The white men had raised a platform on which they place the woman, so that her people could see her and have confidence. When she beheld her people coming, she sang with joy. The factor gave the Chipewyan presents, especially guns, and for each article he told how many skins they must bring him to pay for it. A gun he would hold upright with

accurate in specific detail, it is notable that the story of Thanadelthur as handed down by the Chipewyans emphasized her youth and attractiveness' (41). The Chipewyan historical account recorded by Curtis is not considered by Van Kirk to be the butt on the ground, and explain that a pile of beaver-skins of equal height would pay for it. All day he taught them how to shoot at a mark, how to use axes and files, how to prepare furs. The woman returned with the factor to the fort on Hudson Bay.

'accurate,' to contain the truth of the history of this colonial encounter. Nor is Chipewyan oral tradition 'mythical' in the sense that it is non-historical, a figure of non-truth. The value of this piece of Chipewyan oral tradition is as a resource of references to 'youth' and 'attractiveness.' Van Kirk's privileging of this discursive narrative as a zero degree of reference from which the name 'Thanadelthur' can be extrapolated discloses a metaphysical presupposition about the relationship of Chipewyan oral tradition to a mythic, that is, unmediated, figure of Nature. 'Thanadelthur' derives from a descriptive feature of the 'natural world,' a practice Van Kirk notes as not unusual to indigenous naming processes. However, that does not mean that the names are any more natural or representative of some essential aspect of the person so named. Dissimulation is always at work in the Cree language, for example, where the copulative verb, 'to be,' does not exist in the language as a mark of absolute proximity or simulation.[12]

Van Kirk's use of the name 'Thanadelthur' exceeds its exchange value in the narrative economy of historical truth; as a *mythic prime* its value is exponentially greater inasmuch as it bears the currency of Nature and circulates within a metaphysical opposition between Culture and Nature. The 'oral tradition' is suspended between Nature and Culture and made to orbit around the solidity of European 'writing practice,' even though the source of orality in this case appears as a published document. In relation to a European record of Truth, oral traditions are perceived to be ephemeral instabilities, verbally disseminated and relying on memory as a record of history.

Similar to the appropriation of the name 'Thanadelthur,' the codes of femininity ('youth' and 'attractiveness') function in Van Kirk's assessment of 'Chipewyan oral tradition' as metaphorical tools with which to revise a negative conception of Native women; and to provide a 'naturalized' portrait of Native women as gendered subjects which fit a European patriarchal notion of women's subjectivity. Van Kirk's appropriation of a European patriarchal conception of Native women's subjectivity as a presumably 'positive' and humanistic repre-

sentation of that subjectivity masks the ethnocentrism of 'naturalization': 'If Chipewyan women, in general, failed to conform to the
Englishman's ideal of beauty, Hearne conceded that many were of "a
most delicate make" and "tolerable" when young. Owing to her difficult way of life, a girl's beauty was particularly fleeting. Given in
marriage when very young, the care of a family added to her constant
hard labour rendering even the best-looking woman old and wrinkled
before she was thirty' (41). From which Van Kirk concludes: 'It is
probable, therefore, that Thanadelthur was in her teens when captured
by the Crees' (41). To assume that Native women are 'given away in
marriage,' that their lives consist largely of child-rearing and 'constant
hard labour,' and that the effects of these assumed 'facts' of Native
culture lead to a portrait of ugliness defined by 'wrinkles' is to impose
Eurocentric notions of working-class women's work, ethnocentric
views of social relations between Native men and women, and a
patriarchal and racist standard of 'beauty.' Though Van Kirk may
intend to present a picture of Native women as 'active agents,' she can
only do so within a circumscribed set of eurocentric epistemological
assumptions. Although her appropriation of the name 'Thanadelthur,'
taken from a transcribed source of Native history, would appear to
suggest a margin of attentiveness to an historical source other than the
colonial archive, its usefulness is severely limited by the degree to
which it can be assimilated into a humanistic conception of the name
as a personal and individual signifier as well as by its value in sustain-
ing the currency of Native 'primitiveness.'

   In attempting to prescriptively repair the derogatory connotations in
Knight's nomination 'the Slave Woman,' Van Kirk's supplementary
intervention of a mythic prime of reference veils not only the violence
of Knight's originary colonial discursive framing, but also what
Derrida terms the *arche-violence* of European writing. The violence of
arche-writing Derrida elaborates in *Of Grammatology* as

the violence of difference, of classification, and of the system of appellation ...
For writing, obliteration of the proper classed in the play of difference, is the
originary violence itself: pure impossibility of the 'vocative mark', impossible
purity of the mark of vocation ...
...
... arche-violence, loss of the proper, of absolute proximity, of self-presence
which has never been given but only dreamed of and always already split,
repeated, incapable of appearing to itself except in its own disappearance.
(110, 112)

The search for the proper name in Van Kirk's analysis attempts to reconstitute an absolute proximity between the Native subject and colonial history, to cover over the mediation of 'writing' as that which permits, selectively, the naïve production of a zero degree of reference. That Van Kirk can locate that mythic prime in a Native oral tradition further inscribes an ethnocentrism of the 'naturalness' and primitiveness of Native cultures: their presumed proximity to a conception of Nature where the name 'Thanadelthur' becomes an emblem of discursive purity, a 'naturally' proper name reclaimed. Though the transcribed account of Chipewyan history may be 'inaccurate in specific detail,' its beauty lies in its proximity to a Eurocentric metaphor of Nature.

In Knight's text the Slave Woman figures as an exemplary preceptor in the service of imperialism. Praise for her conduct as 'Chief instrument in finishing of it what has been done' creates an idealized figuration of the Slave Woman. She becomes the ideal Native informant in the colonial encounter, smoothing the way for the expansion of British imperialism. Except for a recollection of conflict between himself and the Slave Woman, written after her death, antagonism is registered in Knight's text largely in the relationship between Indian nations: 'She sayd shee run away w$^{th}$ another Slave Woman from some Indians last fall ... She left her master the North Side of Portnellson River ...' The Slave Woman's position of conflict is in relation to a Cree master. In relation to the colonizer, however, she figures as an ideal delegate, courier, guide, interpreter, peacemaker, and translator – in short, an extraordinary and unique figure, a surrogate master. The abstraction of the Slave Woman into the currency of the extra-ordinary, where any sign of conflict is displaced onto relations between different Indian nations, functions in much the same way as does the stereotype of the Native as an exotic. Like racist characterizations of savageness and primitiveness used to justify Native 'uncooperativeness' with the colonizer, the extra-ordinary or exotic Native is praised precisely for her usefulness as an instrument in the service of colonial exploitation.

Van Kirk reproduces the discursive value of the Chipewyan woman as an exemplary figure of colonial mediation in her own rewriting of Knight's narrative. Van Kirk fashions the Slave Woman, in story-book fashion, as a coherent subject, fully embodied with a European/Euro-Canadian consciousness: 'Thanadelthur, who readily appreciated the importance of her position, soon became the dominating spirit of the expedition' (41); 'Thereafter, Thanadelthur appears to have behaved admirably'; 'Devoted to the traders interests, she instructed her companions ...'; 'Thanadelthur herself was not without duplicity' (44); 'Thanadelthur was enthusiastic about Knight's proposal ...'; 'Thanadelthur refused to let marital duties interfere with this important commission ...' (45). In the process of romanticizing the figure of the Slave Woman / Thanadelthur into an ideal Native informant, the other Native Slave Women whom Knight mentions, along with the young boy mentioned in the entry of 9 May 1716, are forgotten as mediators in the service of imperial expansion. The privileged position 'the' Slave Woman occupies effaces the many women Knight used to expand his imperial project.

As the mythic prime of Native oral tradition 'Thanadelthur' occupies another historical subject-position: a trope of the Native woman as 'active agent' employed to play a role in a postcolonial drama of 'Native' history. In order to perform this postcolonial reading Van Kirk must symptomatically reread the colonial archive; the colonial text appears as captivating a book of knowledge as any that can be read through the specular gaze of a naïve and direct realism, where the universal adequacy of its representational logic is dutifully accepted as transparent. This reading of the archival text attempts to totalize its discursive formation as an empirical disseminator of fully realized representations. But, as Van Kirk's use of the name 'Thanadelthur' demonstrates, any attempt to stabilize a representation of the Slave Woman requires a momentary closing of the text in the interest of epistemological commodification. The text must remain open to the extent that its figures can be appropriated and transformed in order to increase the field of the officially sanctioned knowledge of colonialism. The figure of the Slave Woman / Thanadelthur becomes the labile subject of a multiple set of configurations, a figure of unresolvable uncertainty, vulnerable because of her 'silence,' her 'orality,' her 'naturalness,' to interested forces of representational stability.

In his essay 'Indian, Métis and the Fur Trade' Ron Bourgeault focuses on a passage Knight wrote in his diary the day the Slave Woman died:

Oh Davis, what has he done by his Ignorance & folly w[th] obstinacy It had not been to doo if her but came to his port as he might have done with ease As I have been Writeing about the Salve Woman Deceased it will not be Amiss to Mention one thing Last June She Gave away a Little Kittle as I had given For to carry with her when she went back into her country Again. I tax'd her bout it She said she had not gave it away I sent to the Indian as had it and fetch'd it away & showed it her She told me was a Lyer for he had stole it for she did not give it him & said that her Indians should kill me when I come to Churchill River and did rife in such a passion as I never did see the Like before & I scuffd her Ears for her but the next Morning she came & Cry'd to me and Said She was a Fool & Madd & told me that I was a father to them all & that she and all the Indians would Love me & I should Never come to any harm. She had been very Good ever since In giveing me any Information & always Speaking in our praise to these Indians And her own wee buried her about 4 a Clock I conceald it as Long as I could from these Sick Indians but they Quickly came to Understand it I gave a few odd things to these to Wipe away their Sorrow & all her things She had She desird me to give to her Mother & brother w<sup>ch</sup> she beggd a Little before her death to be given to them & some other of her friends the finest weather we have had any day this Season but the most melancholys't by the loss of her. (5 February 1717)

Produced upon a memory in Knight's chronological journal, the Slave Woman survives as an ongoing metaphysical presence, ideally predicated as the dutiful daughter and the surrogate master. This 'presence' cannot escape the contradictory representation of a Native submissive and an imperial delegate. Knight's self-conscious intervention, 'As I have been Writeing about the Slave Woman Deceased it will not be Amiss to Mention one thing Last June ...,' marks this 'posthumous' passage as a textual misfit, one in a series of misfires in Knight's continuing attempt to totalize a meaning of the Slave Woman for the purposes of developing a useful taxonomy of the imperial signified. Knight's aberrant disclosure unwittingly permits the possibility of continuing to unfold multiple interpretations of the Slave Woman's object/subject-position by postcolonial knowledge.

In Bourgeault's reading of this passage 'the kettle became symbolic of accepting private property and at the same time the conflict around it was symbolic of both colonial and sexual subservience. The Slave Woman's role in Indian society was being used and at the same time her role was being destroyed' (57). Bourgeault reads this passage for what it reveals by way of conflict between colonial and Native conceptions of social relations. For Bourgeault the increasing dominance and success of colonial expansion is demonstrated by the introduction into 'Indian society' of the notion of private property and the imposition of patriarchal values on the Slave Woman by Knight even as the social relations of equality within gatherer/hunter culture place the Slave Woman in a position to act as a useful translator and Native informant. In Bourgeault's argument the figure of the Slave Woman functions as a victim of colonial oppression, and her victimization is com-

plete inasmuch as she is described by Knight as eventually succumb-
ing to his needs and inasmuch as Bourgeault accepts Knight's account
unquestionably.

The possibility of reading the posthumous passage as unambiguously as Bourgeault does cannot sustain itself in the syntactical aberrations
that arise in Knight's text and destabilize its meaning. An elliptical
displacement occurs in Knight's syntax in the following description of
'what happened': 'She said she had not gave it away I sent to the
Indian as had it and fetch'd it away & showed it her She told me was
a Lyer for he had stole it for she did not give it him.' The loss of the
personal pronoun in 'she told me [?] was a Lyer' destabilizes a
monological reading as to who can be identified, definitively, as the
subject engaged in the lying, stealing, and giving. Was the Chipewyan
woman accusing the Indian of being the liar who stole the kettle or is
Knight the liar and the thief – exercising what Marshall Sahlins names
in his *Stone Age Economics* 'negative reciprocity' (191), an exploitive
mode of exchange in which gifts are extracted but not reciprocated – or
is Knight accusing her of lying in insisting that the Indian was a thief
when in fact she did give the kettle to him? This syntactical aberration
challenges a definitive reading of the passage. The Slave Woman's
actions could be interpreted in terms of a resistance to and subversion
of, rather than, as Bourgeault writes, an acceptance of, private property.

The confusion in Knight's text over who has been lying, stealing, or
giving indicates that Knight cannot entirely fix blame nor can he fully
understand what has transpired. Although he coerces the Slave Woman into his perception of the event, the relationship between the Cree
and Chipewyan, or between Chipewyan and Chipewyan, remains
outside, as it were, his realm of control. The Cree and Chipewyan
agree to the peace, and for Knight's purposes this conserves the static
relations required for the expansion of British mercantile wealth. That
the Cree and Chipewyan are operating, in part, in their own interests
is never mentioned in Knight's text. However, his 'posthumous' narrative, in which he discloses an account of physical violence and its
effect in achieving the Slave Woman's submission, would suggest that
Knight's inability to manipulate or control entirely Native exchange
relations and the Slave Woman herself was a source of anxiety.

The narration of resistance and domination can be read allegorically
as a discursive site in which a functional change in sign systems is taking
place: a change from a gatherer/hunter economy of gift reciprocity to a
European mercantile economy, the consequences of which involve for
European mercantile expansion the forced dis-remembrance of any

residual traces of this gatherer/hunter mode of production. Within Knight's posthumous passage, however, the trace of a gatherer/hunter social formation cannot be fully consolidated to the desires of the imperialist.

## A Gift for Languages

'Like the gift, rhetorical usage has the quality of being both deeply gratifying and threatening or anxiety-producing, notably with reference to scientific criteria of meaning (such as univocal definitions of terms)' (39). In this passage from *History and Criticism* LaCapra assimilates Marcel Mauss's notion of antagonistic gift exchange in the Native potlatch to a notion of rhetoric. Translated into a post-structural morphology of textual aberrations, eccentricities, or residual marks of difference, rhetorical peculiarities represent the signs of anxiety, a fear of unassimilable difference. That the 'gift' should figure in LaCapra's textual field as a metaphor of discursive aberration suggests the degree to which this trope upsets certain conventions of exchange and reciprocity in both textual and material economies. In the discursive economy of Knight's text the Slave Woman functions as the bearer of gifts to be exchanged in the process of securing peace. Bourgeault insists that the kettle in Knight's scenario is a symbol of the acceptance of 'private property.' In which case, the 'gift' is no longer a gift in any sense of the forms of gift exchange Marshall Sahlins designates as belonging to a gatherer/hunter economy. Sahlins writes, 'The gift is the primitive way of achieving the peace that in civil society is secured by the State.' And further:

17 June 1715. I gave to the Indians that are going to make peace Powder & shott considerable with flints wch it is particularized in the acc't book there being 5 Mett besides there familys & the Slave Woman & Wm Stewart who I gave likewised wth Severall Quantitys of other things to Distribute amongst some of the leading Indians & her friends for an encouragement for them to come to trade with us by wch they will see those Necessitys they wanted by wch I hope and am well satisfy'd they will not be Ill bestow'd but of great profitt there trade wch are brought to Acc.

The gift, however, would not organize society in a corporate sense, only in a segmentary sense. Reciprocity is a 'between' relation. It does not dissolve the separate parties within a higher unity, but on the contrary, in correlating their opposition, perpetrates it. Neither does the gift specify a third party standing over and above the separate interest of those who contract. Most important, it does not withdraw their force, for the gift affects only will and not right. Thus the condition of peace as understood by Mauss – and as in fact it exists in the primitive societies – has to differ politically from that envisioned by the classic contract, which is always a structure of submission, and sometimes of terror. Except for the honour accorded to generosity, the gift is no sacrifice of equality and never of liberty. The groups allied by exchange each retain their strength, if not the inclination to use it. (169–70)

If we read Knight's passage in terms of Native subversion and colonial exploitation, Sahlins's critique of the differing perceptions of the gift provides a useful conceptual tool. The Slave Woman's struggle over the kettle could suggest a form of gift exchange between the Cree and Chipewyan that subverts Knight's attempt to enforce the codes of a commodity exchange value. If viewed from the epistemology of a political economy of a gatherer/hunter social formation, the Slave Woman no longer figures as a victim of colonial oppression who blindly submits to a violent change in the textual economy of sign systems.[13] Her actions could be interpreted from a gatherer/hunter mode of exchange, in which case Knight's violence can be read as an attempt to obliterate the signs of that economy, particularly as it operates between the Cree and Chipewyan, in an effort to impose the corporate unity of a state form of control, the 'higher unity' of the third party, the Home Office in London.

In the imaginary relations of Knight's textual fantasies such an easy resolution in the form of unremitting love for the Father ('and Said She was a Fool & Madd & told me that I was a father to them all ...') would seem to suggest either failure to the extent that he was unable to entirely obliterate any residual marks of a gatherer/hunter social economy or success accrued

May 1716 ... but the make peace so he pulled out his pipe and Stemm and made a Long Harrangue of the Sacredness of that thing & that it was not to be touched without they were resolved to be true and perform what it was brought there for and smokd in there he Lighted it and handed it about and after everyone had taken so many whiffs as was agreed on and all had takeing it none refusing it her told them they were now to be perpetuall friends with that they all give thanks and a Shoot and Rifed up and strike them all on the head they spent the best part of 2 Days together & made Severall presents of Goods as they had traded with us they reviewed there Hostage by Adopting some of the young men for there sons and so Parted very good Friends. By this success I believe our company may begin to be thought a rich Company in a few through low-intensity coercion, in the form of Knight's brutality towards the Slave Woman. The production of a reading of the Slave Woman's resistance and subversion in the context of Knight's colonial exploitation permits the possibility of a figure of the Slave Woman as neither the unresisting victim of colonial expansion nor the ideal heroine, in control of the construction of her own historical subjectivity as a Native informant. Both of these positions construct History as a fixed script in which the drama of coercive imperialist expansion is accepted as inevitable, entirely successful in its aims, and ultimately undefeatable in its logical and consistent unfolding along the path of progress.

years and if it please God to preserve me with life and health to go through which what I Design ...

In Knight's journal entries the failure of the supply vessel to arrive in the fall of 1716 causes an increasing tension in Knight's accounts. Knight fears the possibility of the ship's absence leading to a precipitous and violent crisis:

wee haveing no news of a ship makes me very much Misdoubt of her Arrivall this Year and I dread the Dismall Consequences of it our Powder being all Spent but 10 barrells so that the Natives that comes next Year to trade will be all dissappointed after they have Spent the whole Summer in Coming down and going back into there Country w$^{ch}$ will Spoil the Next Years Trade all so if a Ship should not come next fall besides many Indians starvd for want of powder & for our Settling at Churchill River it will give such a Check to that trade that I fear it will be a hard matter to keep the Natives in Friendship by being disappointed of a factory & Goods being there it was a very difficult matter to gett the natives in the Humour to make a peace & if done w$^{ch}$ I hope will be is the first as hath been made amongst them since the Confusion of Languages at Babell So I conclude my Journall for this Year w$^{th}$ a Great deal of Sorrow & Grief for the Companys Loss & our Misfortunes. (1 September 1716)

The failure of the supply vessel to reach its destination is an event in Knight's text the discursive and symbolic consequences of which include a very specific chain of displacements. At the centre of Knight's anxiety of impending violence is the metaphor of the 'Confusion of Languages at Babell.' It is as someone in a position to manage the heterogeneity of languages that the Slave Woman gains such importance in Knight's designs. Her death, the loss of her timely 'gift for languages,' produces a state of mourning in Knight's text: a mourning for the potential loss of his epic dreams of colonial expansion to the north at Churchill River, of the search for the infamous Northwest Passage to Asia (10 May 1716), and of the discovery of untold wealth in the form of 'yellow mettle,' which Knight mistakenly thought was gold, but which turned out to be copper (27 July 1716). Knight mourns the loss of his resource in the Slave Woman as a bearer of the imperial signifier. 'If the Slave Woman and Boy should die it would be a great loss to the Company for want of somebody that understands this Country language and English besides the jealousy and suspicion that will be amongst there friends Altho I have taken care as Possible may be I have sent out 2 of the Norward Indians Amongst there here Indians to learn these Indians Speech but how will be treated by them I cannot tell' (27 January 1717).

The figure of the loss of the Slave Woman as a supplementary vessel capable of functioning for Knight as an instrument of discursive mediation represents a critical example of the way in which Native women in the eyes of the colonialist become justifiable and necessary objects of material and discursive violence. The Slave Woman's job, as Knight positions her duties, is to make the peace between the Cree and Chipewyan by way of managing the heterogeneity of discursive 'confusion,' in order to permit the transaction of that discursive exchange into its economic counterpart and bring about the dissolution of disparate tribal entities into a 'higher' political unity controlled by the British state. As a functional instrument in the colonial design her position is ideal and her success predicated upon an idealism; as a failure, as incomplete in bearing the functional reproduction of discursive mediation, she is an unforgivable victim. Van Kirk's and Bourgeault's contributions to postcolonial knowledge continue to position the Slave Woman, to repeat Spivak's quote from 'Subaltern Studies,' in 'the figure of woman, moving from clan to clan, and family to family as daughter/sister and wife/mother, [who] syntaxes patriarchal continuity even as she is herself drained of proper identity. In this particular area, the continuity of community or history, for [Native] and historian alike, is produced on (I intend the copulative metaphor – philosophically and sexually) the dissimulation of her discontinuity, on the repeated emptying of her meaning as instrument' (220).

To propose another reading of this historical archive, to read against the grain of its grammatological necessities, involves a cognitive shift in rethinking the epistemological concepts and metaphors with which colonial confrontation is framed. Sahlins's work produces a critical morphology for an understanding of gatherer/hunter economic exchange. The material violence of imperialism attempts to obliterate and destroy self-sufficient or intrinsic modes of production. This process is carried out not only in the material practices of colonial domination but also in the figures or tropes with which it justifies its low-intensity coercion, in the very structure of its discursive economy. JanMohamed situates the relationship between the discursive and material practices of imperialism as a profoundly symbiotic one in which 'discursive practices do to the symbolic, linguistic presence of the Native what the material practices do to [her] physical presence; the writer commodifies [her] so that [she] can be exploited more efficiently by the administrator ...' (64). Van Kirk and Bourgeault contribute to this reification of the Slave Woman / Thanadelthur in their respective representations of women's history, thereby reproducing, as Newton and Rosenfelt note, a 'static tale of the unrelieved oppression of women or of their unalleviated triumphs' (xxiii).

Certain textual conditions are necessary to the intervention of a critical reading of the Slave Woman's historical constitution as an insurgent in the context of colonial exploitation. The existence of textual remainders such as that of Knight's passage written after her death calls attention to the contradictions and epistemic violence at work in the colonial confrontation. Produced upon her death, this passage continues to unfold the place of the Slave Woman's significance in the imperialist project. Actual death does not foreclose the value of her figuration as an instrument of textual production, nor does death foreclose the imperial task of totalizing the Slave Woman's meaning. Knight takes the opportunity of the Slave Woman's death to circumscribe her subjectivity in a narration of Native resistance and colonial domination.

The epistemic violence of the colonial confrontation inheres in the very structure of its discourse. A violenced textuality emerges in which an instrumental process of low-intensity coercion – assimilation – takes place. In the hegemonic practices of postcolonial knowledge, representations, images, and stereotypes of the Native become the abstract figures of a late-capitalist currency. But within the totalizing logic of late capitalism, within the specific historical structures that determine her exchange value, the subject in question, the Slave Woman, can be figured as actively engaged in her own praxis, in her own 'play' as an 'active agent.' As such, this textual figure can be deployed as an insurgent, an intervention destabilizing the meaning of imperial totalization – a reading of Native women working within the circumstances with which history has confronted them.

The following two chapters bring us back to the contemporary context and the work of writers such as Jeannette Armstrong, Maria Campbell, and Beatrice Culleton. As with the figure of Thanadelthur, the agency of Native writers as makers and unmakers of their own cultural traditions has been ignored; the resulting sanctioned ignorance on the part of the dominant culture, its ethnocentric circumscription of the 'primitive,' the racist and sexist othering of 'the Indian' for the purposes of consolidating the imperialist subject, as well as the general feminization and infantilization of indigenous cultures have served actively to dispossess and marginalize Native modes of cultural production.

The emergence of a new literary object – Native literature – over the past twenty years has drawn attention to the overwhelming 'silencing' of Native cultures, the degree to which their writings have either been denied or made invisible, and their virtual absence from the Canadian mainstream publishing industry. Indeed, the writings of Armstrong, Campbell, and Culleton mark the failure of that industry to sustain its exclusionary practices.

PART THREE

THE CULTURAL POLITICS OF REPRESENTATION

# 5 History Lies in Fiction's Making and Unmaking: Jeannette Armstrong's *Slash*

The performance of these tasks, of the historian and the teacher of literature, must critically 'interrupt' each other, bring each other to crisis, in order to serve their constituencies; especially when each seems to claim all for its own.

Gayatri Chakravorty Spivak, 'A Literary Representation of the Subaltern: A Woman's Text from the Third World,' in *In Other Worlds*, 241

My polemic has as one of its reference points the issue of the relation between history and criticism, including the role of self-reflection that is not autonomized but instead pointedly related to historiographical practice. For many historians at present, history and criticism are two incompatible genres. History is like an owl that in its age-old wisdom knows it must stay close to the ground. Critical theory is like an eagle that soars skyward in quest of its prey. When the eagle tries to mate with the owl, the result is one loud screech.

My love of allegory cannot bring me to endorse this Aesopian fable. Not only can history and criticism co-exist. Their union may engender vital stock. Indeed, in its absence each becomes weaker through excessive inbreeding. Yet the biological analogy is of course itself faulty. Another analogy is perhaps better. It is as acceptable to join history and criticism as it is to have description, dramatic dialogue, and reflective soliloquy in the same novel.

Dominick LaCapra, *History and Criticism*, 136

### Disciplinary Confrontations

Spivak posits the idea of *interruption* as a useful textual strategy for renegotiating the crisis of disciplinary articulations, between, for example, history and literature. This distinction between hegemonic inscriptions of history and literature has recently undergone a crisis in interdisciplinary contamination, as LaCapra's race and gender specific characterization makes explicit. Under the rubric of a new historicism a benign exposure to the post-structural critique in literary theory and philosophy has subjected the notion of an unmediated representation of reality to an interpretive turn, or, on another register, a deconstructive turn. Concurrently, despite American New Critical orthodox claims to the literary purity of self-contained poetic icons, the historicization of the literary event has become a founding principle of a new cultural politics. For the literary critic trained in a New Critical methodology, unlearning and learning takes the form, as Spivak recommends, of 're-think[ing] the notion that fiction derives from truth as its negation' (243), a presupposition produced by an ideological and asymmetric valorization of textual practices that disseminate an 'effect of the Real' – knowledge as Truth. Even so, the disciplinary differences between history and literature, as Spivak also notes, cannot be wiped away, nor can their discursive differences be absorbed into each other. It is precisely because of the difference between them that they can be used to 'interrupt' each other. Alternative critical insights, which would otherwise be ignored, silenced, or suppressed, can emerge in the event of disciplinary confrontations.

Such disciplinary confrontations provide particular insights into Jeannette Armstrong's novel *Slash*. In this discussion of *Slash* I am interested in how the disciplines of literature and history are transformed by Armstrong's own rewriting of Native political history in the 1960s in a fictional mode of address. *Slash* retells the history of Native politics in British Columbia and Canadian Native involvement in the American Indian Movement (AIM) during the 1960s and early 1970s. Armstrong's use of realism in order to recast and problematize borders of official and unofficial histories provides the material for an intervention into the theoretical problematic of history as truth and fiction as untruth. In *Slash* this disciplinary asymmetry is undone by the thematic and formal use of an 'oral Native tradition.' It is important to recognize that traditional Native oral storytelling is a category that already differs from itself in its recent reception in the forms of transcriptions, tapings, translations, and publications. As a figure of Native cultural production it is haunted by a nostalgia, on the part of the colonial critic, for unmediated, closer-to-the-bone, kinds of exchange. And yet the circulation of 'stories,' whether sacred, heuristic, allegorical, or quotidian, under an economic mode of gatherer/hunter production would obviously differ from their function as cultural spectacles under late capitalism. The re-presentation of oral storytelling in *Slash*, the appearance of intratextual stories that interrupt the historical narrative, and the larger historical narrative written in the vernacular combine to contest the boundaries between such oppositions as oral and written, truth and non-truth, history and fiction.

The following section explores the confrontation between history and fiction in *Slash*, the retelling of Native history in a fictional mode. In the next three sections I will elaborate on the themes of race and class in the novel, its textual politics, and use of the Native oral tradition. I will elaborate the particular relationship between the oral and the written through a discussion of the making of a Native literary tradition and the appropriation of Jacques Derrida's critique of the binary opposition oral/written by literary critics working in the area of Native literatures. The last section deals with the construction of women in the text and the implications of that construction for feminist literary criticism.

### Jeannette Armstrong's *Slash*

In *Slash* Armstrong re-presents the socio-political reality of Native involvement in the civil rights movement of the 1960s through an individual, Tommy Kelasket, later renamed Slash for the knife wounds he receives in a barroom fight. Though Slash's travels are not limited to Okanagan territory and the Native politics of British Columbia, this doubly coded area of colonial mapping and Native inscriptions of the earth is the central site of departure and return. *Slash* can be read as a critical reflection on the dominant and official white English-American history of 'sixties' Native politics. It is also a text that addresses the contradictions of Native political practice within the structure of internal colonialism.

Paul Tennant defines the notion of internal colonialism as 'the continued subjugation of an indigenous people in a post-colonial independent nation state. Subjugation will in every case involve restriction of land and resources as well as varying degrees of administrative supervision, social discrimination, suppression of culture and denial of political and other rights and freedoms' (3–4). European colonialism

produces its own specific kind of spurious 'indigenization.' Terry
Goldie uses the term 'indigenization' to delimit the process whereby
aboriginal peoples are 'Other-ed' or 'Not-self-ed' by the dominant
colonial literary apparatus in order to justify an internal process of
patriation. In his book *Fear and Temptation: The Image of the Indigene in
Canadian, Australian, and New Zealand Literatures* Goldie writes:

The importance of the alien within cannot be overstated. In their need to
become 'native,' to belong here, whites in Canada, New Zealand, and Austral-
ia have required a process which I have termed 'indigenization.' A peculiar
word, it suggests the impossible necessity of becoming indigenous. For many
writers, the only chance for indigenization seemed to be through writing about
the humans who are truly indigenous, the Indians, Inuit, Maori, and Aborigi-
nals ... Of course, the majority of writers in all three countries have given brief
or no attention to native peoples. (13)

In the historical process of authenticating its own religious, economic,
and political apparatuses, European colonialism subjects aboriginal
peoples to internal colonialism. Tennant explains that 'in the context
of an English-speaking new world country the concept [internal colo-
nialism] delineates not only the indigenous minority but also the
immigrant majority – that is, the ruling society composed of persons
who are either immigrants or descended from immigrants' (4).

Tennant also warns that the presence of a strong Native political
tradition in British Columbia, the object of his analysis, should not be
allowed to misrepresent the 'enormous burden of indifference, discour-
agement and outright hostility which the dominant society and its
government placed in the way of early Indian political organization.
There may also be a tendency today, *as members of the white majority
continue to be the principal manufacturers of provincial history*, for a spe-
cious satisfaction to be taken in the absence in British Columbia of the
massive dislocation and genocide of indigenous people which has been
so tragically evident elsewhere' (48, emphasis added). I emphasize
Tennant's recognition of the discursive politics involved in who 'constructs' history in order to suggest that *Slash* provides a textual space
for considering an alternative inscription of the history of Native
political organization. If, as Fredric Barth suggests, one response to
internal colonialism is the strategic demarcation of cultural boundaries
which involves 'the codification of idioms' and 'the selection of signals
for identity and the assertion of value for these cultural diacritica, and
the suppression or denial of relevance for other differentia' (quoted in

Tennant, 7), then, in the context of inscribing the history of pan-Indian movements of the sixties from a non-colonial construction, *Slash* represents an important textual formation of the struggle over which 'diacritica' came to be relevant and which did not.

Chapter 1, 'The Awakening,' offers a set of signals that identify a coded idiom of Native difference from the dominant Euro-Canadian culture:

| Metaphors/ Concepts of: | Dominant White Culture | Native Culture |
| --- | --- | --- |
| food | store-bought (29, 39) 'sliced bread and bologna' | 'baked biscuits' 'fried deer meat' (17, 27) |
| health | vitamins (15) hygiene (38) | plant and animal medicines (22) |
| politics | 'white man's leader' (18) Diefenbaker | chiefs/elders (18, 22) Old Pra-cwa |
| law | 'paper laws' (21) | 'real' law (21) (law of the 'good') |
| play | alcohol (20) | hunting (21) |
| language | English (17) | 'talking Indian' (17, 18, 26) |
| education | residential schools (17) | the ranch or bush |
| social value | commodification: houses/ TVs/electricity 'shitters inside their houses' (25, 26) | ritualization: drumming, dancing, sweats (27, 37) |
| economy | charity/capitalism (private property, 25) | exchange/gift-giving (31, 29) |
| knowledge | as truth/fiction (the Sasquatch episode, 35) | 'storytelling' (16, 17, 19, 20) |
| religion | church/Catholicism/ priests (30) | Creator/spirituality (30) |
| gender | white women: 'Hightuned Polly' (19)/teacher, Mrs Hosfah (15) the male 'sissy' who reads (16) | the Mother/gatherer (17); the male 'sissy' who cannot skin a deer (16) |

In the above table traditional conceptions of what foods to eat, what medicines to practise, what language to use, and so forth, are placed in opposition to 'white' cultural values. In the drawing of an imaginary borderline between two cultures, an antagonistic conception of social relations between a subjugated minority and dominant majority comes into play.

Dualistic conceptions of political conflict or 'antagonism' are produced both by the state and Native political organizations, though the nature of the dualisms is defined differently. In a process of internal colonialism antagonistic relations constitute precisely the political space opened up to Native political action and in which Native Indian political organizations in British Columbia, according to Tennant, have participated. The outcome is an exaggerated representation of so-called Native Indian militancy and violence. In *Slash* the instrumental violence of reaction or frustration – 'violence for violence sake' (140) – turns on an ideology of superiority/inferiority:

Just try to explain to them [white ruling class] that respect for all races is the most important thing that some of the so-called militant Indian tribes go by. They demand respect for their own tribe and only give respect to those who respect them. Sometimes, in demanding respect, they're put down. But, it means they don't tolerate things like aggression because they truly believe one race is not superior over another. (140)

### Race and Class

The diacritica mapped out in chapter 1 become, in the emergence of Tommy's critical consciousness in chapter 2, the objects of scrutiny in an analysis of the hierarchical relationship between Native and white cultural values and of the ways in which different cultural valorizations produce an antagonistic social relation. Stereotypes from Hollywood movies, for example, represent a major source of racism, as the following remark by Tommy illustrates: 'Like one teacher, who explained what she wanted in slow Hollywood talk. She said, "You fix'um little story, Tommy, about how you live." To the other kids she had asked, "Please prepare a short biographical sketch of yourself"' (38–9). Tommy becomes critical of the ideology of his education because of his experiences with racism at school (35). In chapter 1 Tommy is integrated into the state school system through many forms of subjective violence inflicted by the seemingly benign institutionalized voice of the school's principal: 'You Indians are lucky to be here.

We'll get along just fine as long as you don't steal from the other kids. I want you all to wait here while the nurse comes to check your heads and ask you some question' (23). White children hand out more overt forms of verbal abuse: 'Humphrey said, "You frigging Injuns are nothing but thieves full of lice, everybody knows that!" ' (24). In chapter 2, after a consciousness-raising discussion with a priest, Tommy interprets Humphrey's derogatory words in the context of racism and discrimination: 'We told them about how a lot of teachers and kids thought we lived in teepees and wore feathers on the reserve. We told them about Monty getting kicked out for fighting with Humphrey even though Humphrey started it by calling us "Injuns" and "full of lice" and stuff' (35). Media stereotypings in Hollywood films (35, 38) and television shows like 'Bonanza' (25, 26) are similarly recalled as promotions of racism. Other colonial ideologies which come under scrutiny include corporate exploitation of the environment (39), 'new-age' philosophical appropriations of Native practices (40), sexism towards Native women (35), and the denigration of Native spirituality as superstition (34). The formation of Tommy's critical consciousness comes with acquiring the hermeneutical skill of interpretation, learning to read the painful experience of negation in residential school as the ideology of racism. The incidents of racism become for Tommy the material of his own storytelling of internal colonialism. His Grandpa Cashmire metaphorizes knowledge as 'You got a little box with a cover. You open it just right so only what you want goes in and not a lot of other junk. When you want to take that thing out again you open the box, just so, and there it is, all by itself, same as when you put it in. That's how you keep things' (38). Tommy's experiences in school become the critical substance, the things, the threads, of his eventual resistance narrative.

Chapter 1 codifies a Native idiom or diacritica in part as a reaction against a sweeping form of cultural assimilation and interpellation determined by the state. Chapter 2, 'Trying It On,' describes the assimilation and alienation produced by an inside/outside figuration of enclosed cultural boundaries. The 'it' in the title is left ambiguous and could refer equally well to a figure of the dominant white culture and its materialism or the traditional Native culture and its pastoral containment of the 'old ways'; in chapter 3 Slash interprets the distinction as the 'split between assimilationists and the traditionalists' (110). Armstrong shows that state policies, enfranchisement (18), taxation (19), regulation of alcohol distribution (20), and the 'white paper' (28) enforce Native assimilation and encourage the dominant culture's indigenization through its appropriation of the subject formation of Native people. The dualism of internal colonialism is rendered in the divisions among Native peoples as to whether or not to become assimilated into the master narrative of development and progress. Some would industrialize reserve lands in the form of grape farming (41); others would commercialize property: ' "I heard that in another reserve they are thinking about turning the reserve into a city – like, you know, part of it anyway." "What do you mean? Are you talking about the houses they want to build and lease out to white people?" ' (41). In both cases the progressives hope to create employment:

This guy looked so neat, almost like a white man, with his grey slacks that had sharp iron creases and a pink button-down shirt and blue polkadot tie ...

He spoke to us about how 'we were living in the twentieth century,' and how 'we had a lot of catching up to do' ... He said, 'We must learn to use new ideas and open up our lands to development, because lack of money is at the bottom of all of our social problems.' (43)

Fighting for equal rights involves, then, fighting for equal access to capitalist expansion and the market economy, what in a colonial context eventually leads to the Andre Gunder Frank paradox, 'the development of under-development': the erosion and destruction of indigenous modes of production, economic exchanges, and socio-symbolic relations in order to produce dependency and ultimately eradicate indigenous cultural practices. In Canada the notorious 'white paper' of 1968 was intended to contain Native struggle within the ideology of equal rights: it was resisted precisely because it was seen as an instrument of assimilation and cultural genocide.

### Textual Politics

As an example of what Barbara Harlow terms 'resistance literature' Slash 'calls attention to itself ... as a political and politicized activity' (28). But more than a writing which contests official history, Slash can also be read for its politics of writing, a politics of writing that leads to a 'third position' beyond the agonistic duel of hegemonic and 'counter-hegemonic ideological production.' A counter-hegemonic ideological position is inscribed by Armstrong in the context of the antagonistic and ultimately insufficient political choices open to the Native struggle for self-determination:

There are all kinds of us from the Native Alliance for Red Power working on this. The Beothucks are a symbol to us. They were a tribe of Indians on the east coast that were wiped out so the land could be open for settlement. You see, there was a bounty placed on them by the government and they were hunted down to the last one. That's how we fit into this society. They just want us out of the way, no matter how. It's called genocide. It's what's happening to our people right now. We are dying off because we can't fit in. Help is offered only to the ones that are so-called progressive. The ones that are just brown white men. The ones that fit in. Soon there will be no more true red men, with their own beliefs and ways. There is nothing wrong with our ways. Just because our people hate to be grabby, just because they don't knock themselves out like robots at nine-to-five jobs, and they don't get too excited about fancy stuff or what I call luxuries, they are looked down on and treated as outcasts and called lazy. Pretty soon, they believe it and they drown in drink. Or else they get like us. They get angry inside and fight back somehow. Usually they end up dead, in prison or drunk. All of these lead to genocide of our people. You see they only give us two choices. Assimilate or get lost. A lot of us are lost. We need to make a third choice. That's what Red Patrol is about. (69–70)

In the textual politics of *Slash* the shift towards a third position is, in part, a result of a battle between the discursive violence of contemporary Western narrative traditions, in which written history constitutes the most viable re-presentation of Truth, and Native oral storytelling viewed by Western ethnocentrism as non-Truth. Official forms of history are received as the definitive word. Written in a 'tell-it-like-it-is' attitude, official history reproduces a Real effect that inscribes its knowledge as *the* truth. Armstrong achieves a third position in her own textual strategies by the use of an intratextual play of stories. I use the term 'intratextual' to draw attention to the layering of storytelling that appears in *Slash*, where not only is there the larger story written in a realist style, but also mini-stories, as it were (either alluded to or actually written down), contained within Armstrong's larger text. These stories within the larger story suggest traditional Native oral 'storytelling.' They call attention to themselves as a signal. They entertain but also unfold other ways of knowing; knowledge-as-truth in the colonial syntax of history becomes knowledge-as-reading or interpretation in the case of Armstrong's 'storytelling,' a rewriting and decolonization of that official historical truth-telling. As stories within a story they also provide an implicit rejection of Native storytelling as either essentially Native or traditional, in the sense of being a historical dinosaur, pure and static in its fossilized figuration. In the midst of the Western narrative of knowledge-as-(un)truth (where the acquisition of knowledge is posed as a struggle to obtain truth or falsify claims to truth) stories intervene to teach the reader to read for the stories within 'the' story, and, on a metanarrative level, to teach the reader to read and interpret knowledge as a historical construction.

### Oral Traditions and Storytelling

The following is an example of an intratextual story that appears within Armstrong's story of decolonization. It is a story which humorously reflects on the 'true' nature of the colonizer's culture:

Once I heard a story, in the early morning, about a woman named Hightuned Polly. She had a dog that she babied like some white women do. She carried it around and made little skirts for it. One time, Hightuned Polly was at a celebration in Omak, during the Stampede Pow-wow. She was staying with some friends in a pow-wow teepee. Her dog got in heat. So all day, there was a big troop of dogs following her wherever she carried her dog. They even sneaked into the teepee under the flaps, while she was inside. Everyone was teasing her as she walked around with fifteen dogs trotting along. Finally, that night, she decided to sew a buckskin pant for her dog, to keep the other dogs from getting to her. Well, in the morning, Hightuned Polly found her dog with many visitors and a hole chewed right through the buckskin. (19)

The are many ways to read this story: as a story about the effects of tampering with nature or the frivolous effects of imitating the dominant culture; or about what happens, for example, when the boundaries of cultural difference are crossed, or in this case 'penetrated,' and imitation becomes a parodic critique by the Native culture of the colonizer's culture. The sexual specificity of this story, its irreverent and carnivalesque humour, add to its subversive criticism of colonial culture, in particular to the ways in which so-called primitive cultures are figured as 'naturally' prone to sexual licence. The narrative allegorizes the 'white man's' attempt to censor, metaphorically, through the use of a buckskin chastity belt what Terry Goldie aptly describes as the 'fear and temptation' experienced by a patriarchal colonial culture in its projected sexualization of Native culture. This story can be read allegorically in order to produce a commentary on the complexities involved in the articulation of a race/gender analysis.

Armstrong's incorporation of an oral Native tradition, or what I am calling 'storytelling,' into a written historical fiction raises two theoretical problems: the use of the term 'storytelling'[1] and the distinction between oral and graphic modes of writing.

## The Making of a Native Literary Tradition

Jeannette Armstrong's *Slash* is a novel that self-consciously explores what it means to be writing as a Native in Canada. The choice of Native political resistance as a theme and the narrative and thematic use of the oral Native tradition are two signs that register this self-consciousness. The use of an oral tradition, in particular, is one way that *Slash* challenges Eurocentric definitions of what constitutes a Native literary tradition. This is especially apparent in the contradiction that emerges with the reference to an oral tradition in a printed text such as Slash. Thomas King notes in his introduction to an anthology of contemporary Canadian Native fiction, entitled *All My Relations*, that arriving at a definition of Canadian Native literature or understanding the essential aspects that define its difference from colonial literature, for example, is an on-going and far from completed project: '... when we talk about contemporary Native literature, we talk as though we already have a definition for this body of literature when, in fact, we do not. And, when we talk about Native writers, we talk as though we have a process for determining who is a Native writer and who is not when, in fact, we don't' (x). In an effort to come to some preliminary understanding of how such a process might be formulated King goes on to say: 'What we do have is a collection of literary works by individual authors who are Native by ancestry, and our hope, as writers and critics, is that if we wait long enough, the sheer bulk of this collection, when it reaches some sort of critical mass, will present us with a matrix within which a variety of patterns can be discerned' (x).

King's formal approach to the making of a Native literary tradition, as that tradition is based on individual writers of Native ancestry, remains uncritically caught within imperial and racial boundaries. Addressing a similar problem of defining an Afro-American literary tradition, Ralph Ellison writes that 'the notion of an intellectual or artistic succession based upon color or racial background is no less absurd than one based on common religious background' (quoted by Gates, 120). In *The Signifying Monkey: A Theory of Afro-American Literary Criticism* Henry Louis Gates, Jr, elaborates Ellison's critique:

Literary succession or influence, rather, can be based on only formal literary revision, which the literary critic must be able to demonstrate. These discrete demonstrations allow for definitions of a tradition. Few definitions of traditions escape the racism, essentialism or nationalism often implicit in rubrics such as 'African' or 'Jewish' or 'Commonwealth' literature. As Ellison argues, 'For the critics there simply exists no substitute for the knowledge of history and literary tradition.' (120)

Gates's historical approach to the formation of an Afro-American literary tradition, based on Ellison's work, is a useful model to follow for dealing with this currently emerging project of defining a Native cultural tradition, a tradition that cannot exist *a priori* of the texts and oral storytelling, written or performed, by Native people. As Gates suggests, 'each literary tradition, at least implicitly, contains within it an argument for how it can be read' (xix–xx). It is important to restate that a literary tradition cannot be based on an uncritical account of an imperial and racially oriented classification such as Native literature. Penny Petrone's *Native Literature in Canada: From the Oral Tradition to the Present* is an initial and important contribution to this emerging field of study, along with the recent volume *Native Writers and Canadian Writing*, edited by W.H. New.

Clifford Geertz, in his *Works and Lives: The Anthropologist as Author*, makes a useful observation about the problem of cultural classifications, derived from the field of ethnography: 'The moral asymmetries across which ethnography works and the discoursive [*sic*] complexity within which it works make any attempt to portray it as anything more than the representation of one sort of life in the categories of another impossible to defend' (144). The attempt by dominant modes of canonization to assimilate the difference of meaning and reference in Native writings into Western classifications such as 'Native literature' is like representing one sort of 'textuality' in the categories of another. The notion of a Native system of classification, however, also presupposes an idealization of Native concepts or metaphors as essentially more proximate than anything the discourse of Anglo-American literary theory, for example, could hope to obtain.

In his essay 'The Imposition of Western Definitions of Literature on Indian Oral Traditions' George L. Cornell criticizes a form of 'literary imperialism' whereby 'definitions of western literature have been, and continue to be, imposed on indigenous oral traditions.' As a result, the 'complicated cultural complex of indigenous ideas, socio-political thought and action, celebration, and spirituality is ... subordinated to formalist treatment' (178). Cornell rereads a Shawnee story, not along the lines of a separation between oral storytelling as untruth or truth-telling but as an *allegory* of a 'socio-political commentary on a prominent period of Shawnee resistance and adaptation' (186). Cornell's application of the formal notion of 'allegory,' a critical term derived from European literary theory and used for rereading Native oral storytelling, could be said to reproduce the same form of literary imperialism Cornell wants to transform. Cornell's criticisms of literary imperialism suggest that it is possible to achieve a 'true' critical language with which to frame an authentic understanding of Native writings. To do so, however, would involve inscribing a pure, uncontaminated, and unalterable discursive space. In the face of colonial conquest and the institutionalization of internal colonialism, the drawing of cultural boundaries is strategically important to the survival of different cultural values. Establishing different cultural diacritica, such as a distinction between colonial mapping and Native inscriptions of the earth, would create a situation whereby deploying the critical language of the dominant culture makes it possible to defend the 'equality' of Native cultures for the dominant colonial culture. As a strategy for cultural survival this position would alleviate the contradictory bind in Cornell's call to an authentic Native critical practice. If Cornell wishes to claim a Native authenticity, then he must also allow for, or at least presuppose, an authentic, essential, and 'true' European or American epistemology that can also be falsified or annihilated. A more strategic approach to Native oral practices than Cornell offers, I would suggest, might be to take the term 'storytelling' and invest it with the same critical force of socio-political meaning Cornell reserves for the notion of allegory; in which case, the very notion of storytelling is recaptured and transformed, rather than left to waste away as an illegitimate mode of knowledge in the context of an Anglo-American colonial literary tradition.

Cross-cultural translations between terms such as 'storytelling' and 'allegory' point to what James Clifford calls the predicament of twentieth-century culture: the unprecedented overlay of traditions and the search for non-essentialist forms of cultural politics. One of the problems with Clifford's position, as he outlines it in his introductory essay to *The Predicament of Culture: Twentieth-Century Ethnography, Literature, and Art*, is that with no recourse to a genealogy of authenticity, land claims, for example, become subject to narratives of diluted blood ties. After three hundred years of cultural confrontation and intermixing who is really an Indian any more?

This loss of cultural specificity becomes transformed for Clifford into a politics of reinvention where 'subjectivities produced in these often unequal [colonial] exchanges – whether of "natives" or of visiting participant-observers – are constructed domains of truth, serious fictions' (10). Clifford's position can be used to call attention to the ideology of extinction or absolute loss deployed at the end of the nineteenth century in such well-known projects as Edward S. Curtis's photographs, designed to record a vanishing race. This ideology ignores the continuity of Native history. It is not static or cut off from colonial culture but actively engaged with colonial culture, although the written historical record may suppress it.

In the negotiation of meaning across cultural boundaries terms such as Cornell's 'allegory,' or my own use of 'storytelling,' indicate not so much competing knowledges as competing narratives about the construction of knowledges whose difference is constituted by a political-social point of view: dominant or oppressed.

In *Slash* the storytelling interruptions into an otherwise conventional Eurocentric or North American narrative of historical fiction create a form specific to, rather than an essential aspect of, Native writing. The use of the vernacular in the syntax of Armstrong's prose, a paradoxical re-presentation of the oral voice within the written, is one such rhetorical strategy of playing upon a written/oral differentiation. A seemingly unmediated re-presentation of direct speech by the central character also produces the effect of oral narration. In the following passage the reader is positioned as a third party addressee in Tommy's testimonial to a Native woman of his experience in the caravan that retraced the infamous 1838 'Trail of Tears' relocation program instigated by the U.S. government:

I'll tell you it was something, that caravan. One night after we made camp and everybody was so tired they all wanted to sleep as soon as they could before facing the next long day, I sat and talked awhile with this girl named Elise. I told her I was from Canada and that I was Okanagan. I told her how things were at home. I said, 'You know we weren't pushed out of our land into another part of the country that was totally alien like some of the people here were.'

I had heard some of the things those old people there described in their stories. I thought it must have been terrifying and horrible to be put in a place where you didn't even know what plants to eat and medicines to use with the weather making everybody so sick all time and lots dying ... (95–6)

Another strategy Armstrong deploys is thematizing the importance of Tommy's Uncle Joe and his grandfather, Pra-cwa, as storytellers:

My special Uncle Joe came to stay with us and help. I went with him every-where and he told me a lot of stories of old Time. He told me about a long time ago, how our people used to live. He sure made it sound like fun. Espe-cially the part about when young boys were allowed to go on long hunting trips for weeks way up in the mountains. We only went hunting one day at a time. (21)

Pra-cwa was still sitting at the table. His long mustache drooped and his thick grey hair stuck out every which way. Every time he laughed, all his wrinkles shook. I knew that they had stayed up all night talking. The good stories came out towards morning. I sometimes stayed up to listen. (19)

In the first passage Uncle Joe's stories are mentioned rather than reproduced. The indirect marking of the stories can be read at least two ways: first as the impossibility of re-presenting the oral in a writ-ten form, and hence preserving the purity of the forms; and/or the re-presentation of the written as supplementary to the oral, in which case the boundary between the two is less distinct though still marked.

Tommy is portrayed as an exemplary literate figure who likes to read and write. In an exchange with his childhood friend, Jimmy, over what constitutes a worse form of sissiness, Tommy's relationship to the written word is positioned as neither conflictual with nor integral to traditional Native practices:

Sometimes, she would let us read if we finished our numbers fast. I liked reading a lot. I could imagine all those places and things just like I was there. Jimmy thought that was kind of sissy-pissy, but I didn't care. Besides, my Dad said boys like Jimmy, who didn't know how to do right things, like skinning a deer, were really the sissies. (16)

This reference designates a liminal point in the transformation of Native oral culture into the written culture. Tommy's ability to read and write, to be literate in the language of the colonizer, gains him the attention of priests and educators, and the praise of his grandfather, for whom the importance of learning English lies in the ability to read and translate government documents for his people (18). To become recognized by the dominant culture as having a legitimate subjectivity

Tommy must be literate, giving voice to his experience as a dispossessed subject. Within Native culture, however, the value of literacy takes on a different meaning as something vital to the survival of his people.

By an inverse process of writing a re-presentation of a Native-speaking subject, images of the Native used in Canadian colonial literature to indigenize the European immigrant also become destabilized. Terry Goldie criticizes the appropriation of Native images in Canadian literature, an operation that allows the author to demonstrate proximity to 'naturalization' by speaking through the Native Indian. Goldie writes, 'A quite appropriate pun is that it is only by going native that the European arrivant can become native' (16). *Slash* theorizes other ways in which the containment of 'Native-ness' is produced: for example, stereotyping in Hollywood movies, and the militarization of Native activism in the 1960s within the political frame of internal colonialism. But *Slash* does more than critique the ways in which representations and re-presentations of Native Indians have been contained in order to cathect the imperialist's self-consolidating other. Armstrong subverts this binary opposition between colonizer and colonized in her use of parodic images such as Hightuned Polly and Uncle Tommyhawks, a name given to Tommy's friend Jimmy when he plays the role of the 'whiteman's Indian.' As parody, these images have a double function; they provide a critique of the colonial culture as well as signalling a rejection of the desire to assimilate to that culture. Both in the case of Armstrong's parodic inversions and her direct criticisms of stereotyping any notion of a definable or confinable 'Native' is destabilized.

As I discuss in more detail in the next section, Derrida's conception of 'writing' is important to understanding the figure of 'storytelling' as a properly oral phenomenon which has been de-legitimized in the master code of colonial history. It cannot be stressed enough how important it is to recognize the legitimacy of the oral mode as part of a heterogeneous conception of 'writing,' in order to combat the Eurocentric attitude that the written word is the universal register of meaning as truth. In *Structural Anthropology* Claude Lévi-Strauss viewed anthropology as a discipline capable of correcting 'the absence of written documents in most so-called primitive societies.' With the development of such a discipline 'it is also possible,' according to Lévi-Strauss, 'to reconstruct the history of peoples who have never known writing' (24). It is in response to this ethnocentric bias that the textual politics of *Slash* must be read as specifically Native critique. Armstrong, along with other Native writers, is realigning the boundaries of what traditional Native oral storytelling means in the context of the written word as the most powerful legitimator of a Eurocentric notion of history; a history that often hides the ravages of imperialism. Armstrong's rhetorical strategies also challenge the ethnocentric view that 'peoples without history' are closer to nature and hence embody an authentic 'primitivism' and innocence precisely because they have a so-called oral (as opposed to written) language.

### Talking to Derrida

As the figure of woman's body has become a sign in the traffic of a primal authenticity, so the figure of 'orality' and the Native oral tradition has come to signify a privileged site for the production of the immediacy, unity, identity, truth, and presence of meaning. Writers such as Arnold Krupat and Gordon Brotherston have taken Jacques Derrida's post-structural critique of the speech/writing binary opposition in European logocentric philosophy, particularly in relation to the work of the anthropologist Lévi-Strauss, as a critical site to investigate the values accorded Native oral traditions.[2]

Gordon Brotherston, in his article 'Towards a Grammatology of America: Lévi-Strauss, Derrida, and the Native New World Text,' takes Derrida to task for failing to acknowledge, along with Lévi-Strauss, that, in Mesoamerica, at least, there exist scripted documents written by Native peoples. Derrida, then, along with Lévi-Strauss, has participated in the production of the myth of peoples without script. Brotherston is engaged in extensive research of what he calls the 'grammatology of America,' Native American and Canadian examples of script. He terms this new geopolitical epistemological terrain the 'Fourth World,' and though he does not cite the use of this term by the elder and chief George Manuel, the phrase evokes similar political issues: the question of 'geographical focus' and 'the political predicament of Native Americans today,' both of which Brotherston laments are ignored to 'the point of agony' (70).[3] Brotherston concludes with the following call to historical specificity: 'With his genealogical Old World obsessions, Derrida likewise denies the native Americans [and Canadians] their historicity and, by ignoring their master texts, reproduces on an intellectual plane the very hegemony he would claim to be combating' (73).

Arnold Krupat, in his essay 'Post-structuralism and Oral Literature,' also charges Derrida with a 'relative lack of interest in historical detail' because of what Krupat understands to be a confusion in post-structuralism between 'orality' and 'openness textuality' (118). Krupat criticizes Derrida and other post-structural critics for their use of the notion of 'textuality,' a notion Krupat insists is itself a textual representation of the performative effectivity and 'openness' already endemic to 'orality.' Unfortunately, Krupat's criticisms of post-structuralism maintain a classical notion of the 'text' as a scripted or printed object, which precisely because of its material substance must therefore constitute a certain 'fixity.' Krupat produces an evolutionary scale from the moment of the oral to the manuscript to the printed book as an increasing movement towards fixing meaning by fixing the word on the page: 'Thus, it came to be recognized that whatever the fixed text found before one – in time this became a printed rather than a manuscript text – it was of the utmost importance for a proper understanding to seek to amplify or alter it on the basis of any and all information available, and in this way to recall that even printed texts derive from manuscript versions, as manuscripts themselves are only the partial record of oral performance' (123).

Although I agree with both Brotherston and Krupat that Derrida fails to acknowledge the symbolic debt his radical philosophy owes to indigenous cultures, I find in Krupat's discussion a reductive misunderstanding of the radical implications of Derrida's critique of the differentiation between the oral and the written for the study of Native oral literature; and in Brotherston, a tendency towards maintaining the separation of the oral from the scripted, and by implication suggesting that the scripted should take precedence over the oral. In which case, his notion of the grammatology of America has yet to adequately theorize 'orality' and the relationship between the scripted and oral modes of writing.

It is important here to review Derrida's argument. In *Of Grammatology* Derrida deconstructs what he holds to be the principal binary opposition in European metaphysics, that of the distinction between speech and writing. In his critique of Lévi-Strauss's 'A Writing Lesson' (in *Tristes Tropiques*) Derrida demonstrates a hidden set of ethnocentric assumptions at work behind an apparent anti-ethnocentrism in Lévi-Strauss's conception of the Nambikwara as a people without writing. The privilege of being a people without writing, a so-called oral culture, is the presumed unimpeded proximity indigenous peoples occupy to the truth of Nature. They are innocent, for Lévi-Strauss, to the corruption that occurs with the use of script as the dominant mode of discursive exchange, the dominant mode of the imperialist European nations. Derrida criticizes Lévi-Strauss for assuming an unqualified power in his ability to corrupt the Nambikwara by supposedly penetrating this imaginary veil of 'orality' and innocence, hitherto intact until the incursion of European imperialism or ethnography:

Another precaution is necessary before the 'Lesson.' I have earlier emphasized the ambiguity of the ideology which governs the Saussurian exclusion of writing: a profound ethnocentrism privileging the model of phonetic writing, a model that makes the exclusion of the *graphie* easier and more legitimate. It is, however, an ethnocentrism in the consciousness of a liberating progressivism. By radically separating language from writing, by placing the latter below and outside, believing at least that it is possible to do so, by giving oneself the illusion of liberating linguistics from all involvement with written evidence, one thinks in fact to restore the status of authentic language, human and fully signifying language, to all languages practiced by *peoples whom one nevertheless continues to describe as 'without writing.'* It is not fortuitous that the same ambiguity affects Lévi-Strauss's intentions. (120)

Derrida coins the notion of *arche-writing* in order to insist that all modes of 'writing,' in such heterogeneous forms as speech, hieroglyphics, weaving, knots, script, self-immolated scarification, and so forth, commit an arche-violence towards any notion of self-presence or absolute proximity in the production of meaning (112); in other words, no mode of language whether written or spoken obtains an unmediated or authentic embodiment of a fully signifying meaning. Implicit to Derrida's critique, then, is the criticism of an ethnocentric naïvety that constructs a representation of Native peoples, collectively, as incapable of resistance or subversion on the basis of their inherent innocence as practitioners of a so-called oral, and therefore natural, language; though such naïvety is perhaps a self-serving and arrogant justification for the colonialist to participate in actions of imperialist violence without fear of reciprocity.

### Imperial Feminism and *Slash*

For colonial feminist literary criticism *Slash* poses another set of classification problems. Armstrong's use of a man as a central character in conjunction with her critique of sexism and racism in the novel has already caused some controversy among Native and non-Native feminists. At the Third Annual Feminist Book Fair conference, held in

Montreal in June 1988, Jeannette Armstrong came under attack from colonial white feminists over her use of a Native man, rather than a Native woman, as her central character. At a reading session held by Native women writers during the conference, Armstrong also spoke in her own defence, stating that she used a male character in order to provide a positive and strong image for the men in her community. I have constructed the following feminist interpretation of *Slash* in order to provide an example of the effects of feminism's blindness to the question of racism within the structure of internal colonialism when the specificity of gender and sexism is removed from a larger social context.

What might such a feminist critique focus on? The following is a demonstration, the limits of which I have demarcated by the use of an indentation:

The figure of Mardi in *Slash*, a political activist, who functions, however, from a distance, as Slash's political mentor, recalls Edward Said's observation about the place of Palestinian women, who, with few exceptions 'seem to have played little more than the role of hyphen, connective, transition, mere incident.'[4] The reader learns about Mardi's political involvement only when Slash runs into her at various political rallies and protests. Otherwise, she circulates in the novel as an underground figure, a floating signifier, always at the centre of AIM's most recent political manoeuvres. Eventually, she 'disappears,' without a trace (195). As a character in the novel she is marginal, and yet, in her absence, she is figured as central to Native political organization. As a silent figure of mediation who bridges the experience and political involvement of Slash, Mardi's character allegorizes the general position of indigenous women in the struggle of decolonization: their work is central but their recognition marginal.

Although I offer up this interpretation with some conviction of its validity – writing as a feminist – its limitations emerge in the context of the following remark made by Slash on the effects of racism in his relations with aboriginal women:

We told them about all that but there were some things that we were too ashamed to even tell. Like all of the white girls laughing at Tony when he asked one of them to dance at the sock-hop. He quit school after that. Also how none of the Indian girls ever got asked to dance at the sock-hops because us guys wouldn't dance with them because the white guys didn't. (35)

A feminist analysis that limits its discussion exclusively to the issue of gender risks displacing racism and assimilation as major determinations in the specific configurations of sexism at any historical moment.

### Textual Weapons

In a dedicatory poem to the novel, Armstrong praises the stories of a friend whose suffering from the violence of alcoholism provided the occasion to take up those stories as weapons, indeed as a strategy in the war on representation and subjectivity:

> We all walk in the shadow of the beast
> so we will step lightly
> All the stories you used to make laughter
> will be told around the tables of your people
> And we will be rich with weapons

The intratextual stories in *Slash* provide the occasion for a critical reflection on the making of fiction and the unmaking of Eurocentric written history. As much as Armstrong is engaged in re-historicizing Native political involvement in the sixties and early seventies from a Native perspective, and hence providing an alternative to what Tennant recognizes as the bias of discursive historical constructions by the European immigrant culture, she is also polemicizing the actual putting-into-writing of Native history. That the written word disseminates the 'truth' of what it means to have a history has become a well-known formulation of European and American ethnocentrism, which suppresses the truth of aboriginal modes of 'writing,' be they oral, hieroglyphic, pictographic, petrographic, syllabic, torn into the flesh, or woven into textiles in a complicated system of knots, in other words, inscribed in systems other than that of a Roman orthography. As I have shown, Armstrong engages with this marker of cultural bias in a number of specific ways.

In the politics of *Slash* the move towards decolonization rests upon refusing the co-optation of Native political action into a cycle of antagonism and aggression. In the final chapter of the novel Native political action has moved beyond a dualistic configuration as Native people begin to argue in the discourse of self-determination rather than the language of 'equal rights.' Slash's own position on self-determination is stated in his refusal to 'negotiate' on state terms, such as in constitutional debates:

They will buy out the land and the billions of dollars worth of resources on it for as little as they can. Then after that they will 'give' you rights in some areas of it within provincial regulations for conservation, if it doesn't interfere with other important things like mining and forestry. But they will hold off agreeing to any of these rights until they buy out all the land claims. They'll continue to 'negotiate' on rights until that is done. Then they'll give us whatever they choose because our greatest weapon will be in their hands. (241)

*Slash* thematizes the involvement of an individual who journeys from a politics of internal colonialism, a politics of the frontier (in no uncertain metaphorical terms), to a politics of self-determination. Self-determination for Slash ultimately means: 'We have our own interpretation as to how we function best' (223). The politics of self-determination are figured in Armstrong's textual politics of decolonization as a reclaiming of knowledge-as-interpretation through the use of 'storytelling': a generic mixture of 'writing' and 'oral' modes that explodes the myth of peoples without history and the ideology of Nativeness produced through a colonial centring of a Native subject-position.

# 6 Occupied Space: Métis and Inuit Writings, Feminist Critique

But it is not enough to stand on the opposite river bank, shouting questions, challenging patriarchal, white conventions. A counterstance locks one into a duel of oppressor and oppressed; locked in mortal combat, like the cop and the criminal, both are reduced to a common denominator of violence. The counterstance refutes the dominant culture's views and beliefs, and, for this, it is proudly defiant. All reaction is limited by, and dependent on, what it is reacting against. Because the counterstance stems from a problem with authority – outer as well as inner – it's a step towards liberation from cultural domination. But it is not a way of life. At some point, on our way to a new consciousness, we will have to leave the opposite bank, the split between the two mortal combatants somehow healed so that we are on both shores at once, and, at once, see through serpent and eagle eyes.

Gloria Anzaldúa, *Borderlands/La Frontera: The New Mestiza*, 78–9

To see through the eyes of the oppressor, to see through the eyes of the oppressed: when we can accomplish this sense of double vision, then we can heal the racial violence that separates us, that separates us from each other. This chapter has a double focus: feminist theoretical investigations into the meaning of cultural difference, and Métis and Inuit writings by women. Of the next four sections, the first one, entitled 'What's the Difference?' addresses the use of the category of difference in feminist discourse as a central metaphor around which to build feminist solidarity. The second section, '"Pagan Authentici-

ties," ' examines two diverse theoretical positions on the figure of the
'aboriginal.' As diverse as the writings of French semiotician Julia
Kristeva and Canadian postmodern novelist Daphne Marlatt are, their
respective fear of and desire for the 'other' turn on an unambivalent
relationship towards the usefulness of an aboriginal authenticity. In the
third section, 'You Are Now Entering the "Wild Zone," ' Elaine
Showalter's pioneering spirit and Teresa de Lauretis's desire for hybridity produce much more ambivalent positions towards the ethnographic subjects of colonialism. For de Lauretis, particularly, this
ambivalence resides in the figure of the Mestiza, a figure whose significance to post-structural theory is not unlike that of the Métis in the
Canadian context. The following two sections discuss Maria Campbell's autobiography, *Halfbreed*, and Beatrice Culleton's novel *In Search
of April Raintree* as two important examples of how Métis women
writers reclaim the derogatory connotations their cultural positions
evoke in terms of biological fears of 'interbreeding,' 'miscegenation,'
and 'racial interbreeding.' I have taken these biological metaphors and
their figural displacements as an occasion to reflect, in the sixth
section, on Derrida's theories of genre intermixing. I read these
(bio)graphic inscriptions of intermixing as signs of a cultural displacement: the fears that adhere to imperial ideologies in their lack of
acknowledgment about the cultural cross-overs or incorporations
which those ideologies have exploited and denied. The last section,
'Silly Cry,' includes a reading of a passage from Minnie Aodla Freeman's *Life among the Qallunaat*. Written by an Inuit woman, *Life
among the Qallunaat* discloses some of the contradictions between
feminism and decolonization. And I read this text – in order to bring
to crisis the investigating subject of postcolonial feminism – as a story
in which the tension between Freeman and her female Qallunaat
room-mate parallels the feminist investigations of the 'other.' In Freeman's text, however, the investigating subject actually comes into
conflict with an Inuit woman. It is precisely this conflict that postmodern feminism has closed off in a text such as Freeman's, which
describes its own silencing.

### What's the Difference?

The analytical categories of race, class, and gender currently represent
the historical and political axes through which women's relations are
constituted; however, the contradictions within and among these terms
are often resolved simply by evoking the referential and unifying

power of the sign of Woman, be it women of colour, white women, Native women, working-class women, middle-class women, lesbian or heterosexual women. It is precisely the clashes and conflicts of class exploitation, and racist and sexist oppression, that are subsumed under a seemingly all-inclusive, and yet I would argue, ultimately exclusive, category of Woman. While feminists gather together out of concern for the political ethics of exclusivity, it is more the case that the frontiers of inclusivity are being extended to manage the crisis of categories that can no longer contain the minds and spirits of their victims.

One response to the fear of perpetuating the crime of subject exclusion has been to place a great deal of value in the idea of difference. But difference, here, is a metaphysical construction and one that is being forged in the figure of Woman, specifically, in the figure of the female body, or what I have been calling a Woman/Body. There are concrete determinations, oppositions, and contradictions among women that cannot be covered over by a universalizing concept such as difference. Nowhere are the problems in this theoretical move made more apparent than in the vexed dynamic of feminist theory's relationship to Native women's critique of colonialism. Decolonizing feminist theory, then, involves rethinking the practical and theoretical implications of how gender is both constructed and contained by notions of 'sexual difference' in feminist semiotic theory, for example, as well as in the marxist-feminist language of a 'sexual division of labour.' The process of rethinking feminism involves reading and listening to Native women's discourses.

### 'Pagan Authenticities'

aboriginal: 'First or earliest so far as history or science gives record; primitive; strictly native, indigenous. Used both of the races and natural features of various lands.'

*The Oxford English Dictionary*

I want to discuss a general process of the feminization of 'aboriginal' cultures in relation to the very concept of ab/orginality; a term in which is contained the Nature/Culture opposition of European epistemology. I will do so with a demonstration from the spectacle of the ethnographic society as ab/original trace in Julia Kristeva's essay 'The Ethics of Linguistics' (in her *Desire in Language*).

In this essay Kristeva will find the spectacle of the ethnographic society a cause for celebrating the semiotic rhythm pulsing through the discourses of Western reason. However, in her critique of a formalist approach to linguistic analysis Kristeva will insist that study directed towards the ethnographic society is anachronistic. 'The ethical foundations for this [systemic approach] belong to the past: in their work, contemporary linguists think like seventeenth century men, while structuralist logic can be made to work only with primitive societies or their surviving elements' (24). Ethnographic societies would appear to belong to a purely delineated past, and any study of this unyielding and resistant authenticity is itself a sign of the inability of the linguist to enter the modern world and to face 'the contemporary mutations of subject and society.' Kristeva makes this point in order to insist that a semiotic approach is needed to think through the poetry of such Russian futurists as Mayakovsky or Khlebnikov: to think through, in Kristeva's words, 'the rhythm of Mayakovsky through to his suicide or Khlebnikov's glossolalias to his disintegration' (24). In her discussion of Khlebnikov glossolalias is described as a technic of infantilism, a pagan attitude regarding words. What constitutes this pagan language? According to Kristeva, rhythm, infantile regression, instinctual drives, and, of course, a lessening of sexual semantic tension. Pagan language is structurally equivalent to an original and innocent site of Nature, a woman's body, for example. Indeed, Kristeva dismisses 'pagan mythology' as 'probably nothing more than rhythm become substantive: this *other* of the linguistic and/or social contract, this ultimate and primordial leash holding the body close to the mother before it can become a social speaking subject' (30).

Kristeva's rejection of a historically situated ethnographic subject, her 'othering' of Native oral narrative as a pre-symbolic childhood from which to trace the maturity of Western civilization, subordinates and contains Native cultural productions as ab/original. Always coming from a beginning – a site of Nature, the reproductive woman/ body – Native cultural histories, including their orality, are subsumed. It would be interesting to know what Kristeva would make of the current transcription of Native oral narratives into print culture. Would this merely be their entry into the symbolic order of a late-capitalist mode of production in which the Native 'social speaking subject' is no longer, in Marie Annharte Baker's words, 'frozen Indians and frozen conversations'?[1] While for Kristeva the ab/original fulfils the function of an original and natural resource and in its anarchic formulation is to be feared, infantilized, and feminized, in postmodern feminism the figure of the aboriginal fulfils the desire for the 'other.'

Two brief passages from Daphne Marlatt's *Ana Historic: A Novel* demonstrate the overdetermination of the aboriginal figure to Euro-Canadian literary production. The novel is about a bourgeois British woman, Mrs Richards, and her precarious place as an agent of her own historical making in Canadian History writ large. Her situation is problematized by the narrator, Anna Richards [a.k.a. Ana Historic], who must locate her own praxis in the process of writing Mrs Richards's 'history':

in the dark (i imagine her writing at night, on the other side of a day in England she already knew) she can overlook the stumps, the scarred face of the clearing that surrounds her, and see herself ab-original in the new world (it is the old one she is at the end of). (30)

to be born in, enter from birth that place (that shoreline place of scarlet maples, since cut down) with no known name – see it, risen in waves, these scarlet leaves, lips all bleeding into the air, given (birth), given in greeting, the given surrounds him now. surrounds her, her country she has come into, the country of her body.
to be there from the first. indigene. *ingenuus* (born in), native, natural, free(born) – at home from the beginning.
*
she longed for it. (127)

A partial reading of *Ana Historic: A Novel* might investigate how the figure of the aboriginal and the indigene negotiate what is quickly becoming in Canadian postcolonial discourse an impassable fissure between a national/colonial opposition. In striving to become naturalized, the national citizen appropriates that which re-presents the wholly natural. *Ana Historic* contextualizes the gender specificity in an English-Canadian woman's relationship to the officially sanctioned record of Canadian national history. The historical figure of Mrs Richards as 'imperial mother' (117) completes the transatlantic circuit of exchange in Europe's trade routes. She is the vessel of imperialist ideology, the mother of the British 'race': 'the vessel she is – (full)-filling her destiny' (118). Imperialism has a foreign face in the novel, a global and external dimension: 'teas. pickles. currants. ex Star of Jamaica. ex, out of' (117). Economic imperialism in a pre-Confederation Canada does not enter the sphere of Marlatt's naturalization of the bourgeois female subject.

While two Siwash men appear in the text (41–2) as victims of white racism, which takes the form of fear and loathing of stereotypical drunken Indians, crazy and irrational, it is a Siwash woman named Ruth who becomes the object of the imperial gaze: 'As I was straightening books and the children's things, I observed Ruth to pass her fingers slowly over the slate, as if the letters marked thereon might leap into her very skin. Our Magic is different from theirs, I see – And yet it cannot capture them – the quiet with which each seems wrapt, a Grace that – the Grace of direct perception, surely, untroubled by letters, by mirrors, by some foolish notion of themselves such as we suffer from. I cannot find the words for this the others would dismiss as Pagan – perhaps our words cannot speak it' (69). 'Magic' and 'Pagan' signify the ideological difference between the illiterate letters and the unmediated essence of an aboriginal language of the flesh ('as if the letters marked thereon might leap into her very skin'). The Native woman is an embodiment of an essential and authentic language. At the same time as a Woman/Native language is figured as different ('Our Magic is different from theirs'), it is a key metaphorical displacement of the very 'unconditioned language' (75) Marlatt is seeking to reproduce for the disenfranchised female bourgeois subject.

Both Marlatt and Kristeva, then, rely on the centrality of a notion of the 'authentic' aboriginal, beyond language, to develop their respective feminist critiques, thereby displacing a range of colonized 'others' such as Native women. This displacement vitiates their critique because it serves to transfer relations of oppression onto a Native Woman/Body.

## You Are Now Entering the 'Wild Zone'

The antagonistic break with Anglo-American feminist theories of gender determination on the part of Native women writers and activists in recent years discloses a struggle over the production of meanings and values spoken for and by women. The value of the female body as concept and metaphor in postcolonial feminist critique suggests that the Woman/Body is a central overdetermination in feminist critical practice. When Teresa de Lauretis notes in her essay 'Eccentric Subjects: Feminist Theory and Historical Consciousness' that 'feminist theory came into its own, or became possible as such – that is, became identifiable as feminist theory rather than a feminist critique of some other theory or object-theory – in a postcolonial mode' (131), she refers to the metaphorical appropriation of woman's body as the site of colonial conquest: 'We spoke of ourselves as a colonized population and conceived of the female body as mapped by phallic desire or territorialized by Oedipal discourse' (131).

Elaine Showalter's frequently anthologized essay 'Feminist Criticism in the Wilderness' exemplifies this homologous conflation of 'penetration is to woman's body' what 'imperial conquest is to the land.' The very title 'Feminism in the Wilderness' is enough to invoke the pioneering frontier spirit and the avengers of unruly, out-of-control land masses. Indeed Showalter's claim to a 'wild zone' for women's literary textual production was clearly a reaction to a potentially explosive fragmentation of the women's movement, if not the fear of its dissolution. The threat of an elite French feminist theory, the African-American critique of racism in a predominantly white middle-class women's movement, the sexuality debates ('Did S/M dikes belong in a liberal women's movement ?*!#'), and the articulation of marxism and feminism (unhappily called the 'unhappy marriage of ...'), all of these challenged Showalter's liberal paradigm. And we should note that this liberal paradigm also gives rise to an alternative totality of gender difference. The figure on which this last gasp for a greater unity was being produced – going global seemed a good idea at the time – was that of the 'colonized.' For Showalter, the answer to feminism's 'tumultuous and intriguing wilderness of difference' lies in cultural anthropology. Women constitute a separate culture, whose beliefs, rituals, and artistic expressions can be deciphered by an ethnographer. The true sphere of women's culture exists in a spatial abstraction called the wild zone, 'literally no-man's-land.' Showalter would repopulate this no man's land with women, thereby displacing indigenous cultures in the so-called wilderness. On the one hand, Showalter parallels women with indigenous cultures as objects of ethnographic study; on the other hand, she expropriates the territory of indigenous people and turns non-Native women into upwardly mobile feminist pioneers replete with Amazon Utopias and Dark Continents. Either way her gynocentric criticism effectively exiles the internally colonized, both Native women and men, who constitute the original and proper inhabitants of a strangely unpopulated wilderness.

De Lauretis, however, subverts the way in which colonialism has become a metaphorical substitution for the Woman/Body through the notion of the 'eccentric subject' – the subject ex-centric to the totalizing figures of body and territory, the totalities of heterosexism and imperialism. The Mestiza and the lesbian become, for de Lauretis, the inappropriate/d subjects of an articulated difference. I agree with de Lauretis's argument about the centrality of the female body to a postcolonial critical mode; however, this particular textual relationship needs further discussion – we are not out of the woods yet. What is productive about the figure of the Mestiza is, at best, ambiguous. The Mestiza is the impure social formation which bastardizes the totalizing theory of kinship and its traffic in female gender-value; in a similar way the figure of the lesbian situates herself ex-centric to a heterosexist reduction of women to exchange commodities.[2] The Mestiza, thus, becomes an exemplary figure of a fertile political and cultural discursive territory in which to explore metaphors such as hybridity and difference. The figure of the Mestiza is in many ways comparable to that of the Métis in Canada. The figure of the Métis is also made to contain the racial ideology of mixed-blood (Ojibway/French, Cree/Scottish) as well as functioning as a figure for theories of cultural cross-over.

The Métis, like de Lauretis's use of the Mestiza, figure as the dream tropes of postcolonial discourse – fulfilling the desire for the other, hybridity is manifested in the very flesh of language: the (m)other of the race comes home to roost and the frame of a Woman/Body bears the ideology of racism.[3]

What is at stake in Showalter's and de Lauretis's ambivalent use of the metaphors of colonialism is the feminization of indigenous cultures: the slide from body to land, mother to homeland, figure to territory, penetration to colonization, and so on. The centrality of the Woman/Body to these homologous relations naturalizes the relationship between the colonized and women. Power is dispersed through the capacity of this spatial figure to contain continual deformations.

The following discussion of *Halfbreed* and *In Search of April Raintree* examines the ways in which the textual figure of the Métis provides a fertile political and cultural territory in which to explore the meaning and effects of assimilation, integration, hybridity, and difference.

## Halfbreed

Kate Vangen reads Maria Campbell's *Halfbreed* as a reclaiming of a third cultural position distinct from the two worlds of the 'Indian' or the 'White':

Historically, the term 'half-breed' has been used (rather sloppily) to refer to almost any kind of racial mixture. In other contexts, the term half-breed typically suggests those between two worlds – the 'economic middlemen, intercultural brokers, and interpreters.' However, as Harold Beaver notes, the non-Native travellers and agents of the previous century vituperate in their assessments of 'half-bloods as "designing," "fickle," "credulous" – in a word, as mischievous bastards.' To the non-Native, then, the person who is said to be caught 'between two worlds' is illegitimate to both. To the Native people, on the other hand, to people like Campbell's Cree relatives, half-breeds are simply allowed half-status – they are 'awp-pee-tow-koosons' or 'half people.' (191)

The distinction between the 'two worlds' emerges in Campbell's text through the use of opposition: 'The Halfbreeds who came were self-sufficient trappers and hunters. Unlike their Indian brothers, they were not prepared to settle down to an existence of continual hardship, scratching out a scanty living from the land' (7). In the following passage, Halfbreed and Indian are set against each other in a disturbing use of oppositions such as passive and active that become interchangeable for 'good' and 'bad' Indian; however, both the terms are deployed, in contradictory fashion, against the Indians:

There was never much love lost between Indians and Halfbreeds. They were completely different from us – quiet when we were noisy, dignified even at dances and get-togethers. Indians were very passive – they would get angry at things done to them but would never fight back, whereas Halfbreeds were quick-tempered – quick to fight, but quick to forgive and forget.

The Indians' religion was very precious to them and to the Halfbreeds, but we never took it as seriously. We all went to the Indians' Sundances and special gatherings, but somehow we never fitted in. We were always the poor relatives, the *awp-pee-tow-koosons*. They laughed and scorned us. They had land and security, we had nothing. As Daddy put it, 'No pot to piss in or a window to throw it out.' They would tolerate us unless they were drinking and then they would try to fight, but received many sound beatings from us. However, the old people, 'Mushooms' (grandfathers) and 'Kokums' (grandmothers) were good. They were prejudiced, but because we were kin they came to visit and our people treated them with respect. (25)

In contrast to the German and Swedish immigrants, who 'looked cold and frightening, and seldom smiled,' the Halfbreeds 'laughed, cried, danced, and fought and shared everything' (27). Vangen suggests that it is Campbell's use of humour, 'making faces,' as it were, at the absurdity of cultural and racist stereotyping, that retrieves *Halfbreed* as an exemplary text which surpasses the discursive antagonisms of biculturalism. The following is an additional example, to those Vangen calls attention to, of 'making faces':

When I was still quite young, a priest came to hold masses in the various homes. How I despised that man! He was about forty-five, very fat and greedy. He always arrived when it was mealtime and we all had to wait and let him eat first ... my brother Robbie and I decided one day to punish him. We took Daddy's rabbit wire and strung it across two small green trees on either side of the footpath. The wire was tight as a fiddle string ... It was almost dusk. Soon the Father came striding down the path, tripped on the first wire and fell to the ground, moaning. He scrambled up, only to hit the second wire and crash head first to the ground again. There was silence for a few seconds and then he started to curse ... Years later, Daddy told us that Mom had prayed for a week afterwards because she had laughed so much. The Father never dropped by again to eat our Sunday dinners and we left the strawberry patch to God. (29–30)

As Vangen notes, ironically, the violence of the tormented is turned back on the tormentor (191). The intratextual stories in *Halfbreed* evoke parodic subversions similar to such as those of 'Hightuned Polly' and 'Uncle Tommyhawks' found in Jeannette Armstrong's *Slash*. These parodic figures destabilize and subvert the 'law of representation,' in which an authentic Native subjectivity must be claimed in order to maintain uncontaminated cultural differences between Native and white, or Indian and Métis. These moments of textual aberrancy signal a threshold of difference, a point at which the hierarchical position contained by an ideology of the subject-of-oppression (Native subjectivity contained as 'oppressed people,' and dominant white subjectivity contained as 'the oppressor') is overturned. By overtly wearing the mask of the stereotypical image, the Native no longer resembles the stereotypical image of the 'Native'; thus, the image is shown to be different from itself, to be nothing more nor less than, what James Clifford calls, a 'serious fiction' (10).

*Halfbreed* also reconstitutes the position of the 'counterstance' and inscribes an ambivalent rhetorical agonism. The third position of the Métis is produced upon a position of cultural difference. The subject-position of the Métis is cleared only at the expense of producing a binary set of oppositions between categories of the 'Indian' and the 'White.'

In *Halfbreed* what might appear to be formal imitation, reinscription, and repetition of colonial violence, a farcical reversal of the Métis as a silent, bastardized figure of mediation, exemplifies what Homi Bhabha calls 'hybridity.' In his essay 'Signs Taken for Wonders: Questions of Ambivalence and Authority under a Tree outside Delhi, May

1817' Bhabha writes: 'The display of hybridity – its peculiar "replica-tion" – terrorizes authority with the *ruse* of recognition, its mimicry, its mockery' (157). The stories that 'make faces' at the dominant cul-ture, that mock the re-presentations of the Indian or Métis as 'lazy,' 'passive,' 'drunken,' etc., become, in Bhabha's words, not metaphorical substitutions of self-contained 're-presentations' but metonymies of presence. Bhabha, after Franz Fanon, further describes this ambivalent play of difference as stemming from an agonistic rather than antago-nistic experience; the aim of [colonial violence], Fanon writes, 'is rather a continued agony than a total disappearance of the pre-existing cul-ture' (156, as quoted in Bhabha). Bhabha's notion of hybridity permits the possibility of reading textual agonism as a mode of resistance to the unifying pressures of colonial subject effacement and constitution.

### In Search of April Raintree

In *In Search of April Raintree* the social and economic dispossession of the Métis is figured in the re-presentation of two Métis sisters: April, whose skin is white enough to permit her entry into the middle class, and Cheryl, whose brown skin produces an identification with the dispossessed Indian:

There were two different groups of children that went to the park. One group was the brown-skinned children who looked like Cheryl in most ways. Some of them even came over to our house with their parents. But they were dirty-looking and they dressed in real raggedy clothes. I didn't care to play with them at all. The other group was white-skinned and I used to envy them, especially the girls with blond hair and blue eyes. They seemed so clean and fresh, and reminded me of flowers I had seen. Some of them were freckled but they didn't seem to mind. To me, I imagined they were very rich and lived in big, beautiful houses and there was so much that I wondered about them. But they didn't care to play with Cheryl and me. They called us names and bullied us.
    We were ignored completely only when both groups were at the park. (15)

April is a textual figure with a split subjectivity – 'I felt torn in differ-ent directions ... Did I ever feel sorry for myself' (53). She gives voice to her abjection and self-negation through repetitions of white racism: 'Métis and Indians were inclined to be alcoholics. That's because they were weak people' (49); 'Poor Cheryl. She would never be able to disguise her brown skin as just a tan' (49); 'Being a half-breed meant being poor and dirty ... when I got free from being a foster child, then I would live just like a real white person' (49). Whereas in *Halfbreed*, in which the figure of Maria contains 'hybridity,' in *In Search of April Raintree* the narrative of ambivalence is split into two figures, Cheryl and April. Cheryl laments the lack of a unified, coherent subjectivity: 'I wish we were whole Indians' (45). April, however, internalizes the split between two totalities of difference that do not intersect.

The situating of hegemonic racist discourse within the figure of a Métis woman, April, produces a dislocation in the re-presentation of a unified, coherent subjectivity. To borrow a critical term from Mikhail Bakhtin and to deploy it in the area of subjectivity, a 'dialogism' breaks open in the figure of April. Writing about the double-directed voicedness of the dialogic imagination in the use of parody, Bakhtin argues: 'The second voice, once having made its home in the other's discourse, clashes violently with its primordial host and forces him [*sic*] to serve directly opposing aims. Discourse becomes an arena of battle between two voices' (193). April enters, as it were, the primordial host of the dominant racist discourse, forcing it to serve directly opposing aims, forcing it to speak its racism in order to expose its violence. To do so in the body of a Métis woman destabilizes the origin of racism – racism is placed precisely at the site of its effects.

*In Search of April Raintree* concludes by reconstituting a totality in the figure of 'a people': 'As I stared at Henry Lee, I remembered that during the night I had used the words "My people, our people" and meant them. The denial had been lifted from my spirit. It was tragic that it had taken Cheryl's death to bring me to accept my identity. But no, Cheryl once said, "All life dies to give new life"' (228). In the figure of April, Culleton reclaims 'identity' over difference. Cheryl's death assures the effacement of difference April could never accept. If authenticity can no longer be claimed in the figure of the 'Indian' for the Métis, it can be claimed in the production of another sphere of identity, a third position, a new synthesis of the split narratives of subjectivity constituted in Cheryl and April: the Métis. But this synthesis ultimately produces a new order of unification and reconciliation in which the 'Indian-ness' of Cheryl is absorbed into the 'whiteness' of April. Cheryl's death is, in fact, sacrificial; her irreducible difference as a figure who is made to occupy the vacancy of 'Indian' is cut out in Culleton's signifying space.

*Halfbreed* does not conclude with the inscription of a new totality of identity. Campbell opens up the signifying space of difference:

For these past couple of years, I've stopped being the idealistically shiny-eyed young woman I once was. I realize that an armed revolution of Native people will never come about; even if such a thing were possible what would we achieve? We would only end up oppressing someone else. I believe that one day, very soon, people will set aside their differences and come together as one. Maybe not because we love one another, but because we will need each other to survive. Then together we will fight our common enemies. Change will come because this time we won't give up. There is growing evidence of that today.

The years of searching, loneliness and pain are over for me. Cheechum said, 'You'll find yourself, and you'll find brothers and sisters.' I have brothers and sisters, all over the country. I no longer need my blanket to survive. (184)

In Julia Kristeva's terms, as written in her essay 'Women's Time,' Campbell inscribes in this passage a 'demassification of the problematic of *difference*, which would imply, in a first phase, an apparent de-dramatization of the "fight to the death" between rival groups and thus between the sexes [and the races]' (52). Setting aside difference instead of effacing the irreducibility of difference produces a configuration of political praxis that involves a process of articulation. From being silent figures of mediation situated between the spheres of 'rival groups,' women writers have become the negotiators, the brokers, of a non-hierarchical alignment of differences, dismantling cultural, racial, and sexual boundaries as hegemonic, and class forms of containment and divisiveness. Both *Halfbreed* and *In Search of April Raintree* demonstrate that the hegemonic management of cultural, racial, and sexual differences maintains class differences. In the specific instance of Native women neocolonialism is maintained although the society of the spectacle has further displaced questions of political economy into a postcolonial discourse in which images, re-presentations, 'authenticities,' and the 'experience of marginality' circulate as the currency of exchange.

### 'Genres Should Not Be Mixed'

In the hegemonic discourse of racism the 'host' contains the re-presentation of the 'Indian' as a parasite; in the figure of April the parasitical relation is reversed and turned back on the discursive monstrosity of racism's rhetorical agonism. April is a textual figure of agonism who 'lives' Artaud's formulation of cultural dismemberment: 'I am not dead but I am separated.'

The construction of Métis subjectivity as internally 'hybridized' destabilizes the law of representation in which hegemonic inscriptions of subjectivity are unified around a white centring of the subject. The genre of realism, in which *Slash, Halfbreed*, and *In Search of April Raintree* are presumably written, is also subject to the same process of destabilization; 'realism,' as a discursive form which bears an effect of 'reality,' can no longer sustain the coherence of its presumed re-presentation of a given reality. In his deconstruction of *les genres des genres* Jacques Derrida deploys an etymological play between the terms 'gender,' 'genes,' and 'genre' in order to demonstrate the racist implications of European 'classifications.' He introduces the urgency of the law against 'intermixing' and 'interbreeding' through the opening interdiction, 'genres should not be mixed,' and further, 'genres should not intermix' or there will be a risk of 'impurity, anomaly, or monstrosity' ('The Law of Genre,' 56, 57). Derrida also positions the question of the *origin* of genre corruption within an etymological logic of the *ab-orgine* and the *ab-ortion* (58).

What are the implications of a critical morphology that uses terms such as 'hybridity,' 'bastardization,' and 'mixed gen(r)es' for a discussion of two texts which narrate the lives of two Métis women? The line between theory and practice becomes somewhat blurred. The Métis, specifically Métis women, have lived the aberrancy of socio-symbolic dispossession that the morphologies of critical theory valorize as a textual mode of intervention into the colonial ruses of power, knowledge, Truth, and History. Does the post-structural move in Derrida's philosophy owe a symbolic debt to what George Manuel called the 'Fourth World,' in the same way such modernist writers as Joseph Conrad, Virginia Woolf, and D.H. Lawrence and the artist Pablo Picasso owe one to the 'Third World'? This question marks the contradiction of reading literary criticism which uses Derridean post-structural theory, for example, in order to abstract indigenous knowledges of interpretation into a First Worldist discursive consumption.[4] There is an implied narrative in which 'marginal' experience becomes abstracted into a critical theory, in which the spectacle[5] of marginality gains a certain currency in commodity exchange and is then returned to the Native, the marginal, the ethnic, as a legitimation of value: you are valuable precisely because of your labour as a sign. Human 'value' has been surpassed by abstracted commodity value.

If the hegemonic management of genre/gene boundaries is not maintained, the result, as Derrida notes, is the production of 'an internal division of the trait, impurity, corruption, contamination, decomposition, perversion, deformation, even cancerization, generous proliferation, or degenerescence. All of these disruptive 'anomalies' are engendered – and this is their common law, the lot or site they share – by repetition' (57–8). To substitute 'reproduction' for 'repetition' in the above formulation would call attention to a displacement in Derrida's racial narration since 'reproduction' (or repetition and difference) would seem to follow better the chain of signifiers – genetics, hereditary traits, diseases, deformation, etc., – and since it is only through a process of 'invagination'(79) that a genetic/genre corruption could possibly occur: through the metaphysics of ab/original women's bodies: through the feminization of critical theory in which the body of ab/original women functions as a silent, hyphenated figure of mediation.

Another example of how the ab/original Woman/Body becomes a site of contested and conflicted meanings, values, and desires appears in Minnie Aodla Freeman's Inuit feminist anthropological and autobiographical account, *Life among the Qallunaat*.

### 'Silly Cry'

Minnie Aodla Freeman's *Life among the Qallunaat* is an autobiographical text in which Freeman tells the story of her relocation to the south as a young woman to work as an interpreter for the then Department of Northern Affairs and National Resources. The definitions given for the Inuktituk word *Qallunaat* are revealing for what they tell us about Inuit perceptions of their encounter with white women and men. The parallel between English-Canadian feminist theory and the history of male-dominated colonialism can be seen to be played out in the definitions:

Qallunaaq (singular); qallunaat (plural): literally 'people who pamper their eyebrows'; possibly an abbreviation of qallunaaraaluit; powerful, avaricious, of materialist habit, people who tamper with nature. (13)

The passage I am going to discuss is entitled 'Silly Cry,' and it is about an exchange between Freeman and her room-mate over the significance of a pair of baby-doll pyjamas. I take the liberty of quoting the passage at length:

#### Silly Cry

My *qallunaaq* and I celebrated our birthdays on the same date. In our first year as roommates we gave ourselves a party. By this time she and I could talk to each other about our problems, sorrows, wishes and dreams and share our female to female secrets. We got along very well, mainly because I did not argue or disagree with her suggestions or plans. I went along with everything she did and enjoyed it as well.

Someone had given me a pair of baby-doll pyjamas for my birthday. They were the new fad that year. Every girl was daring to wear them. They were beautiful. Because I was brought up by my grandmother, I inherited some of her idiosyncrasies. She treasured anything that she thought was beautiful, no matter what it was. When I got into her trunk or suitcase, I would find a single necklace bead, a broken ironstone plate with flower prints on it, an old dress she picked up from her neighbours, a brand new ashtray with scenes on it, a slip that she had put away because it was too pretty to wear. So it was with these baby-doll pyjamas. I kept them in a drawer among other things that I treasured. They were very pretty to me and too pretty to wear. My other reason for not wearing them was because of my shyness.

My *qallunaaq* and I shared one dresser and one closet. She used one side and I, the other. Every time one of us opened our drawers we saw the other's things. Both of us knew about everything we owned. She went to bed in baby-dolls and I went to bed in my long-legged flannelette pyjamas. Neither of us really noticed or mentioned to the other what we wore to bed. It was something that was not important, so we took it for granted as one of our habits. But one evening, while she was sitting at the dresser attired in her baby-dolls, combing her hair and looking in her mirror, I opened the drawer where I kept my treasures. Whatever I needed at that moment was not in that drawer. Seeing my baby-dolls, she remembered that I had never worn them. 'Do you not like those? How come you have never worn them? They are too beautiful, just to leave them in a drawer. Are they too big? Are they too small? Why don't you try them on?' What could I say to all her questions? She would not understand my reasons and besides, they were not important. I followed her suggestion. I knew that if I argued my side she would become all worked up, so I tried them on.

I felt very naked, very flashy. She became excited just the same: 'Oh, how beautiful! The colour just suits you! You look so cute in them! I don't think you appreciate the girl who gave them to you! I think it's terrible to leave them in the drawer! Why don't you wear them? Are you shy? I would give anything to have nice brown skin like yours! Are you shy about your legs? Look at my legs, and I wear baby-dolls!' I began to cry. 'How silly of you to cry, it's so stupid! Whoever heard of crying over baby-dolls?'

We both became very quiet. How could I explain that I did not cry over the baby-dolls? I wanted to tell her my feelings but I could not. I wanted to tell her that I treasured them because they were too pretty to wear in an old bed, that I was afraid that they might get all wrinkled, and that I did not want to wash them for fear they would lose their prettiness. I wanted to tell her that I appreciated the person who gave them to me very much and that I showed my appreciation by trying to make them last as long as possible. I wanted to tell her that I was not brought up to show off my body, that showing off the body where I came from is described as *anguniattuk*, fishing for a man, the word also used for dogs who are in heat. Where I come from, a lady does not show off what she has.

My *qallunaaq* finally broke the silence by saying, 'I did not realize you were so shy. I did not mean to hurt you. I am awfully sorry. You don't have to wear them if you don't want to. After all they are yours.' I wished she would just keep quiet about the whole thing. I cried because she gave me too much notice and she insulted by baby-dolls for not understanding that they were my treasures. That was the first time my *qallunaaq* and I had had unhappy feelings since we met. It was the first time I stood up for my beliefs without following hers. It made me wonder how many times we would have had unhappy feelings if I had not followed her and if instead I tried to explain my beliefs to her. (58–60)

This section structures the significance of a pair of baby-doll pyjamas between two conflicting cultural ideologies. The clearest site of conflict occurs over what the baby-doll pyjamas signify in terms of gift exchange. To the Qallunaat reverence for the fashion cycle and the rapid reproduction of the 'new' demand that this sacred object of fashion be worn, if for no other reason than to wear out its value as the latest spectacle of commodified femininity; the baby-dolls as feminine fetish in the discourse of the Qallunaat is not disconnected from the reification of the female body in general. To Freeman the baby-dolls signify an object not to be worn, but to be treasured as an aesthetic object. Here the baby-dolls re-present their value as an object of beauty and not as an article of clothing.

Under a great deal of pressure to explain why she does not wear the baby-doll pyjamas Freeman remarks: 'I wanted to tell her that I appreciated the person who gave them to me very much and that I showed my appreciation by trying to make them last as long as possible. I wanted to tell her that I was not brought up to show off my body, that showing off the body where I came from is described as *anguniattuk*, fishing for a man, the word also used for dogs who are in heat. Where I come from, a lady does not show off what she has.' Freeman combats the pressure to conform to a Qallunaat system of gender formation with her own declaration of Inuit gender formation. Under a marxist-feminist rubric of the universal oppression of women the question might be asked of Freeman's text, Does her account of women's sexuality in Inuit culture represent an indigenous form of gender containment? And further, what do the relations of gift-exchange among the Inuit constitute by way of gender determination? We have to be careful in imposing a language of repression onto Freeman's stricture. One way of reading this text would be to acknowledge anthropological, including feminist anthropological, research, which stresses the non-repressive, particularly the sexually non-repressive, social relations in gatherer/hunter societies, such as the Inuit. Following this interpretation, we might read Freeman's remarks as a sign of the influence of non-Native religion. And this begs the question, what *is* properly indigenous? Having marked this possible interpretation and indicated the problems with it, I would like to suggest that I can only go so far as to register my own discomfort with Freeman's moralism. These questions aside, the passage illustrates a series of interjections she wanted to make but did not. My purpose in focusing on this passage is to demonstrate how she is silenced by the seemingly benign generosity of her room-mate, and how Freeman strategically displaces this silencing in the writing of this text as an explication of that silence.

Freeman's room-mate, the investigating subject in the text, and I would also suggest, an imaginary marxist-feminist critic, is in crisis. Listen to Freeman's room-mate's hysterical interrogation: 'Seeing my baby-dolls, she remembered that I had never worn them. "Do you not like those? How come you have never worn them? They are too beautiful, just to leave them in a drawer. Are they too big? Are they too small? Why don't you try them on?"' and later, '"Why don't you wear them? Are you shy? I would give anything to have nice brown skin like.yours! Are you shy about your legs? Look at my legs, and I wear baby-dolls!" I began to cry. "How silly of you to cry, it's so stupid! Whoever heard of crying over baby-dolls?"'

'What could I say to all her questions? She would not understand my reasons and besides, they were not important.' 'We both became very quiet. How could I explain that I did not cry over the baby-dolls?' These questions are posed by Freeman in response to the interrogation she receives. Her questions represent the unspeakable knowledge of the investigated subject. Freeman takes up the vacancy of her subject-position under colonialism as the voice of the unspeakable: 'We got along very well, mainly because I did not argue or disagree with her suggestions or plans.' 'It made me wonder how many times we would have had unhappy feelings if I had not followed her and if instead I tried to explain my beliefs to her.' Freeman reverses the investigator/investigated relation of exchange between herself and a Qallunaat woman. But she does not fully occupy the space of the investigator as an imperial subject, with a sovereign disposition towards the empire of signs. Freeman uses the written text and the commodity book form to write and print the unsayable; that is, she writes in a narrative and technological form the limits of what she can say given the gender containment to which she is subject.

(iii) *The equivalent form*[6] We have seen that a commodity A (the [text]), by expressing its value in the use-value of a commodity B of a different kind (the [book]), impresses upon the latter a form of value peculiar to it, namely that of the equivalent. The commodity [text] brings to view its own existence as a value through the fact that the [book] can be equated with the [text] although it has not assumed a form of value distinct from its own physical form. The [book] is directly exchangeable with the [text]; in this way the [text] in fact expresses its own existence as a value [*Wertsein*]. The equivalent form of a commodity, accordingly, is the form in which it is directly exchangeable with other commodities. (147)
...
The body of the commodity which serves as the equivalent always figures as the embodiment of abstract human [birthing], and is always the product of some specific useful and concrete [birthing]. This concrete [site of origin-ality] therefore becomes the expression of abstract human [ab/origins]. If the [book] is merely abstract human [birthing]'s realization, the [imprinting] actually realized in it is merely abstract human [origins]'s form of realization. In the expression of value of the [original], the usefulness of

The marxist-feminist critic is both different from the text's investigating subject and similar to her: different in that she is able to perform a critique of the commodity femininity which determines the antagonistic and aggressive interrogation to which Freeman is put. And yet questions remain and are symptomatically reproduced: if the essential feminity of late-capital exchange overdetermines relations among Qallunaat women, can we say that the gift-exchange of kinship relations also overdetermines relations among Inuit women? Is the figure of the 'baby-doll' pyjamas, over which this antagonistic exchange takes place, a metonymic displacement of the baby-doll-functioning in the kinship versus capitalist exchange between two between-women? Alternatively, trafficking in the symbolic status of a pair of baby-doll pyjamas, are we interpreting a symbolic displacement of their respective gender-value differences or a struggle over meaning/truth/re(-)presentation?

[ab/originalizing] consists, not in
making [aboriginals], and thus also
people, but in making a [represen-
tation] which we at once recognize as
relations of value, as a congealed
quantity of [blood], therefore, which
is absolutely indistinguish-able from
the [birthing] objectified in the value
of the [original]. In order to act as
such a mirror of value, [aborigin-
alizing] itself must reflect nothing
apart from its own abstract quality of
being [birthing]. (150)

Situating ourselves as cultural critics somewhere in the proximity of
these thresholds of valuation might make it possible to ask questions
which unfold the contradictions within feminist practice, in order to
understand, for example, the reproduction of the imperial violence of
knowledge within the neocolonial discourses of an imperial feminist
postmodernism, such as that exemplified in *Ana Historic* and the text of
the marxist-feminist investigating subject.

This passage in Freeman's book stages the contradictions and tensions
at issue in the relationship of Native and non-Native women. This relationship cannot be subsumed under abstract categories such as difference. In approaching Native women, feminism cannot adopt a language
of authenticity in order to 'naturalize' or verify its own practice/theory.
Finally, we must be wary of critique that displaces the historical specificity of colonialism through a metaphorical domestication. An analysis of
a strategically placed subject-position such as that of Native women
allows us to rethink the wild zone as the limit of the Woman/Body
metaphor and its work as a central and centralizing mode of social,
political, and cultural critique.

# Notes

1 I have no intention of 'covering' the broad theoretical terrains of feminism and postcolonialism, or of even staking out the full limits of these various disciplinary domains. My interest here is not cartographic and circumscriptive; rather it approximates the spirit of the wanderer. And the difference between the cartographer and the wanderer is something like the difference between the imperialist and the nomad, who is neither aimless nor containable. The revalorization of the nomadic in critical theory increasingly holds out a promise of redemption with which to immunize the 'West' from greater social, environmental, and political atrocities. It is an attractive proposition and one that I take seriously, however cautiously (the parasitical injection in the process of immunization being penultimately therapeutic). Whatever use or value is left in rethinking the figure of the nomad in a gatherer/hunter society I take up so as to investigate a set of determinations arrested in the conceptual (and not intrinsic) essence of the 'feminist triangle': race, class, and gender.

2 For an excellent history of post-Saussurian intellectual thought see Rosalind Coward and John Ellis's *Language and Materialism: Developments in Semiology and the Theory of the Subject.*

3 On the small *m* in marxism, I take my lead from Rosalind Coward's *Patriarchal Precedents: Sexuality and Social Relations.* The effect of the lower case can be registered as an implicit critique of the unequal textual relationship between feminism and marxism.

4 The Lone Ranger, an imperial trope in industrial fiction media, meets an indefatigable adversary in the figure of Ariel Dorfman. See Ariel Dorfman, *The Empire's Old Clothes: What the Lone Ranger, Babar, and Other Innocent Heroes Do to Our Minds.*

5 The bracketed reference to 'hetero' before 'sexism' is intended to be suggestive of the way in which sexism is often interpreted within the oppositional antagonism between 'women' and 'men.' I would displace this opposition by focusing on the way in which sexism divides women from 'women.' In the case of sexism the relations between women and men are privileged over relations among and between women. To de-privilege the antagonism between women/men would allow for the possibility of a 'positive' collective practice, even as I recognize that, on a practical level, antagonistic relations remain between the subject articulations of 'race,' 'colonialism,' and 'gender,' and that this antagonism is irreducible. The following passage is from Rosario Morales's 'We're All in the Same Boat,' published in *This Bridge Called My Back: Writings by Radical Women of Color*, edited by Cherrie Moraga and Gloria Anzaldúa. I quote it here because I think that the problem Morales outlines is indicative of the divisiveness of heterosexism for women: 'My experience in the Puerto Rican communist & independent movements has made me suspicious of and angry at Puerto Rican (& other Latin American) activist women. They have been sexist and supported the macho line that we *needed to fight against imperialism first – only later could we think about women as women.* I desperately want Latina women in the feminist movement while I fear the entry of hispanic & often black women because I fear they will play an anti-feminist role' (91).

6 For an excellent discussion of how Derrida has been misread as 'some kind of transcendental solipsist who believes that nothing "real" exists outside the written text' see Christopher Norris, *Derrida,* especially 142.

7 Further to the antagonism between feminism and marxism, see Michèle Barrett, *Women's Oppression Today: Problems in Marxist Feminist Analysis.*

8 Insofar as national designations of feminist traditions are useful, a more grounded approach to the question of marxism for feminist practice has been claimed for British and Scandinavian feminist practice. Toril Moi writes in her essay 'Feminism, Postmodernism, and Style: Recent Feminist Criticism in the United States' that

socialist feminism in Britain and the Scandinavian countries 'is much more mainstream than in the U.S. I think it is correct to say that since the 1960s, socialist feminism in its various forms has been the *dominant* trend in British and Scandinavian feminism, both inside and outside academic institutions' (4). Feminism in Canada also has a well-founded history of socialist feminism, particularly in the social sciences, although, unlike its British counterparts, its importance has been at the expense, at times, of accepting the site of cultural productions as a constitutive force in political movement. However, the publications of collected essays, such as *Gynocritics/La Gynocritique: Feminist Approaches to Canadian and Quebec Women's Writing*, edited by Barbara Godard, *A Mazing Space: Writing Canadian Women Writing*, edited by Shirley Neuman and Smaro Kamboureli, and *Work in Progress: Building Feminist Culture*, edited by Rhea Tregebov, indicate that feminist cultural studies in Canada are indeed a growth industry that can no longer be ignored.

9 The notion of *redemption* as a driving force through which forgiveness of past events can lead to future 'happiness' is one of the contributions to a critical understanding of history which Walter Benjamin makes in his essay 'Theses on the Philosophy of History': 'Social Democracy thought fit to assign to the working class the role of the redeemer of future generations, in this way cutting the sinews of its greatest strength. This training made the working class forget both its hatred and its spirit of sacrifice, for both are nourished by the image of enslaved ancestors rather than that of liberated grandchildren' (260). A materialist feminist position is one, like Benjamin's understanding of marxism, that must remain true to its knowledge of past experience. A deconstructive approach makes possible the unfolding of historical violence, whereas a liberal feminist pluralism circumscribes existing choices which constitute a range of utopian (im)possibilities.

10 For an extended critique of Weedon's 'reductive opposition' between feminism and post-structuralism see Teresa de Lauretis's 'The Essence of the Triangle or, Taking the Risk of Essentialism Seriously: Feminist Theory in Italy, the U.S. and Britain.'

11 For a detailed discussion of the ways in which these terms are deployed in the social and political sciences see Peter Kulchyski, 'Towards a Theory of Dispossession: Native Politics in Canada,' especially chapter 6, 'The State and Native Peoples in Canada: Totalization and Dispossession.'

CHAPTER ONE  Gender and the Discourses of Orientalism

1 In Said's bio-graphic representation of Palestinian women the metonymic value attributed to the hymen as the displaced object of loss is an unacknowledged textual agent for bearing the movement of Said's syntax. Like the verb 'to be' as the indicator of absolute proximity, the very question of being is taken somewhat for granted; it has lost its metaphorical force and become in Nietzschean terms, 'natural (i.e., gendered), fixed, canonic, and binding.'

2 As an example of a counter-productive move to reinscribing the hegemonic Woman, Gilbert and Gubar's *The Madwoman in the Attic: The Woman Writer and the Nineteenth-Century Literary Imagination* is exemplary. Gilbert and Gubar supplement the narrative of male (af)filiative aesthetic production with a female version of Harold Bloom's 'plot for poetic history': a male narrative of the son killing off the literary father in order to make his place in the patriarchal canon of literary history. Gilbert and Gubar's revisionary shift uses a metaphysics of women's reproductive capacity to engender the female writer's right to creative dominance. While Said moves towards an increasing secularization in the filiative/affiliative contradiction, Gilbert and Gubar produce a feminine theology of the primacy of the mother. As an emerging feminist theocracy, their position fails to recognize its complicity in genteel history, in the insertion of women writers into a bourgeois canon.

CHAPTER TWO  Engendering Textual Violence

1 De Lauretis critiques Michel Foucault, Jacques Derrida, and René Girard for their failure to acknowledge the gender specificity of their critical readings into the Western socio-historical, literary, and philosophical canon. Spivak directs her charge of sanctioned ignorance towards Louis Althusser as well as Michel Foucault.

2 For an elaboration of Spivak's notion of the 'gendered subaltern' see her essay 'A Literary Representation of the Subaltern: A Woman's Text from the Third World,' in *In Other Worlds*, particularly pages 253–8. And for her critique of Antonio Gramsci's work on the 'subaltern classes' see 'Can the Subaltern Speak?' 283 ff.

3 See Soraya Antonius, 'Fighting on Two Fronts: Conversations with Palestinian Women,' 65.

4 See Sarah Kofman's *The Enigma of Woman*, especially 50–65, for a relevant discussion of female narcissism.

5 'An Interview with Nawal el Sadaawi [*sic*],' 176. See also Leila Ahmed, 'Feminism and Cross-Cultural Inquiry: The Terms of Discourse in Islam' for an extended discussion of how the current orthodox version of Islam emerged in relation to other, lesser known, and to some extent suppressed interpretations of Islam such as those of the Sufi and Qarmati movements, which have questioned the so-called 'inferiority of women.'

6 'A mosque built in memory of the Prophet Mohamed's daughter Zeinab. Sayeda is a term of respect used for women' (author's note, 79).

7 As Spivak writes: 'In seeking to learn to speak to (rather than listen to or speak for) the historically muted subject of the subaltern woman, the postcolonial intellectual *systematically* "unlearns" female privilege' ('Can the Subaltern Speak?,' 295).

8 Spivak deploys the notion of 'consciousness' *strategically*, as in the following explanation: 'I am suggesting, rather, that although the group [subaltern studies] does not wittingly engage with the post-structuralist understanding of "consciousness," our own transactional reading of them is enhanced if we see them as *strategically* adhering to the essentialist notion of consciousness, that would fall prey to an anti-humanist critique, within a historiographic practice that draws many of its strengths from that very critique' (206–7).

9 Those 'effects' are both debilitating and productive. The Cape Dorset artist cooperative, established during the 1950s by James Houston while he was employed by the federal Department of Indian Affairs and Northern Development (currently the Ministry of Indian and Northern Affairs), then in charge of the development of arts and crafts programs in the North, produced prints and soapstone sculptures which have gained national as well as international acclaim. This artistic venture brought much-needed material security to some of the Inuit population, whose nomadic way of life had become threatened by diseases brought in by Europeans and Euro-Canadians, and by government relocations of large groups of Inuit people for the purpose of creating settlements in the North. Pudlo Pudlat is one such artist whose works have been shown nationally and internationally. Commenting on his stature as a famous 'Canadian' artist, Pudlo remains uncompromised by the material necessity of his cultural productions. To paraphrase a comment he made in a *Globe and Mail* newspaper article in July 1990, Pudlo draws for a commercial market. He does it for the money. See also Marie Routledge and Marion E. Jackson, *Pudlo: Thirty Years of Drawing*.

10 This is, of course, Marx's familiar point in his 'The Eighteenth Brumaire of Louis Bonaparte,' where he writes: 'Nor indeed must one imagine that the democratic representatives are all *shopkeepers* or their enthusiastic supporters. They may well be poles apart from them in their education and their individual situation. What makes them representatives of the petty bourgeoisie is the fact that their minds are restricted by the same barriers which the petty bourgeoisie fails to overcome in real life, and that they are therefore driven in theory to the same problems and solutions to which material interest and social situation drive the latter in practice. This is the general relationship between the *political and literary representatives* of a class and the class which they represent' (176–7).

CHAPTER THREE   (De)constructing Affinities

1 At Women and Words / Les Femmes et les mots, also a ground-breaking conference in Canadian feminist studies, held in Vancouver, British Columbia, 30 June–3 July 1983, Jeannette Armstrong, Beth Brant, and Beth Cuthand delivered papers. Perhaps the difference between the Women and Words Conference and the International Feminist Book Fair could best be characterized in terms of 'naming.' Under the name of 'Woman,' Armstrong, Brant, and Cuthand were positioned to speak against a 'double colonization,' thereby invoking the metaphorical power of a universal representation of women's bodies as a site of 'territorial conquest.' At the International Feminist Book Fair, Native women were to speak directly to the historical and experiential aspects of colonialism, to speak to the fractures of their colonized subjectivity, rather than as additional representations of feminism's representative subject, Woman.

2 *The Oxford English Dictionary* as cited in de Lauretis, 'The Essence of the Triangle,' 5

3 'An Act for the Gradual Enfranchisement of Indians, the Better Management of Indian Affairs, and to Extend the Provisions of the Act 31st Victoria, Chapter 42, s.c. 1869, s. 6, c. 6,' in *Indian Acts and Amendments: 1868–1950*, 2d ed. (Treaties and Historical Research Centre, Research Branch, Corporate Policy, Department of Indian and Northern Affairs Canada, 1981), 7. See Kathleen Jamieson's excellent essay 'Sex Discrimination and the Indian Act' for an outline of these discriminations. See also her extended discussion of these issues in *Indian Women and the Law in Canada: Citizens Minus*.

4 *The Quest for Justice: Aboriginal Peoples and Aboriginal Rights*, ed. Menno Boldt and J. Anthony Long in association with Leroy Little Bear. See especially Appendices E and F, 363–5.

5 The Canadian Charter of Rights and Freedoms was passed in the Constitutional Act of 1982 and took effect 17 April 1985.

6 For an earlier and more optimistic account of the relationship between feminism and Native women see Caroline LaChapelle, 'Beyond Barriers: Native Women and the Women's Movement.'

7 As quoted in Barbara Harlow, 'Commentary: "All That Is Inside Is Not Center": Responses to the Discourses of Domination,' 162

8 See also Anne Cameron, 'A Message for Those Who Would Steal Native Traditions,' for Cameron's own commentary on appropriation in connection with spirituality.

9 Unpublished as far as I know and enclosed in a letter to the author, 27 November 1989

10 The text in question here is now in print: *Writing the Circle: Native Women of Western Canada*, ed. Jeanne Perreault and Sylvia Vance. In the foreword the editors argue convincingly for the importance of this publication: 'The work of compiling and editing this book has been very exciting, because of the people we have met and the friends we have made and because of the *intrinsic value* of this collection' (xiv). It is a truism that emancipatory politics exists within the double bind of having to make use of dominant social formations, such as those of liberal pluralism, at the same time as the very categories, classifications and discriminations that determine the scope of that liberal plurality are open to subversion. The notion of an intrinsic value, however, is an essentialist concept to which race and sex differences are enjoined as the exchange values mediating the current circulation of difference under late capitalism.

Emma LaRoque's preface to the collection, entitled 'Preface or Here Are Our Voices – Who Will Hear?' provides the occasion for deconstructing the social relations which inhere in the text's publication. Her essay is a brilliant account of the importance of 'giving voice,' not simply as an admittance into the publishing domain but also in having control over what is and is not said, in other words, admittance into the editorial decision-making process. Both editors make a point of clarifying their own process; however, it still must be said that the 'hand's off' approach they take does not solve the contradictions of their positions *vis-à-vis* the material they include. Refusal to dialogue with these texts, to acknowledge that, whatever our positions, we can never simply take an indifferent position with respect to questions of aesthetic value, is to reproduce the contradictions of a supposedly neutral free culture and its attendant subject-positionings.

11 It is important to note that during the course of the book fair participants were informed of the escalating conflict emerging between the federal government and the Province of Quebec, on one side, and the Kanienkehaka (Mohawk Nation), on the other, concerning what the federal government considered to be the illegal selling of contraband cigarettes. On 1 June 1988 the Royal Canadian Mounted Police, armed with handguns and automatic weapons, raided Kahnawake to confiscate documents in an effort to put an end to the 'cigarette dispute' and to undermine Mohawk sovereignty, so that tax revenue from cigarette sales could be recovered for the Canadian government. The most recent event to mark this set of conflicts occurred at Oka on 11 July 1990, when the Kanienkehaka of Kanesatake put up barricades to prohibit the municipality of Oka from using their lands to expand a golf course.

CHAPTER FOUR  'A Gift for Languages'

1 Hudson's Bay Company Archives, 'York Factory Journals, 1714–17,' B. 239/a/1–3. All further references to these journals, which are cited by their entry date, are included in the text.
2 See Alison Prentice et al., eds., *Canadian Women: A History*, 24–5.
3 For the use of the psychoanalytic term 'transference' as a way of understanding relations between the present and the past in historiographic practice see Dominick LaCapra, *History and Criticism*, 72ff; and his *Soundings in Critical Theory*, 37ff.
4 I have maintained as direct a transcription of the archival document as possible, leaving the differences in spelling, punctuation, word usage, etc. That these differences pose problems for the contemporary reader in deriving clear and unambiguous meanings is irreducible and, at least, demonstrates the degree to which historical rereadings of archival documents often tend towards effacing textual differences and contradictions in order to produce a coherent and monological reading.
5 For an excellent discussion of the effects of feminist theory on the discipline of history see Arlette Farge, 'Women's History: An Overview,' in *French Feminist Thought*, ed. Toril Moi, 133–49.
6 See E.E. Rich, *The History of the Hudson's Bay Company: 1670–1870*, vol. 1, especially 435–41. See also J.F. Kenney, *The Founding of Chur-*

*chill: Being the Journal of Captain James Knight, Governor-in-Chief in Hudson Bay, from 14th July to 13th of September, 1717* for an account of William Stewart's eventual insanity and death, especially 49ff.

7 Abdul JanMohamed's work in the area of discursive economy I take to be a reworking of Marx and Engels's discussion of the social forms of thought in *The German Ideology*: 'The production of ideas, of conceptions, of consciousness, is at first directly interwoven with the material activity and the material intercourse of [women], the language of real life. Conceiving, thinking, the mental intercourse of [women] appear at this stage as the direct efflux of their material behaviour. The same applies to mental production as expressed in the language of politics, laws, morality, religion, metaphysics, etc. of a people' (47). JanMohamed, however, elaborates a post-structural critique of the social production of meaning, taking into account the commodification and by extension fetishization of the material signifier. 'The Slave Woman,' for example, has been endowed with a mystical and reified status, both within Knight's text and subsequent historical reworkings.

8 Peter Kulchyski observes that 'what was said about the Indian often played a role in the struggle over meaning that was related to the European class struggle' ('Towards a Theory of Dispossession: Native Politics in Canada,' 16). The assimilation of the Native to a Eurocentric mode of classification not only works in the interest of containing Native subjectivity within European class lines but also reflects the way in which the image of the Indian served to maintain the positional superiority of a colonial ruling class at home as well as abroad.

9 For another example of the status-and-prestige argument in relation to gender and power in indigenous societies see Sherry Ortner's essay 'Gender Hegemonies.' Ortner's essay makes a strong case for the necessity of an analysis of prestige as a significant aspect of power relations in gatherer/hunter societies. However, her argument deploys the Gramscian notion of hegemony, a critical term that emerged in response to a capitalist mode of production, to explain a gendered division of power in a gatherer/hunter mode of production. A hegemonic approach, then, appears to be somewhat misplaced in this context. While I am convinced that feminist research into status and prestige in gatherer/hunter modes of production is important, Ortner's particular use of hegemony does not offer the kind of critical approach that can take feminist research beyond the liberal feminist ideal of the universal oppression of women.

10 For a discussion of the state and Native politics see Peter Kulchyski, ' "A Considerable Unrest": F.O. Loft and the League of Indians.'

11 See Edward S. Curtis, *The North American Indian*, 18:8–11.

12 I am indebted to Judy A. Bear, a Cree language instructor with the Native Cultural Centre in Saskatoon, Saskatchewan, for providing me with this knowledge.

13 The notion of a violent change in sign systems is elaborated by Gayatri Chakravorty Spivak: 'A functional change in sign-system is a violent event ... The site of displacement of the function of signs is the name of reading as active transaction between past and future' ('Subaltern Studies: Deconstructing Historiography,' 197–8).

CHAPTER FIVE  History Lies in Fiction's Making and Unmaking

1 In Cree, for example, there are two types of 'stories': those that belong to sacred ceremonies and those that belong to the 'everyday,' including anecdotes, historical accounts, allegories, and fictional tales. See H. Christoph Wolfart, *Meet Cree: A Guide to the Cree Language* for a fuller description of the distinction.

2 Different approaches to the question of Native oral modes of cultural production have been taken up by Dennis Tedlock in 'On the Translation of Style in Oral Narrative,' in *Smoothing the Ground*, edited by Brian Swann. See also Barbara Godard's essay 'Talking about Ourselves: The Literary Productions of Native Women in Canada.'

3 The use of the term 'the Fourth World' signals the formation of a political unity of indigenous peoples; a Fourth Worlding that homogenizes, as in the use of the term 'the Third World,' a diverse body of people. In Brotherston's article the phrase remains at best ambiguous, both as a sign of a transformative political unity and, because of the desire for 'unity,' a site of ideological containment.

4 See *After the Last Sky: Palestinian Lives*, 16.

CHAPTER SIX  Occupied Space

1 Marie Annharte Baker, 'One Way to Keep Track of Who Is Talking,' in *Being on the Moon*, 78

2 One of the most influential explications of this problematic is Gayle Rubin's essay 'The Traffic in Women: Notes on the "Political Economy" of Sex.' Theoretically, Rubin's notion of sex/gender sys-

tems demands comparison with the larger matrix of feminist-marxist debates, such as those between Eleanor Leacock and Michèle Barrett, on the current contextualization of indigenous gender formation.

3 On Native lesbian and gay culture see *Living the Spirit: A Gay American Indian Anthology*, edited by Will Roscoe; and Walter L. Williams, *The Spirit and the Flesh: Sexual Diversity in American Indian Culture*.

4 See, for example, the collection of essays *Narrative Chance: Postmodern Discourse on Native American Indian Literatures*, edited by Gerald Vizenor, in which various postmodern theories are *applied to* a series of texts written by Native Americans.

5 See Guy Debord, *The Society of the Spectacle*: 'In societies where modern conditions of production prevail, all of life presents itself as an immense accumulation of *spectacles*. Everything that was directly lived has moved away into a representation' (sect. no. 1).

6 The text in the left-hand column represents deformations of passages from Marx's *Capital: A Critique of Political Economy, Volume 1*, translated by Ben Fowkes. In the section which follows the one I have just discussed, entitled 'Gifts to Take North,' Freeman records taking fabric to her grandmother, while her friend buys herself new clothes. The relationship between this fabric and the new clothes uncannily reproduces the central metaphors in Marx's analysis of the commodity form in chapter 1 of *Capital*. The relationship between exchange value and use value in Marx's discussion is elaborated through a difference between the ten yards of linen and a coat, a difference that is not unlike the difference between the labour of weaving and that of tailoring, is not unlike the difference between textuality and print commodities, the difference between human reproduction and cultural production, between the original and the ab/original, voice and the sayable, meaning/truth, evidence/the verifiable. What is assumed to be a raw material is, in fact, already cooked, already consuming, already part of a process of consumption.

# Bibliography

Ahmed, Leila. 'Feminism and Cross-Cultural Inquiry: The Terms of
  Discourse in Islam.' In *Coming to Terms: Feminism, Theory, Politics.* Ed.
  Elizabeth Weed. New York: Routledge 1989
Allen, Paula Gunn. *The Sacred Hoop: Recovering the Feminine in American
  Indian Traditions.* Boston: Beacon Press 1986
Althusser, Louis. 'Ideology and Ideological State Apparatuses.' In *'Lenin and
  Philosophy' and Other Essays.* Trans. Ben Brewster. London: Monthly
  Review Press 1971, 127–86
Amadiume, Ifi. *Male Daughters, Female Husbands: Gender and Sex in an
  African Society.* London: Zed Books 1987
Amos, Valerie, and Pratibha Parmar. 'Challenging Imperial Feminism.'
  *Feminist Review*, no. 17 (July 1984), 3–19
Antonius, Soraya. 'Fighting on Two Fronts: Conversations with Palestinian
  Women.' In *Third World / Second Sex.* Ed. Miranda Davies. London: Zed
  Press 1983
Anzaldúa, Gloria. *Borderlands / La Frontera: The New Mestiza.* San Francisco:
  Spinster / Aunt Lute 1987
Armstrong, Jeannette. *Breath Tracks.* Vancouver: Williams-Wallace / Theytus
  Books 1991
– 'Cultural Robbery, Imperialism: Voices of Native Women.' In *Trivia: A
  Journal of Ideas* 14 (Spring 1989), 21–3
– *Slash.* Penticton, BC: Theytus Books 1985
Atwood, Margaret. *Survival: A Thematic Guide to Canadian Literature.*
  Toronto: House of Anansi Press 1972
Baker, Marie Annharte. *Being on the Moon.* Winlaw, BC: Polestar Press 1990

Bakhtin, Mikhail. *Problems of Dostoevsky's Poetics*. Ed. and trans. Caryl Emerson. Minneapolis: University of Minnesota Press 1984

Bannerji, Himani. 'But Who Speaks for Us? Experience and Agency in Conventional Feminist Paradigms.' In *Unsettling Relations: The University as a Site of Feminist Struggles*. Ed. Himani Bannerji et al. Toronto: Women's Press 1991, 67–107

Barrett, Michèle. *Women's Oppression Today: Problems in Marxist Feminist Analysis*. London: Verso 1980. Reprinted with a new introduction and new subtitle 1988

Benjamin, Walter. 'Theses on the Philosophy of History.' In *Illuminations*. Ed. Hannah Arendt. New York: Schocken Books 1969, 253–64

Bhabha, Homi K. 'DissemiNation: Time, Narrative, and the Margins of the Modern Nation.' In *Nation and Narration*. Ed. Homi K. Bhabha. New York: Routledge 1990, 291–322

– 'Signs Taken for Wonders: Questions of Ambivalence and Authority under a Tree outside Delhi, May 1817.' *Critical Inquiry* 12 (Autumn 1985), 144–65. Reprinted in Gates, 1986, 163–84

– 'Difference, Discrimination and the Discourse of Colonialism.' In *The Politics of Theory*. Ed. Francis Barker et al. Colchester, England: University of Essex Press 1983, 194–211

– 'The Other Question – the Stereotype and Colonial Discourse.' *Screen* 24, no. 6 (Nov./Dec. 1983), 18–36

Boldt, Menno, and J. Anthony Long. *Pathways to Self-Determination*. Toronto, University of Toronto Press 1984

Boldt, Menno, and J. Anthony Long in association with Leroy Little Bear, eds. *The Quest for Justice: Aboriginal Peoples and Aboriginal Rights*. Toronto: University of Toronto Press 1985

Bourgeault, Ron. 'Indian, Métis and the Fur Trade: Class, Sexism and Racism in the Transition from "Communism" to Capitalism.' *Studies in Political Economy* 12 (Fall 1983), 45–80

Brant, Beth. *A Gathering of Spirit: A Collection by North American Indian Women*. Toronto: Women's Press 1988. Originally published by Sinister Wisdom in 1984 in the United States

Brotherston, Gordon. 'Towards a Grammatology of America: Lévi-Strauss, Derrida, and the Native American World.' In *Europe and Its Others, Volume Two*. Ed. Francis Barker et al. Colchester, England: University of Essex Press 1985, 61–77

Brown, Jennifer, and Jacqueline Peterson. *The New People: Being and Becoming Métis*. Winnipeg: University of Manitoba Press 1988

Cameron, Anne. 'A Message for Those Who Would Steal Native Traditions.' *Moccassin Line*, Summer 1987, 3

– *Daughters of Copper Woman*. Vancouver: Press Gang 1981

Campbell, Maria. *Halfbreed*. Toronto: Goodread Biographies 1983. Originally published by McClelland and Stewart, 1973. Published in a Seal Books edition in 1979

*Canadian Woman Studies / Les Cahiers de la femme* 10, nos. 2–3 (1989) [Special issue: Native Women]

Chrystos. *Not Vanishing*. Vancouver: Press Gang 1988

Cixous, Hélène. 'Castration or Decapitation?' Trans. Annette Kuhn. *Signs*, 7, no. 1 (1981), 41–55

Clifford, James. *The Predicament of Culture: Twentieth Century Ethnography, Literature, and Art*. London: Harvard University Press 1988

Cornell, George L. 'The Imposition of Western Definitions of Literature on Indian Oral Traditions.' In *The Native in Literature: Canadian and Comparative Perspectives*. Ed. Thomas King, Cheryl Calver, and Helen Hoy. Oakville, Ont.: ECW Press 1987, 174–87

Coward, Rosalind. *Patriarchal Precedents: Sexuality and Social Relations*. London: Routledge and Kegan Paul 1983

–, and John Ellis. *Language and Materialism: Developments in Semiology and the Theory of the Subject*. London: Routledge 1977

Culleton, Beatrice. *April Raintree*. Winnipeg: Pemmican 1984

– *In Search of April Raintree*. Winnipeg: Pemmican 1983

Curthoys, Ann. 'Women and Class.' In *A Double Colonization: Colonial and Post-Colonial Women's Writing*. Ed. Kirsten Holst Petersen and Anna Rutherford. Oxford: Dangaroo Press 1986, 11–17

Curtis, Edward S. *The North American Indian*. Vol. 18. New York: Johnston Reprint Corporation 1928

Cuthand, Beth. *Voices in the Waterfall*. Vancouver: Lazara Press 1989

Davies, Miranda, ed. *Third World / Second Sex: Women's Struggles and National Liberation*. London: Zed Press 1983

Dearborn, Mary. *Pocahontas's Daughters: Gender and Ethnicity in American Culture*. Oxford: Oxford University Press 1986

Debord, Guy. *The Society of the Spectacle*. Detroit: Black & Red 1983

de Lauretis, Teresa. 'Eccentric Subjects: Feminist Theory and Historical Consciousness.' *Feminist Studies* 16, no. 1 (Spring 1990), 115–50

– 'The Essence of the Triangle or, Taking the Risk of Essentialism Seriously: Feminist Theory in Italy, the U.S. and Britain.' *differences: A Journal of Feminist Cultural Studies* 1, no. 2 (1989), 3–37. Revised as 'Upping the Anti (sic) in Feminist Theory.' In Hirsch and Fox Keller, 255–70

– *Technologies of Gender: Essays on Theory, Film, and Fiction*. Bloomington: Indiana University Press 1987

– *Alice Doesn't: Feminism, Semiotics, Cinema*. Bloomington: Indiana University Press 1984

Deleuze, Gilles, and Félix Guattari. *A Thousand Plateaus: Capitalism and*

*Schizophrenia*. Trans. Brian Massumi. Minneapolis: University of Minnesota Press 1987

de Lotbinière-Harwood, Susanne. 'Interview with Lee Maracle.' *Trivia: A Journal of Ideas* 14 (Spring 1989), 24–36

Delphy, Christine. *Close to Home: A Materialist Analysis of Women's Oppression*. Ed. and trans. Diana Leonard. Amherst: University of Massachusetts 1984

Derrida, Jacques. *Limited Inc*. Trans. Samuel Weber and Jeffrey Mehlman. Evanston, Ill.: Northwestern University Press 1988

– *The Ear of the Other, Otobiography, Transference, Translation*. Ed. Christie V. McDonald. New York: Schocken Books 1982

– *Positions*. Trans. Alan Bass. Chicago: The University of Chicago Press 1981

– 'The Law of Genre.' Trans. Avital Ronell. *Glyph* 7 (Spring 1980), 55–81

– *Margins of Philosophy*. Trans. Alan Bass. Chicago: University of Chicago Press 1979

– *Writing and Difference*. Trans. Alan Bass. Chicago: University of Chicago Press 1978

– 'Signature Event Context.' Trans. Samuel Weber and Jeffrey Mehlman. *Glyph* 1 (1977), 172–97. Reprinted in *Limited Inc.*, 1–24

– *Of Grammatology*. Trans. Gayatri Chakravorty Spivak. Baltimore: Johns Hopkins Press 1976

Dorfman, Ariel. *The Empire's Old Clothes: What the Lone Ranger, Babar, and Other Innocent Heroes Do to Our Minds*. New York: Pantheon Books 1983

el Saadawi, Nawal. *The Fall of the Imam*. Trans. Sherif Hetata. London: Methuen 1987

– *She Has No Place in Paradise*. Trans. Shirley Eber. London: Methuen 1987

– *Two Women in One*. Trans. Osman Nusairi and Jana Gough. Seattle, Wash.: Seal Press 1986

– *God Dies by the Nile*. Trans. Sherif Hetata. London: Zed Press 1985

– *Memoirs from the Women's Prison*. Trans. Marilyn Booth. London: Women's Press 1983

– *Woman at Point Zero*. Trans. Sherif Hetata. London: Zed Press 1983

– 'Arab Women and Western Feminism: An Interview with Nawal el Sadaawi [sic].' *Race and Class* 22, no. 2 (Autumn 1980), 175–83

– 'Creative Women in Changing Societies: A Personal Reflection.' *Race and Class* 22, no. 2 (Autumn 1980), 159–73

– *The Hidden Face of Eve: Women in the Arab World*. Trans. Sherif Hetata. London: Zed Press 1980. Reprinted by Boston Beacon Press. Foreword by Irene L. Gendzier, 1980, 1981

Emberley, Julia. 'The Pain of the Text – Anger: Intertextuality: Gender.'

*Tessera*, no. 4. In *Contemporary Verse* 2 11, nos. 2–3 (Spring/Summer 1988), 125–35

– Review of *Enough Is Enough: Aboriginal Women Speak Out. Canadian Woman Studies/Les Cahiers de la femme*, 9, nos. 3–4 (Fall/Winter 1988), 138–40

Etienne, Mona, and Eleanor Leacock, eds. *Women and Colonization: Anthropological Perspectives*. New York: Praeger 1980

Fanon, Franz. *Black Skin, White Masks*. New York: Grove Press 1967

Farge, Arlette. 'Women's History: An Overview.' In *French Feminist Thought*. Ed. Toril Moi. Oxford: Basil Blackwell 1987, 133–49

*Fireweed*, no. 22 (1986) [Special issue: Native Women]

Foucault, Michel. 'The Order of Discourse.' In *Untying the Text: A Post-Structural Reader*. Ed. Robert Young. London: Routledge and Kegan Paul 1981, 48–78

– *The Order of Things*. New York: Random House 1970. Originally published as *Les Mots et les choses* by Editions Gallimard, France, 1966

–, and Maurice Blanchot. *Foucault/Blanchot*. Trans. Brian Massumi and Jeffrey Mehlman. New York: Zone Books 1987

Freeman, Minnie Aodla. *Life among the* Qallunaat. Edmonton: Hurtig 1978

Freire, Paulo. *Pedagogy of the Oppressed*. New York: Seabury 1970

Gates, Jr, Henry Louis. *The Signifying Monkey: A Theory of Afro-American Literary Criticism*. New York: Oxford University Press 1988

–, ed. *'Race,' Writing, and Difference*. Chicago: University of Chicago Press 1986

Geertz, Clifford. *Works and Lives: The Anthropologist as Author*. Stanford: Stanford University Press 1988

Gilbert, Sandra M., and Susan Gubar. *The Madwoman in the Attic: The Woman Writer and the Nineteenth-Century Literary Imagination*. New Haven: Yale University Press 1979

Godard, Barbara, ed. *Gynocritics/La Gynocritique: Feminist Approaches to Canadian and Quebec Women's Writing*. Toronto: ECW 1987

– 'Voicing Difference: The Literary Production of Native Women.' In *A Mazing Space: Writing Canadian Women Writing*. Ed. Shirley Neuman and Smaro Kamboureli. Edmonton: Longspoon/NeWest 1986, 87–107

– *Talking about Ourselves: The Literary Productions of Native Women in Canada*. CRIAW paper no. 11. Ottawa: CRIAW 1985

Goldie, Terry. *Fear and Temptation: The Image of the Indigene in Canadian, Australian, and New Zealand Literatures*. Kingston and Montreal: McGill-Queen's University Press 1989

Green, Joyce. 'Sexual Equality and Indian Government: An Analysis of Bill C–31 Amendments of the Indian Act.' *Native Studies Review* 1, no. 2 (1985), 81–95

Green, Rayna. 'Native American Women: Review Essay.' *Signs* 6, no. 2 (1980), 248–67

Griffiths, Linda, and Maria Campbell. *The Book of Jessica: A Theatrical Transformation*. Toronto: Coach House Press 1989

Haraway, Donna. 'A Cyborg Manifesto: Science, Technology, and Socialist Feminism in the Late Twentieth Century.' In her *Simians, Cyborgs, and Women: The Reinvention of Nature*. New York: Routledge 1991, 149–81

Harlow, Barbara. *Resistance Literature*. New York: Methuen 1987

– 'Commentary: "All That Is Inside Is Not Center": Responses to the Discourses of Domination.' In *Coming to Terms: Feminism, Theory, Politics*. Ed. Elizabeth Weed. New York: Routledge 1989, 162–70

Hartmann, Heidi. 'The Unhappy Marriage of Marxism and Feminism: Towards a More Progressive Union.' In *Women and Revolution: A Discussion of the Unhappy Marriage of Marxism and Feminism*. Ed. Lydia Sargent. Montreal: Black Rose Books 1981, 1–41

Hirsch, Marianne, and Evelyn Fox Keller, eds. *Conflicts in Feminism*. New York: Routledge 1990

Hogan, Linda. 'New Shoes.' In *Earth Power Coming*. Ed. Simon J. Ortiz. Tsaile, Ariz.: Navajo Community College Press 1983, 3–20

hooks, bell [Gloria Watkins]. *Feminist Theory: From Margin to Center*. Boston: South End Press 1984

*Indian Acts and Amendments: 1868–1950*. 2d ed. Ottawa: Treaties and Historical Research Centre, Research Branch, Corporate Policy, Department of Indian and Northern Affairs Canada 1981

Irigaray, Luce. 'Plato's *Hystera*.' In her *Speculum of the Other Woman*. Trans. Gillian C. Gill. Ithaca: Cornell University Press 1985, 241–364

Jameson, Fredric. 'Architecture and the Critique of Ideology (1985).' In his *The Syntax of History*. Vol. 2 of *The Ideologies of Theory, Essays 1971–1986*. Minneapolis: University of Minnesota Press 1988, 35–60

– 'Postmodernism, or the Cultural Logic of Late Capitalism.' *New Left Review* 146 (July/August 1984), 53–92

– *The Political Unconscious: Narrative as a Socially Symbolic Act*. Ithaca: Cornell University Press 1981

Jamieson, Kathleen. 'Sex Discrimination and the Indian Act.' In *Arduous Journey: Canadian Indians and Decolonization*. Ed. J. Rick Ponting. Toronto: McClelland and Stewart Ltd. 1986, 112–36

– *Indian Women and the Law in Canada: Citizens Minus*. Ottawa: Ministry of Supply and Services Canada 1978

JanMohamed, Abdul. 'The Economy of Manichean Allegory: The Function of Racial Difference in Colonialist Literature.' *Critical Inquiry* 12 (Autumn 1985), 59–87

Jayawardena, Kumari. *Feminism and Nationalism in the Third World*. London: Zed Press 1986

Joe, Rita. *Song of Eskasoni*. Charlottetown: Ragweed Press 1988

Johnston, Gordon. 'An Intolerable Burden of Meaning: Native Peoples in White Fiction.' In *The Native in Literature*. Ed. Thomas King et al. Oakville, Ont.: EWC Press 1987, 50–66

Kane, Marlyn (Osennontion) and Sylvia Maracle (Skonaganleh:rá). 'Our World.' *Canadian Woman Studies / Les Cahiers de la femme* 10, nos. 2–3 (Summer/Fall 1989) [Special issue: Native Women], 7–19

Kenney, J.F. *The Founding of Churchill: Being the Journal of Captain James Knight, Governor-in-Chief in Hudson Bay, from 14th July to 13th of September, 1717*. London: J.M. Dent & Sons 1932

King, Thomas, ed. *All My Relations: An Anthology of Contemporary Canadian Native Fiction*. Toronto: McClelland and Stewart 1990

– 'Introduction: An Anthology of Canadian Native Fiction.' *Canadian Fiction Magazine* 60 (1987), 4–10

–, and Cheryl Calver, and Helen Hoy, eds. *The Native in Literature: Canadian and Comparative Perspectives*. Oakville, Ont.: EWC Press 1987

Knight, Governor James. 'York Factory Journals, 1714–1717.' Hudson's Bay Company Archives

Kocsis, Loretta Meade. Review of *Enough Is Enough: Aboriginal Women Speak Out*. *Canadian Woman Studies / Les Cahiers de la femme* 10, nos. 2–3 (Summer/Fall 1989), 159

Kofman, Sarah. *The Enigma of Woman*. Trans. Catherine Porter. Ithaca: Cornell University Press 1985

Kristeva, Julia. 'Women's Time.' In *Feminist Theory: A Critique of Ideology*. Ed. Nannerl O. Keohane, Michelle Z. Rosaldo, and Barbara C. Gelpi. Chicago: University of Chicago Press 1981, 31–53

– *Desire in Language*. Trans. Thoman Gora, Alice Jardine, and Leon Roudiez. Ed. Leon S. Roudiez. New York: Columbia University Press 1980

Krupat, Arnold. 'The Dialogic of Silko's Storyteller.' In *Narrative Chance: Postmodern Discourse on Native American Indian Literature*. Ed. Gerald Vizenor. Albuquerque: University of New Mexico 1989, 55–68

– 'Post-structuralism and Oral Literature.' In *Recovering the Word: Essays on Native American Literature*. Ed. Arnold Krupat and Brian Swann. Berkeley: University of California Press 1987, 113–28

– *For Those Who Came After: A Study of Native American Autobiography*. Berkeley: University of California Press 1985

–, and Brian Swann, eds. *Recovering the Word: Essays on Native American Literature.* Berkeley: University of California Press 1987

Kulchyski, Peter. 'Primitive Subversion: Totalization and Resistance in Native Canadian Politics.' *Cultural Critique* 12 (Spring 1992), 171–96

– 'The Postmodern and the Palaeolithic: Notes on Technology and Native Community in the Far North.' *Canadian Journal of Political and Social Theory* 12, no. 3 (1989), 49–63

– ' "A Considerable Unrest": F.O. Loft and the League of Indians.' *Native Studies Review* 4, nos. 1–2 (1988), 95–117

– 'Towards a Theory of Dispossession: Native Politics in Canada.' PHD York University 1988

LaCapra, Dominick. *Soundings in Critical Theory.* Ithaca: Cornell University Press 1989

– *History and Criticism.* Ithaca: Cornell University Press 1985

LaChapelle, Caroline. 'Beyond Barriers: Native Women and the Women's Movement.' In *Still Ain't Satisfied: Canadian Feminism Today.* Ed. Maureen Fitzgerald, Connie Guberman, and Margie Wolfe. Toronto: Women's Press 1982

Laclau, Ernesto. 'Metaphor and Social Antagonisms.' In *Marxism and the Interpretation of Culture.* Ed. Cary Nelson and Lawrence Grossberg. Chicago: University of Illinois Press 1988, 249–67

–, and Chantal Mouffe. *Hegemony and Socialist Strategy: Towards a Radical Democratic Politics.* Trans. Winston Moore and Paul Cammack. New York: Verso 1985

Landry, Donna, and Gerald MacLean. *Materialist Feminisms: An Introduction.* Oxford: Basil Blackwell (forthcoming)

Lévi-Strauss, Claude. *Structural Anthropology.* Trans. Claire Jacobson and Brooke Grundfest Schoelf. New York: Basic Books 1963

Lorde, Audre. 'The Master's Tools Will Never Dismantle the Master's House.' In *This Bridge Called My Back: Writings by Radical Women of Color.* Ed. Cherrie Moraga and Gloria Anzaldúa. New York: Kitchen Table / Women of Color Press 1981, 98–101

Lugones, Maria C., and Elizabeth V. Spelman. 'Have We Got a Theory for You! Feminist Theory, Cultural Imperialism, and the Demand for "The Woman's Voice." ' *Women's Studies International Forum*, 6, no. 6 (1983), 573–81

Lukács, Georg. *The Meaning of Contemporary Realism.* Trans. John and Necke Mander. London: Merlin Press 1963

MacLean, Gerald M. 'Citing the Subject.' In *Gender and Theory: Dialogues on Feminist Criticism.* Ed. Linda Kauffman. London: Basil Blackwell 1989, 140–57

McGrath, Robin. 'Oral Influences in Contemporary Inuit Literature.' In *The Native in Literature*. Ed. Thomas King et al. Oakville, Ont.: ECW Press 1987, 159–73

*The Magazine to Re-establish the TRICKSTER* 1, no. 1 (1989)

Manuel, George, and Michael Poslums. *The Fourth World: An Indian Reality*. Toronto: Collier-Macmillan 1974

Maracle, Lee. *Sojourner's Truth and Other Stories*. Vancouver: Press Gang 1990

– 'Moving Over.' *Trivia: A Journal of Ideas: Part II: Language/Differences: Writing in Tongues* 14 (Spring 1989), 9–12

– *I Am Woman*. North Vancouver, BC: Write-On Press 1988

– *Bobbi Lee: Indian*. Foreword by Jeannette Armstrong. Ed. Viola Thomas. Toronto: Women's Press 1990. Originally published as *Bobbi Lee, Indian Rebel: Struggles of a Native Canadian Woman*. Ed. Don Barnette and Rick Sterling. LSM (Liberation Support Movement) Press 1975

Marlatt, Daphne. *Ana Historic: A Novel*. Toronto: Coach House Press 1988

Marx, Karl. *Capital: A Critique of Political Economy, Volume One*. Trans. Ben Fowkes. New York: Vintage 1977

– 'The Eighteenth Brumaire of Louis Bonaparte.' In *Surveys from Exile*. Ed. and Introd. David Fernbach. New York: Vintage Books 1974

–, and Fredric Engels. *The German Ideology, Part 1*. New York: International Publishers 1970

Mohanty, Chandra Talpade. 'Under Western Eyes: Feminist Scholarship and Colonial Discourse.' *Boundary* 2 12, no. 3–13, no. 1 (1984), 333–58. Reprinted in *Feminist Review* 30 (1988), 61–88. A revised version appears in Mohanty, Russo, and Torres, 51–80

–, Ann Russo, and Lourdes Torres, eds. *Third World Women and the Politics of Feminism*. Bloomington: Indiana University Press 1991

Mohsen, Safia K. 'New Images, Old Reflections: Working Middle-Class Women in Egypt.' In *Women and the Family in the Middle East: New Voices of Change*. Ed. Elizabeth Warnook Fernea. Austin: University of Texas Press 1985, 56–71

Moi, Toril. 'Feminism, Postmodernism, and Style: Recent Feminist Criticism in the United States.' *Cultural Critique* 9 (Spring 1988), 3–22

– *Sexual/Textual Politics: Feminist Literary Theory*. London: Methuen 1985

Moody, Roger, ed. *The Indigenous Voice: Visions and Realities, Volumes One and Two*. Atlantic Highlands, NJ: Zed Books 1988

Morales, Rosario. 'We're All in the Same Boat.' In *This Bridge Called My Back: Writings by Radical Women of Color*. Ed. Cherrie Moraga and Gloria Anzaldúa. New York: Kitchen Table / Women of Color Press 1981

Mulvey, Laura. 'Visual Pleasure and Narrative Cinema.' In *Feminism and*

*Film Theory*. Ed. Constance Penley. New York: Routledge 1988. Originally published in *Screen* 16, no. 3 (Autumn 1975), 6–18

New, W.H., ed. *Native Writers and Canadian Writing*. Vancouver: University of British Columbia Press 1991

Newman, Shirley, and Smaro Kamboureli, eds. *A Mazing Space: Writing Canadian Women Writing*. Edmonton: Longspoon/NeWest 1986

Newton, Judith, and Deborah Rosenfelt, eds. *Feminist Criticism and Social Change: Sex, Class, and Race in Literature and Culture*. New York: Methuen 1985

Nicholson, Linda. 'Feminism and Marx: Integrating Kinship and the Economic.' In *Feminism as Critique*. Ed. Seyla Benhabib and Drucilla Cornell. Minneapolis: University of Minnesota Press 1987, 16–30

Nietzsche, Friedrich. 'On Truth and Falsity in Their Ultramoral Sense.' In *Complete Works of Nietzsche*. Vol. 2. Ed. D. Levy. London 1911

Norris, Christopher. *Derrida*. London: Fontana Press 1987

O'Brien, Mary. *The Politics of Reproduction*. London: Routledge and Kegan Paul 1981

Ortner, Sherry. 'Gender Hegemonies.' *Cultural Critique* 14 (Winter 1989–90), 35–80

Perreault, Jeanne, and Sylvia Vance, eds. *Writing the Circle: Native Women of Western Canada*. Edmonton: NeWest 1990

Petrone, Penny. *Native Literature in Canada: From the Oral Tradition to the Present*. Toronto: Oxford University Press 1990

Philip, Marlene Nourbese. 'Journal Entries against Reaction.' In *Work in Progress: Building Feminist Culture*. Ed. Rhea Tregebov. Toronto: Women's Press 1987, 65–76

Poulantzas, Nicos. *Political Power and Social Classes*. Trans. Timothy O'Hagan. London: Verso Editions 1968

Prentice, Alison, et al., eds. *Canadian Women: A History*. Toronto: Women's Press 1987

Routledge, Marie, and Marion E. Jackson. *Pudlo: Thirty Years of Drawing*. Ottawa: National Gallery of Canada 1990

Rich, Adrienne. *On Lies, Secrets and Silence: Selected Prose 1966–1978*. New York: Norton 1979

Rich, E.E. *The History of the Hudson's Bay Company: 1670–1870*. Vol. 1: 1670–1763. London: The Hudson's Bay Record Society 1958

Roscoe, Will, ed. *Living the Spirit: A Gay American Indian Anthology*. New York: St Martin's Press 1988

Rubin, Gayle. 'The Traffic in Women: Notes on the "Political Economy" of Sex.' In *Toward an Anthropology of Women*. Ed. Rayna R. Reiter. New York: Monthly Review Press 1975, 157–210

Ryan, Michael. *Marxism and Deconstruction: A Critical Articulation*. Baltimore: Johns Hopkins University Press 1982

Sahlins, Marshall. *Culture and Practical Reason*. Chicago: University of Chicago Press 1976

– *Stone Age Economics*. New York: Aldine-Atherton 1972

Said, Edward. *After the Last Sky: Palestinian Lives*. With photographs by Jean Mohr. New York: Pantheon Books 1985

– 'Ideology of Difference.' In *'Race,' Writing and Difference*. Ed. Henry Louis Gates, Jr. Chicago: University of Chicago Press 1985, 38–58

– 'Orientalism Reconsidered.' *Race and Class* 27 (1985), 1–15

– *The World, the Text, the Critic*. Cambridge, Mass.: Harvard University Press 1983

– *Orientalism*. New York: Pantheon Books 1978

Sartre, Jean-Paul. *Critique of Dialectical Reason*. Vol. 1. Trans. Alan Sheridan-Smith. London: New Left Books 1976. Originally published as *Critique de la raison dialectique* by Editions Gallimard, Paris 1960

Showalter, Elaine, ed. *The New Feminist Criticism: Essays on Women, Literature and Theory*. New York: Pantheon 1985

– 'Feminist Criticism in the Wilderness.' In *Writing and Sexual Difference*. Ed. Elizabeth Abel. Chicago: University of Chicago Press 1980, 9–35

Silman, Janet. *Enough Is Enough: Aboriginal Women Speak Out*. Toronto: University of Toronto Press 1987

Silverman, Kaja. *The Subject of Semiotics*. New York: Oxford University Press 1983

Slipperjack, Ruby. *Honour the Sun*. Winnipeg: Pemmican 1985 (Extracted and revised from the diary of the Owl)

Smith, Barbara, ed. *Home Girls: A Black Feminist Anthology*. New York: Kitchen Table / Women of Color Press 1983

Smith, Dorothy. *The Everyday World as Problematic: A Feminist Sociology*. Toronto: University of Toronto Press 1987

– *Feminism and Marxism: A Place to Begin, a Way to Go*. Vancouver: New Star Books 1977

Smith, Paul. *Discerning the Subject*. Minneapolis: University of Minnesota Press 1988

Spivak, Gayatri Chakravorty. 'Can the Subaltern Speak?' In *Marxism and the Interpretation of Culture*. Ed. Cary Nelson and Lawrence Grossberg. Chicago: University of Illinois Press 1988, 271–313

– *In Other Worlds: Essays in Cultural Politics*. New York: Methuen 1987.

– 'Imperialism and Sexual Difference.' *Oxford Literary Review* 8 (1986), 225–40

– 'The Rani of Sirmur.' In *Europe and Its Others, Volume One: Proceedings of*

*the Essex Sociology of Literature Conference, July 1984.* Ed. Francis Baker et al. Colchester, England: University of Essex Press 1985, 128–51
– 'Displacement and the Discourse of Woman.' In *Displacement: Derrida and After.* Ed. Mark Krupnick. Bloomington: Indiana University Press 1983, 169–95
– 'French Feminism in an International Frame.' *Yale French Studies* 62 (1981), 154–84
– 'Revolutions That as Yet Have No Model: Derrida's *Limited Inc.' Diacritics* 10 (Dec. 1980), 29–49
– 'Three Feminist Readings: McCullers, Drabble, Habermas.' *Union Seminary Quarterly Review* 35, nos. 1–2 (Fall/Winter 1979–80), 15–34
– 'Subaltern Studies: Deconstructing Historiography.' In her *In Other Worlds: Essays in Cultural Politics,* 197–221
Tarabishi, Georges. *Women against Her Sex: A Critique of Nawal el Saadawi.* Trans. Basil Hatim and Elizabeth Orsini. London: Saqi Books 1988
Taussig, Michael. 'Violence and Resistance in the Americas: The Legacy of Conquest.' In *The Nervous System.* New York: Routledge 1992, 37–52
Tedlock, Dennis. 'On the Translation of Style in Oral Narrative.' In *Smoothing the Ground.* Ed. Brian Swann. Berkeley: University of California Press 1983, 57–77
Tennant, Paul. 'Native Indian Political Organization in British Columbia, 1900–1969: A Response to Internal Colonialism.' *BC Studies* 55 (Autumn 1982), 3–49
Tregebov, Rhea, ed. *Work in Progress: Building Feminist Culture.* Toronto: Women's Press 1987
Vangen, Kate. 'Making Faces: Defiance and Humour in Campbell's *Halfbreed* and Welch's *Winter in the Blood.*' In *The Native in Literature.* Ed. Thomas King el al. Oakville, Ont.: ECW Press 1987, 188–205
Van Kirk, Sylvia. 'Towards a Feminist Perspective in Native History.' In *Papers of the Eighteenth Algonquin Conference.* Ed. William Cowan. Ottawa: Carleton University 1987, 377–89
– '*Many Tender Ties': Women in Fur-Trade Society in Western Canada, 1670–1870.* Winnipeg: Watson and Dwyer Publishing Ltd. 1980
– 'Thanadelthur.' *Beaver* (Spring 1974), 40–5
Vizenor, Gerald, ed. *Narrative Chance: Postmodern Discourse on Native American Indian Literatures.* Albuquerque: University of New Mexico Press 1989
Wallace, Michelle. *Invisibility Blues: From Pop to Theory.* New York: Verso 1990
Weedon, Chris. *Feminist Practice and Poststructural Theory.* Oxford: Basil Blackwell 1987
Williams, Walter L. *The Spirit and the Flesh: Sexual Diversity in American Indian Culture.* Boston: Beacon Press 1986

Wimsatt, W.K. *The Verbal Icon: Studies in the Meaning of Poetry.* Lexington:
   University of Kentucky Press 1954
Wolfart, H. Christoph. *Meet Cree: A Guide to the Cree Language.* Lincoln:
   University of Nebraska Press 1981
Woodhull, Winifred, 'Unveiling Algeria.' *Genders* 10 (Spring 1991), 112–31

# Index